MAX SCHE

ON FEELING, KNOWING, AND VALUING

SELECTED WRITINGS

Edited and with an Introduction by

HAROLD J. BERSHADY

THE UNIVERSITY OF CHICAGO PRESS

Chicago and London

HAROLD J. BERSHADY is professor of
sociology at the University of Pennsylvania.

The University of Chicago Press, Chicago 60637
The University of Chicago Press, Ltd., London
© 1992 by The University of Chicago
All rights reserved. Published 1992
Printed in the United States of America

01 00 99 98 97 96 95 94 93 92   5 4 3 2 1

ISBN (cloth): 0–226–73670–9
ISBN (paper): 0–226–73671–7

Library of Congress Cataloging-in-Publicaton Data

Scheler, Max.
    On feeling, knowing, and valuing : selected writings / Max Scheler;
  edited and with an introduction by Harold J. Bershady.
      p.   cm.—(The Heritage of sociology)
    Includes bibliographical references and index.
    1. Emotions (Philosophy) 2. Knowledge, Sociology of. 3. Social values.
  4. Sociology—Philosophy.   I. Bershady, Harold J.
  II. Title. III. Series.
  B3329.S481063   1992
  121—dc20   92-2976
                                                        CIP

Contents

Acknowledgments

Charles Bosk, Victor Lidz, and, shortly before he died, Talcott Parsons encouraged me to do this book. Ever since I decided to do it, Charles and Victor have given me generous intellectual, personal, and stylistic counsel. Barney M. Dlin and the "Saturday Morning Group" were invaluable in bolstering my resolve to pursue, and in aiding me to clarify, psychological issues. Stuart Bogom, Richard Farnum, Sy Leventman, and Pamela Spritzer read and made useful comments on an earlier version of the introduction. Peter Haley gave me able assistance in translating chapter 7. E. Digby Baltzell was helpful in matters of substance and style. Donald Levine was a kind and thoughtful editor who deftly facilitated bringing this book to completion. Not least, my wife, Suzanne, was a constant source of moral and personal support.

Introduction

Max Scheler, whose life spanned the years 1874–1928, was acclaimed
in Europe after the First World War as one of the leading minds of the
modern age and Germany's most brilliant thinker—no mean praise
considering the caliber of his German contemporaries, such as Troeltsch, Sombart, Meinecke, and, above all, Max Weber, with whom he
was being compared.[1] But within a few years of his death Scheler became, at least publicly, a forgotten man. His reputation did not so
much decline as it was virtually extinguished by the political upheavals
in Germany and the war that engulfed all of Europe. His once-famous
books were banned form publication in the country of his birth. Certain of his eminent former champions, Heidegger in particular, tacitly
endorsed the ban, and European commentary on his work practically
ceased. The enforced silence on Scheler's work, however, did not result
in permanent amnesia. When his books were brought out again at the
conclusion of the Second World War, they were greeted with revived if
tempered interest by a wide range of Continental scholars. The mood
had of course shifted, become more sober. But Scheler's reputation did
not again ascend to its former lofty heights; doubtless it never will. In
the aftermath of the war scholarly attention soon turned to more
pressing questions, and interest in Scheler's work receded—more naturally and slowly this time—to rest mainly on his philosophy of religion, where it lingers to the present. Scheler is now generally remembered as one of the intriguing but minor figures on the Weimar
landscape, a philosopher who dealt chiefly with metaphysical and religious subjects and occasionally with sociological ones as well.[2]

If the current appraisal of Scheler is more just than the exaggerated
claims made of him earlier, it is nevertheless based on too fleeting an
acquaintance with the variety and extent of his thought. Scheler was
not a genius, nor was he merely a man of some talent. He was a pioneer in terrain that is not wholly familiar to us yet. The nature and
sources of positive and negative sentiments and their relation to communal life, phenomenology of the emotions, philosophy of religion
and culture, sociology of knowledge, theory of value—these are areas

1

in which he blazed new trails and found rich though barely charted ground.

Although several of Scheler's works have been translated into English over the past twenty-five years, his thought is not well known among English-speaking social scientists.[3] This is peculiar, in view of the fact that the fields he pioneered have become well established in the United States. I see two reasons for this anomaly. For one thing, certain areas to which Scheler made original contributions have long been associated with other European founders—most notably, the sociology of knowledge with Karl Mannheim and phenomenological sociology with Alfred Schutz. These men were almost a generation younger than Scheler. When they escaped the Nazi occupation— Mannheim to England, Schutz to the United States—they had hardly entered their most productive years. They had the good fortune to reestablish their careers and remain productive well beyond the conclusion of the Second World War. They wrote and taught with seriousness, originality, and force. An aura surrounded these scholars. They were not only living representatives of a foreign tradition of learning that, if not widely understood, was respected, but were also refugees of the common enemy. This last fact perhaps especially quickened the sympathy of several young American scholars who were themselves not too far removed from needing to flee European oppression. However novel their ideas may have appeared initially, Mannheim and Schutz soon found vigorous Anglo-American champions. Their versions of the sociology of knowledge and phenomenological sociology were promulgated in major universities in England and America decades before Scheler's work became accessible to a largely English-reading audience. Thus, when Scheler's writings began to appear, the "paternity" of these areas and the characteristic idiom in which their problems were expressed had already become well defined. Scheler's innovations, precisely because they were pitched at so different an angle, were more often seen as curiosities, somewhat exotic, but in any case not easily assimilable to prevailing views. Such differences have contributed to the obscurity in which Scheler's thought remains.

What is more, Scheler wrote from an avowedly religious standpoint all of his adult life. The social sciences, on the other hand, whatever may have been their original religious animation, are now thoroughly secular in orientation and most of their practitioners "religiously unmusical." the metaphysical and transcendental notes that resound throughout Scheler's entire corpus must embarrass many such practitioners. Indeed, this was very much my own response when I first read Scheler in the mid-1950s at the suggestion of a respected teacher. Several of his ideas piqued my interest, but I was at a loss at how to deal with the open expression of religious sentiments in the work of a modern social thinker. Nor was my consternation due merely to the fact that Scheler had any kind of religious views at all, which I, in common with most American scholars, believed should best be kept a private matter. It was due as much to the fact that Scheler's views were Catholic in outlook and thus foreign, indeed antagonistic, to the major assumptions that have shaped our own largely Protestant culture. Scheler stressed the existence of hierarchies: of kinds of persons, of values, of feelings, of knowledge. This stress is part of his endeavor to see the whole, to find the place of particular elements in a larger scheme. But to the more egalitarian and individualistic moorings of most American scholars, Scheler's stress upon hierarchy is as deeply unsettling as the religious origins from which it sprang. Thus, although Mannheim acknowledged his debt to Scheler many times, and Schutz published three commentaries in English on Scheler's work, the American followers of Mannheim and Schutz have by and large ignored Scheler.[4]

Max Scheler's Life and Work

Max Scheler struggled constantly to gain mastery over contradictory impulses that raged within him—a mastery that he projected in his intellectual work but never achieved in his personal life. Born in Munich of a Protestant father and a Jewish mother, Scheler was attracted to Catholicism as an adolescent. His father had been an administrator of farmlands to the duke of Saxe-Coburg, a post he resigned in order to move to Munich. Scheler knew his father mainly as a man depressed, retired on his small savings while still young, longing to return to the countryside, withdrawn. Scheler's mother, born and raised in Munich, was dependent on her wealthy brothers for support in the reduced circumstances of her marriage. She indulged Scheler's every whim, favoring him over his younger sister, but had only contempt for the failings of his father, whom she taunted and upbraided at every turn.[5]

Although raised as a Jew until he entered a Catholic high school shortly before his father died, Scheler found the conception of brotherhood, community, mercy, and love conveyed to him by the chaplain immensely appealing. It was a conception that promised to dispel the oppressive, hateful atmosphere of his household. And in the public celebrations of holy days when the large Catholic population of Munich crowded the streets in candlelight processions, in the fellowship of the choral devotions to the Virgin Mary, Scheler felt the promise in some part fulfilled. He converted to Catholicism at the age of fourteen.[6] But his character was already stamped, caught between the press of his powerful spiritual strivings and equally powerful sensual desires.

Soon coupled to his apostasy was a failing school performance, either of which would have been enough to provoke his mother's wrath. At this point, however, a maternal uncle intervened in a role that such relatives sometimes assume with rebellious younger members of their families. To encourage Scheler in his efforts to break out of the confines of his family in ways the family might find less objectionable, the uncle gave him Nietzsche to read and promised to finance his further schooling. Bolstered by this support, Scheler completed his high school studies and enrolled at the University of Munich in 1893 at the age of nineteen.

Scheler intended at first to study medicine. Biology interested him; indeed, in all of his writings Scheler refers to the latest biological research. But hardly before he had begun at the university, philosophy and less sublimated matters claimed his attention.

While on vacation in the Austrian Alps the summer before he was to enter college, Scheler met Amélie von Dewitz, an alluring woman eight years his senior, married and the mother of a child. Against her enticements his moral qualms gave way. The liaison seemed to come to an end when she returned to her home in Berlin and Scheler returned to Munich to begin his university studies. But just as the grasp of his intelligence began to quicken and was recognized by his fellow students and teachers, so too did his lusts spring forth. Brilliant and debauched by turns, able in one moment to engage in complex, elevated arguments and in the next to pursue the first women who met his eye, Scheler became too confused to devote himself to medical studies. Ridden with guilt and suffering at the breach of the tenets of his Catholic faith, by year's end Scheler had determined to take himself in hand, to find some clarity by studying ethical and moral philosophy, subjects for which he had shown considerable aptitude.

And this was in fact a pattern Scheler followed for the remainder of his life: the greater his moral transgressions the more he seemed compelled to turn, as in recompense, to the study of morality. Augustine is perhaps the greatest exemplar of this pattern. In none of Scheler's actions, however, was he able to reconcile the two extremes. The intellectual results were sometimes astonishing, however tortured the life.

Scheler left Munich and enrolled for his second year at the Univer-

sity of Berlin. He studied philosophy and sociology with Dilthey and
Simmel, went to the theater and saw the plays of Ibsen and Hauptmann, roamed the streets of the great industrial metropolis whose
mood and pace were the antithesis of countrified Munich, and of
course sought out and found Amélie von Dewitz. Doubtless her presence in Berlin influenced Scheler's move to that particular university.
After several months Dewitz divorced her husband, and Scheler, in an
apparently precipitate act, married her outside the church in a civil
ceremony. Henceforth he held to his faith unsteadily, vacillating between near abandonment and renewed affirmation until near the end
of his life when, in a period of acute crisis, he broke with the church
altogether.

Scheler decided to leave the city at the end of the year. Berlin re-
pelled him. The ruthless competition in the market that he saw everywhere, the zones of poverty and blight to which failures in the competitive struggle were consigned, the calculating outlook, self-
interestedness, impersonality, and strife of the inhabitants of the city—
all this seemed to him to be the very concentration of the evils of modern times, the place where his communitarian ideals were gravely en-
dangered. Scheler was hardly unique in this view. Many eminent
nineteenth- and twentieth-century figures of the most diverse political
and religious persuasions have assessed modernity in much the same
way. In part, the assessment is an expression of romantic nostalgia.
But in some part, too, the assessment is rooted, as was German romanticism generally, in the Lutheran ethos that had pervaded all of Germany and tinged Catholic Bavaria as well as secular Berlin. The spirit
of charity and brotherliness extolled by Luther and held to be embodied in close-knit, sanctified communities was believed by many to be
scarcely possible in the colossal enterprises of the modern world. Such
enterprises were, in their cold and mechanical operations, a kind of
living death that continually isolated human beings from one another.
Scheler's personal history surely made him receptive to this negative
view, and Berlin as a symbol of modernity very likely also stood as a
metaphor for his early family experiences. When in later years he was
able to formulate the view more fully, his personal involvement undoubtedly lent great passion to the formulation, but he spoke in a
voice that was authentically German—not only personally or as a
Catholic thinker—and was widely and enthusiastically heard as such.
Scheler in this respect stood alongside Weber, Tönnies, and countless
others as an inheritor of the Lutheran legacy.[7] In any case, it was his
encounter with Berlin, as much as with the sociologists at the univer-

sity, that awoke in Scheler a concern for social questions. But the university was of a piece with the city, emphasizing scientific subjects and positivist philosophy, and thus also not to Scheler's liking.

At the age of twenty-one, he set out for Jena with his wife and adopted daughter to study with the well-known moral philosopher, Rudolph Eucken. It was through Eucken's personal example as well as in his teachings that Scheler was to find his own vocation in philosophy and to begin to make his mark.

Eucken's aim was to discern the single, unchanging ground by which human life, in all its historical and cultural variety, is distinctly human.[8] This ground is metaphysical, Eucken taught, and consists of a realm of timeless spiritual values through which the meaning and unity of human life are derived. Historical periods, particular religions and cultures, personal experiences are so many different expressions of the one imperishable human spirit. The task of the philosopher is to find the permanent that is disguised within the flux, to see beyond any one of its incarnations the absolute itself. To this end the duty of the philosopher as a social being is critical: to assess the society and all the manifestations of value of his time against the transcendental values to which the society stands as a part to the whole. Indeed, after the First World War Eucken lectured widely in Europe and America on the spiritual unity of humankind in an effort to divert modern civilization from its self-destructive course. For this effort he was awarded the Nobel Peace Prize. This man, who sought to heal the breaches of modern life, adopted Scheler as his protégé.

Galvanized by Eucken's conceptions, perhaps also finding in them a source of relief from the guilt of his religious transgressions, Scheler completed his doctoral dissertation in a scant two years, in 1897 at the age of twenty-three. It was an extraordinary achievement. The topic of the dissertation was the relation of logic to ethics. Two years later, with the completion of his habilitation on the transcendental and psychological methods, he was admitted to the faculty of the University of Jena as a junior member and began to teach.[9]

In the two dissertations written under the influence of his teacher, Scheler began to sound out themes to which he returned many times in the course of his life. He retained Eucken's conception of an independent realm of values embodied in particular things and historical periods. But how, Scheler asked, are such values discerned? The truths of logic are qualities of judgments and are apprehended by our intellect. Values are qualities of things and apprehended only by the state of our feelings. It is through our feelings for things, in our loves and our hates, that we can glean their value. The logic of the heart, Scheler argued following Pascal, Augustine, and others, cannot be assimilated to the logic of the intellect; goodness and truth reside in entirely separate domains whose objects are incomparable. The scientific mentality that has encroached upon all aspects of modern life has threatened to obliterate the distinction between the domains by reducing psychology and philosophy merely to mechanistic principles, such as instincts, drives, and the like. What is required is a method truly congenial to the transcendental domain that will permit the objects of the spirit to be appreciated as they exist, independent of all psychophysical determinants. The nature of this method in Scheler's early treatment of it remained little more than a programmatic restatement of Eucken's view. Its clarification was to come later. However, the relations of the various domains to one another, of the emotions and the intellect, remained in his understanding as they were in his life, glimpsed but never fully ordered.

The intimate yet cosmopolitan milieu of Jena proved to be the natural element for the ardent young Scheler. His stimulating lectures and involvement in university life soon won him a circle of admirers. Word of the promising philosopher began to spread. In 1901 he was invited to a party in the nearby city of Halle, where he met another philosopher, Edmund Husserl, fifteen years Scheler's senior. The meeting was fateful, one that Scheler later was to recall as marking a turning point in his intellectual life.[10]

Scheler had been attempting, especially since his second book, to characterize the method through which spiritual objects are ascertained. He considered Eucken's version of the method to be inadequate, indeed, perilously close to psychophysical reductionism. In Eucken's view experience is limited to sensuous contents, which it is the philosopher's task to reconstruct into unified wholes. But such reconstructions, however well carried out, never yield moral objects, Scheler held, only further sensuous contents. Our intuitions of the world, our experiences, are actually far richer in their makeup than the sensuous elements of which they are only partly composed. Not until the concept of intuition was clarified, Scheler believed, would the method for which he was searching be found.

In discussing these matters with Husserl, Scheler discovered that he was speaking not only to a sympathetic intelligence but to a philosopher whose own work had proceeded along somewhat parallel lines. Husserl had to this point taken up the question of intuition mainly with respect to mathematical and logical objects. The characteristics of such objects, for example, the *necessity* and *universality* of the law of noncontradiction, can never be derived from our sensuous experiences of them alone, Husserl argued, for sensuous experiences are variable and therefore are relative. Each of us has had a history in which we have sooner or later come to learn that $2 \times 2 = 4$. But that history is independent of the logical certainty that $2 \times 2 = 4$. To understand the nature of a mathematical or logical intuition, therefore, the philosopher must eliminate from consideration all prior experiences and focus his attention exclusively on the intuition at hand. The causal—psychological or anthropological—analysis of experiences is obviously valuable for many purposes but irrelevant to phenomenology, which aims to investigate experiences—intuitions—as they are given immediately in our consciousness.

Scheler returned to Jena excited by his discussion with Husserl and determined to study his new friend's writings.[11] In them he would find an example that would be useful, if not fully assimilable, to his own concerns. For Husserl's ideal, from which he never wavered, was utterly rational, his approach analytical, and his manner that of sustained, ascetic devotion to scholarly tasks. To a nature as volatile as Scheler's, for whom nothing less than an all-embracing view would provide containment and stability, Husserl's path was far too rigorous and confining, however many genuinely new vistas it opened. It was in Bergson, whom Scheler had also begun to read at this time—amplified slightly later by study of Indian philosophy—that he discovered a breadth of vision and sensitivity, an aspiration to understand life in its fullness, that was much more akin to his own. Here was an openness to the world like that of the child, one that went far beyond the desire rationally to comprehend it, but stood ready, without judgment, to receive the world as it is. The natural aim of this inclination, with its many affinities to mysticism, is to surrender oneself to the variety and value of the world and to reach harmony and peace.[12]

As Scheler pondered these views, he began to think of intuition not as a method or set of procedures, nor as consisting of conceptual or symbolic processes. He wanted to resist submitting intuition to scientific and rational dogmas that disfigure the true nature of our experiences. Intuition is, he believed, an integral part of each of our experiences, from the most visceral to the most rarefied, in which we commune with things directly and behold their essences. Only by attending to the full range of our intuitions will we flower and the world become a garden for us all.

Scheler was to hold to these sentiments far beyond his phenomenological phase, express them in many different formulations, and yearn to overcome a sense of alienation all his life. Indeed, however disparate in subject matter and approach his works appear when considered together, the theme of an alienation to be overcome imparts a kind of coherence of mood to all of his works that makes of them a distinctive whole. Thus, Scheler initially put together his own view and his own particular brand of phenomenology from the teachings of Eucken, Husserl, and Bergson. Intuition is a central element along with values and emotions. The intellect, too, has an important place, but not a dominant one. All too soon, however, the period of burgeoning creativity was interrupted.

Scheler's marriage had from the beginning not been happy and in a few years had become filled with bitterness and recrimination. A son born to the Schelers did little to improve matters. The more Scheler tried to extricate himself from a worsening situation, the more possessive became his wife. One evening at a party attended by many university officials and faculty, Amélie Scheler, unable to contain her jealousy and anger, slapped the wife of Scheler's publisher and charged her with having an affair with Scheler. Whether the charge was true or not, the scandal of the public episode could not be smoothed over, and Scheler was forced to resign his post. Through Husserl's influence, however, he was able to find a new post at the University of Munich, his old school, which he took up in the fall of 1907.

For a short time almost all went well with Scheler. He again quickly gained a reputation as a popular teacher, lectured on ethics and psychology, and attracted an enthusiastic following of students. Munich was a larger and livelier city than Jena, with a well-developed tradition of artistic culture and scores of social circles in which intellectuals, artists, writers, and members of established society mixed. Still living with his wife, but in a state of increasing enmity, Scheler avidly entered the social life of the city where his brilliance, passion, and erotic charm, all coupled with an intense spirituality, made him a much sought-after guest. It was at one of these gatherings that he was to meet his future wife. But within two years of his move to Munich everything came tumbling down, and his life was to take a completely unanticipated course.

Under the burden of what had become an essentially nominal marriage, Amélie Scheler finally agreed to a separation. To the editor of the city's socialist newspaper she confided that her husband's many affairs and the debts he had accumulated to finance them had left her and the children penniless—in fact, destitute. The first of the stories was published in the fall of 1909. Scheler treated the accounts merely as malicious gossip and ignored them. The university, however, becoming alarmed at the scandal that was brewing, ordered a full-scale investigation. Scheler then sued the newspaper for libel. The newspaper's lawyers countered by recovering a hotel register that showed he had checked in with a woman, a shopgirl it turned out, whom he had passed off as his wife. (Rumors that he had borrowed money from students without repayment could not be substantiated but were also damaging.) The university requested Scheler's resignation. Far worse, by formal decree that declared him to be morally unfit, he was stripped of the right ever again to teach at a university in the German Empire. By 1910, after a promising start, Scheler's academic career was at an end. There have of course been notable American scholars—W. I. Thomas and Thorstein Veblen among them—who for similar reasons suffered a like fate.

Without money, job, tangible prospects, or hope of support from his long-estranged Munich family, Scheler moved to Göttingen, where Husserl had gathered around him a lively group of young phenomenologists. Their roster now reads like a who's who of the founding circle of phenomenology—Hedwig Conrad-Martius, Theodor Conrad, Moritz Geiger, Jean Hering, Roman Ingarden, Fritz Kaufmann, Alexandre Koyré, Adolph Reinach, Edith Stein. In Munich he left behind Maerit Furtwaengler whom he loved and would later marry. But at the heart of the phenomenological movement in Göttingen he might find a place; even if he could not teach at a university, he could maintain scholarly contacts and through these, perhaps, find a way again to earn a living. He moved in with a friend, Dietrich von Hildebrand, who had gone off a year earlier to study with Husserl. Von Hildebrand, loyal and eager to help, set out to rent a hall and round up students to whom Scheler could lecture privately for a fee.

Phenomenology was a bold philosophical undertaking that sought an enduring foundation for all of consciousness and therefore did not look for its end in natural causes, which are contingent and unstable, or in history, which consists of a welter of arbitrary standpoints. The prize was to be found only by searching consciousness itself, penetrating to its innermost recesses, extracting its ingredients, and testing its qualities and structure. Anything not essential to consciousness proper, not immanent to any consciousness, would be ruthlessly discarded. Phenomenology in this sense was to be a "first science" that would ground and illuminate each of the sciences. For as the sciences consist of knowledge, they too are a vein of consciousness and share with each other consciousness certain common features. But phenomenology was also to be a "first science" in the sense that this effort, foreshadowed by thinkers in the past, particularly Descartes and Kant, had never before been undertaken with as much clarity of purpose and rigor of means.

In the excited atmosphere of the Göttingen group, generated by the daring and novelty of its intellectual venture and heightened by attacks from rival philosophical quarters, Scheler rose like a new star. It was not simply that he was enthusiastic—everyone in the group was enthusiastic—but that the reach and subtlety of his thought seemed to encircle vast regions of human experience that Husserl, until then preoccupied with sifting rational structures, had as yet hardly touched. Scheler turned his sights to the phenomenological aspects of communal relations, friendships, valuations, love, shame, and hate as well as knowledge. Beyond such academic questions, Scheler dwelt on personal and social issues that were troubling Germans and Europeans in general at the time—the dislocations, loneliness, anxieties, and doubts of the modern experience—and evoked in his audience a powerful emotional response, which spurred him to animate his views with electrifying intensity. Unbound by the constraints of a formal academic manner, he thundered freely on the themes of the restoration of man and human solidarity—in the rented lecture hall, at private gatherings and clubs, in cafés, and on the streets. He created a sensation in Göttingen and left an unforgettable mark.[13]

But perhaps this very success worked against him. Husserl, for one, was not dazzled and remained aloof. Scheler was all glitter and flash, he felt, and merely leaped at insights when painstaking labor was required for lasting results. To be sure, there was some truth in Husserl's views, yet for all Scheler's disorderliness and unworkmanlike manner, he caught glimpses of things that more deliberate quarrying might never reach. Indeed, Husserl's gaze was steadfastly trained on a timeless vision, and in the bulk of his path-breaking work he remained programmatic; whereas Scheler, notwithstanding many a sidelong glance at eternity, was deeply engaged in the life of his time and in each of his works attempted to take its measure. The two men were separated by differences in temperament and stance that were perhaps too great ever to be fully joined.[14] The sordid aroma of the recent Munich affair clung to Scheler also and to a character as sternly moralistic as Husserl would be forever repellent. Perhaps most serious, Scheler was beginning to attract many of Husserl's followers, and even slight signs of a shift in their leanings were likely seen by Husserl as a personal betrayal and a threat to the further development of the phenomenological movement he was struggling to build. There was no place for Scheler in Göttingen. After six months he returned to Munich.

Scheler was now at a crossroad. The loss of Husserl's confidence must have been especially defeating. Husserl's authority, which he had too obviously challenged, remained intact, and Scheler's last ties to an intellectual community were severed. But although deeply shaken, he was not left entirely without resources. He had won an undoubted mastery of a complex subject matter, a modest intellectual reputation, and not least, devoted friends and a new love. In 1911, set adrift, but helped by his friends and Furtwaengler without whose support he may well have foundered, Scheler attempted to put the pieces of his life together and strike out in a fresh direction. He turned to free-lance writing and continued in this line for several years. It was a career that would culminate in his becoming a national figure with a large and eager following.

By the end of the first year of free-lance work Scheler had completed several essays, including a book-length essay that was translated into English in 1961 as *Ressentiment.*[15] This book brought him to the attention of a wider literate public and earned the praise of Werner Sombart and Ernst Troeltsch, among the leading historians and philosophers in Germany. Troeltsch called him the "Catholic Nietzsche," and in this epithet irony and admiration were combined. Irony, for Nietzsche was one of the most famous atheists of the nineteenth century, *the* anti-Christ by his own proud admission, whereas Scheler held up Christianity as the highest of values. But admiration too, for on the subject of *ressentiment* at which Nietzsche had fired a savage and brilliant blast twenty-five years earlier, Scheler now leveled his own attack, equally brilliant, equally deadly. Troeltsch's paradoxical praise served to make the book and the man who wrote it all the more intriguing.

The originality of Scheler's study lay in his analysis of the social origins of *ressentiment* and the variety and extent of its manifestations. He kept the main feature of Nietzsche's account of *ressentiment* as a negative sentiment expressed by persons who aim to devalue, but at the same time secretly covet, the achievements of others. The English term "sour grapes" conveys the meaning of *ressentiment* precisely. Several factors in combination, he observed, produce this negative sentiment. One factor is a continual repression of emotions associated with revenge, hatred, malice, envy, and spite. Such emotions by themselves are normal parts of human nature. When not released—say, by the shaking of a fist, verbal abuse, an act that is genuinely avenging, or work that acquires the envied possession—the emotions course through the psyche with an explosive potential that grows with each addition to their store. It is possible that by an act of true forgiveness a desire for vengeance, for example, will be morally conquered and the corresponding emotions checked. But when the emotions are powerful and joined to a sense of impotence, to the feeling that they cannot be expressed because of physical or mental weakness or fear, *ressenti-ment* will erupt. *Ressentiment* is thus the attitude of weaker parties who place themselves on the same level as their injurer.

The psychological state favorable to *ressentiment* will spread inexorably, Scheler maintained, with the discrepancy between the social standing of a group and its factual power. *Ressentiment* will be slight in a democracy that is social as well as political and has promoted a certain equalization of property among its members. Very much the same is true of a society of castes, such as India, in which the prerogatives and position of each caste are fixed. But in his own society, Scheler argued, and indeed throughout the West, *ressentiment* is rampant. In the societies of the West, which emphasize the formal equality of their members, there are nevertheless vast substantive differences in achievement of wealth, power, honor, and prestige, and these achievements too are valued or they would not be sought. Consequently, although one is encouraged to compare oneself with others, the comparisons are frequently unfavorable. To those who fall short the discrepancies are more keenly felt the more permanent they appear to be—among members of political parties confined solely to an opposition role, among groups such as women who feel their low standing as a destiny, among the aged who can no longer compete with the young, among the physically and mentally handicapped, among all persons and groups who believe their very existence is an injury and calls out for revenge.

It seems that no action will relieve the crushing sense of inferiority that is the outcome of such comparisons. However, two responses may lighten the pain. The first is an attitude of resignation to one's lot in life. Persons who select this alternative are linked to society not merely as lesser parts, Scheler argued, but also as full-fledged members, for they share with others the general standards that allow particular value judgments of each one's lot to be made. Partaking in a social and moral entity greater than themselves enables such persons to bestow value upon the things of the world, including their own meager qualities, and be sustained. The choice of resignation requires at minimum a stable scale of values. But in the modern societies of the West, captivated by an ideal of progress that converts each attainment into a mere way station, a means to another receding end, virtually all scales of value have become transitory. The first alternative is therefore scarcely possible any longer.

The other alternative is an attitude that belittles the qualities against which one has been compared, lowers all values to the level of one's abilities, and seeks to construct an illusory scale of values—as Scheler put it—in keeping with one's wishes and goals. Yet, while providing immediate relief, this attitude of *ressentiment* begins a process of self-isolation and embitterment that—if a blocked impulse for revenge is involved—may lead to withering away and death. Minor officials, artisans, and petty bourgeoisie are more susceptible to *ressentiment* than the proletariat, Scheler believed, since these groups are more powerless. *Ressentiment* is a prominent feature of modern bourgeois societies, Scheler concluded, generated by their very structure, shattering the solidarity of their members and overturning their most cherished values.

Scheler's analysis was, in part, directed to Nietzsche's charge that "the most delicate flower of *ressentiment*" had bloomed as the idea of Christian love—an idea whose covert purpose in elevating the weak was to exact vengeance on the strong.[16] Nietzsche's error, Scheler argued, was to confound the true meaning of Christian love with its degraded form, its transvaluation, in the modern age. Genuine Christian love is an expression of values not sensual but spiritual; their measure cannot be taken by worldly standards of any kind. The modern love of humanity, on the other hand, has assimilated the concern with salvation into the concern with material well-being. Although masquerading as a pure passion of the heart, the leveling sweep of humanitarian love as well as the abstract character of its object—not persons, observed Scheler, but a category of persons—betray another, nonloving impulse at work. When seeking its climax in a socialism that would annihilate the powerful and rich in order to transfer their holdings to the poor, the hate to which such love has been secretly coupled from the beginning, and thus the *ressentiment* of which it is in large part animated, stands revealed. Nietzsche's view, in Scheler's judgment, is applicable to humanitarianism and its various offshoots, but not to Christianity.

The humanitarian and Christian attitudes have nothing in common, Scheler declared. The spiritual values extolled by Christianity involve no diminution of any kind, nothing that resembles the cost-accounting mentality that reckons one's gain against another's loss. The act of Christian love is a reaching out to persons poor and sick of soul by nobler beings whose love is freely given in full confidence of its inexhaustible abundance and strength. The exemplary manifestation of such love was the descent of the deity to man in the palpable form of the Savior. Because spiritual values reside on a higher plane than material values, Christianity properly understood could be, indeed was, integrated with little conflict into the aristocratic societies of medieval times. Moreover, Christianity recognizes a hierarchy of spirit in the distinction between the saved and the damned. To speak of Christian socialism or communism in a worldly sense, insisted Scheler, is a contradiction of terms. Christianity in its full intention aims at a solidarity of spirit, a participation in the invisible kingdom of God. But with the appearance of an egoistic individualism heralding the rise of the bourgeois age, medieval society as well as Christian values were subverted, and in their stead was erected an illusory value conception limited solely to this world. The gauging of each individual's worth exclusively in earthly terms has been the breeding ground of a *ressentiment* that will end in defaming the world and all its values. Thus in his first important work did Scheler sum up his time.

Scheler did not offer specific remedies for *ressentiment*—he limited himself to criticism. Although his view of Christianity derived from Catholic sources, he was no mere Catholic apologist. He was alert, for example, to the lurking *ressentiment* of priests who, because they must show a face of unflagging love to the world, are prohibited from expressing their hate. Nor did he yearn nostalgically for a return to medieval life. The medieval age—however dubious his characterization of it—was over and done with, passed into history. The most pressing need of modern life, in his view, was to restore humanity's spiritual and moral solidarity. To this end, an understanding of the true order of values was indispensable, would indeed help point the way.

Scheler's voice was not the only one in Europe raised in criticism and alarm. In France, Émile Durkheim had for decades been warning of the pathologies of modern life in terms somewhat akin to Scheler's, through analyses of an individualism that was veering towards egoism and the weakening of normative orders. Scheler did not know Durkheim's work at this time and was unsympathetic to the positivism of the French sociologist when he later became acquainted with his writings. In any case, Scheler's treatment of the generation and release of *ressentiment* tapped deep experiential dimensions of this negative sentiment, which made his analysis more resonant with a wide, educated public.

With this one stroke Scheler gained national recognition as a social critic of power and promise. He thus joined a growing number of intellectuals—theologians of several faiths, political theorists of the Right and the Left, expressionist playwrights and painters, mystic poets—who, despite their differences, had in common a revulsion at what they deemed to be the moral decay of their age. For this was a time—two years before the start of the First World War—when the rumbling discontent of preceding decades was beginning to flare into open, barely contained enmities among nations, classes, and political and religious groups, a time when a mood of apprehension and bewilderment was sweeping across Europe, a time searching to make sense of itself and thus ripe for the favorable reception of Scheler's book.

Encouraged by his success, Scheler decided to move with Maerit to Berlin where opportunities for free-lance writing were more plentiful and access to a large cosmopolitan community was virtually assured. He also hoped that Sombart would help him find an academic post—the only one of his hopes not realized until the war was over and Wilhelmine Germany dissolved. Just before embarking he divorced Amélie Scheler and regained religious legitimacy by marrying Maerit Furtwaengler, in December 1912, in the Catholic church near the University of Munich. He was in the ascending phase of the cycle around which he moved all his life, having swung from disgrace and banishment to rectitude and acclaim.

If Munich was renowned as the "arts city" of Germany, Berlin had become by 1912 one of the major intellectual and commercial capitals of Europe, attracting scholars, students, artists, and businessmen from all parts of the globe. Scheler's second sojourn in the metropolis was utterly unlike the first. Now he entered as a mature man of the world, self-confident and ready to act. He quickly made his way through the clamor of the city to find those persons whose communitarian ideals, like his own, were religiously and spiritually framed. Among his new associates who would achieve international repute were Max Brod, perhaps best known today in Anglo-American countries for introducing Franz Kafka to the world; Martin Buber, the Jewish theologian and utopianist; Gustav Landauer, the anarcho-Communist later assassinated and chiefly remembered as a martyr to the Communist ideal; Georg Lukács, the Hungarian aesthetician and philosopher; Werner Sombart, the economist and social critic; Ernst Troeltsch, the Protestant theologian and historian; and, peripherally, Max Weber, teaching at Heidelberg and already famous as a scholar of religion and politics. Scheler was accepted by these men on an equal footing, as someone who had much to say. Again he had found a worthy community of which to be a part.

Sustained by his Berlin friends as he had been sustained by Eucken almost twenty years earlier, Scheler's creative energies were fired into a blaze of writing and speaking that hardly again diminished, even after he left Berlin, until his death. Within weeks he had contracted to write for several journals on a wide variety of philosophical and social topics. The themes he had begun to develop in *Ressentiment,* the several perspectives he had blended together and employed with such facility, reappeared in practically everything he wrote. In addition to many articles and reviews, in his first year in Berlin he published two monographs that were to solidify his standing as a philosopher and link his name more prominently to phenomenology than Husserl's.

The first of his studies, *The Nature of Sympathy*,[17] was a subtle, penetrating analysis of identification, empathy, vicarious feeling, fellow feeling, emotional infection, egoism, love, and hate, and the bearing of these psychological states on ethical and social life. The book remained for many years a source of inspiration for kindred investigations by other scholars.[18]

The second, far more ambitious work, the first part of *Formalism in Ethics and Non-formal Ethics of Values*,[19] was an attempt to clarify the scale of values to which he had referred in his other books and found dangerously obscured in the modern West. Here Scheler went much farther than he had gone under Eucken. He still held to the conception of a realm of values, immutable and eternal, that can be grasped by the emotions but are not emotions themselves. The elements of this realm are ordered by two principles. The first is a principle of generality according to which the narrowest values of pleasure, pertaining to organisms, stand at the lowest point of the scale and the most encompassing values of the holy, pertaining to the universe, at the highest. The second, a principle of energy, is the inverse of the first. According to this principle, values of least energy stand at the highest point of the scale and values of most energy at the lowest. Pleasure impels us with the mightiest force but does not take us very far. For the more general the values, the greater the range of ethical conduct they can guide. To act under the direction of higher values thus requires a painful sacrifice of the lower ones—as was revealed with incomparable fullness by the Buddha, Scheler observed, in his meditations on suffering thousands of years ago. But this truth is accessible to human beings the world over, for no one is exempt from suffering, in the experience of which preference for a higher value and loss of a lower one are always to be found. Each age has its own perspective, in terms of which it interprets the hierarchy of values that towers above us all. Yet the structure of values and their various modes can be seen, however incompletely, by each of us. Each perspective yields a partial truth, an aspect of values that would not be possible if the full truth and independence of values were not to exist. Values and their hierarchy, therefore, are not merely subjective, a matter of value judgments, nor are they relative, based solely on historical experience. However, confusion of the goods through which values are realized with the values themselves, or inflation of a lower value to occupy the entire realm of values, produces disorientation and impairs our ability to act ethically. Both types of malaise have afflicted the West. The great surge of vitality that propels modern industry to its stupendous growth and the positive sciences to their conquest of nature—all this is important and of value, to be sure, but not the be-all and end-all of values as so many proclaim. Vital values have triumphed in the West, without doubt, but at the expense of the spirit. The triumph is a hollow one. A similar complaint over the spiritual nullity of modern life was made by Weber ten years earlier in the concluding pages of *The Protestant Ethic and the Spirit of Capitalism*[20] and is heard in many quarters today. Scheler's *Ethics*, the second part of which was published in 1916, was the most systematic of his efforts and central to his thinking for many years. It adumbrated themes that occupied much of his later work on the philosophy of religion and the sociology of knowledge.

Also foreshadowed in Scheler's *Ethics* was a rudimentary notion of the cybernetic ordering of elements in a system (the "realm of values") in which elements higher in information but lower in energy, spiritual values, govern elements lower in information but higher in energy, pleasure values. Analogous conceptions of the influence of values upon social conduct were developed by several of Scheler's contemporaries, notably Durkheim, who viewed morality as the disciplining agent of desire, and Weber, who analyzed religious orientations as constraining the scope of rationalization of economic and practical activity. A more nearly cybernetic view was developed by Freud, who cast the informed ego as moderating the blind id—comparable to a discerning but weak rider controlling a powerful horse. Each of these scholars apparently proceeded independently of the others. More recently, an explicit cybernetic conception, in some ways parallel to Scheler's, was elaborated by Talcott Parsons, in which normative culture is conceived to be at the apex of the system of social action, shaping and guiding all the other elements—in descending order of "information," these are the social, personality, and behavioral systems.[21] (Selections from Scheler's *Sympathy* and *Ethics* are included in the present volume.)

When war was declared in August 1914, Scheler, like many Germans, responded with patriotic ardor. Forty years old and having astigmatic vision, he rushed to enlist and was, of course, rejected. He then turned to the nearest weapon, his pen, and dashed off a fiery essay entitled "The Genius of War." The war, he urged, was the mechanism through which the community of Europe, long torn and in agony, could be made whole again. Against the autocratic eastern Christendom of Russia, the utilitarian egoism of England, and the corrupt rationalism of France, Germany with its penchant for the spirit would rise and prevail—an attitude not uncommon in the fervid atmosphere of the day. Scheler's essay, however, shocked certain of his friends, pacifists like Brod, Buber, and Landauer, who had met with Scheler only a few days before the essay appeared and apparently received Scheler's agreement—at least, tacit agreement—with their pacifist views. Scheler's deception was an unconscionable breach of trust that estranged these friends from him ever after.[22]

By October 1914 it was clear the war was no short-lived skirmish but likely to be protracted. Over the next two months Scheler expanded his brief essay into a book of several hundred pages that was published under the same title early in the following year.[23] By spring of 1915 Scheler's name was known in every educated household in Germany. Within weeks his book reached heights of popularity that no other book on the war, among the many hundreds written—some by notable authors—would achieve. Although he had forsaken an intimate circle of friends, he was now nationally famous.

It is doubtful that Scheler intended this outcome, however much he welcomed it. He certainly could not have anticipated that he would become famous, but wrote the book in an effusion of feeling he was unable to contain. The book is a peculiar document whose tone—as distinct from its contents—is unlike anything Scheler had written before or would write again. It fit in well, of course, with the mentality of the times. And, as usual with everything Scheler wrote, it contains insights into what we might call questions of national culture. But the book is utterly unrestrained, not so much impassioned as frenzied. An emotional outburst teeming with grotesque metaphors, it pictures war as part of the natural metabolism of social life, with the power to cleanse and to heal, to bring forth the spirit and to make nations and men one. This savage rhapsody was not merely evidence of an emotional infection caught from the nation's mood; the book exacerbated the nation's mood. The tone of the book reveals—to use Scheler's language—that the lowest, coarsest elements within him had overpowered the sublimated elements of intellect and spirit and were masquerading in their guise. He continued the moral descent begun with the disgraceful deception of his friends, shattering that intimate community he had so often held up as his most prized earthly ideal; with the essay and the book he plunged more deeply into the negative side of his nature, compelled to destroy and reveling in the destruction at the same time.

Because of the acclaim the book received and Scheler's reputation as an inspirational speaker, the German Foreign Office invited him to join their propaganda department.[24] He took up the work with zeal. His lectures to officers, common soldiers, prisoners of war, and German nationals in Austria, Switzerland, and Holland were highly effective in maintaining morale. But although he continued to work as a propagandist to the end of the war, his views soon began to change. For if the loss of a lower value produces suffering, the loss of a higher value is nevertheless a loss and must also bring suffering in its train. Increasingly gripped by remorse, Scheler slipped away in the winter of 1915 to a retreat at the Benedictine abbey of Beuron. There he confessed and took up again the sacraments of the church.[25]

Purified, Scheler returned to the fray, but no longer to sing the praise of war. His second book on the war was published in 1916, the same year the concluding portion of his *Ethics* appeared.[26] He did not recant the first book. And he directed several sharp blows against France. But his attitude toward war—not merely this war, but war in general—was completely reversed. War was a destructive force, pure and simple, in which no hope for spiritual rebirth could be found. Moreover, Germany must bear with the other nations of Europe full responsibility for the destruction released. Europe was, in truth, more like a family in discord for which assignment of blame to this member or that was far less important than reconciliation. The only hope for lasting harmony in Europe was for each nation to repent and affiliate with the others in a supranational community founded on principles of Christian solidarity.[27] This did not mean socialism, of course, for socialism was no more than the nether side of capitalism, bound inextricably to the very bourgeois outlook that was at the root of all the trouble—as Scheler had pointed out in his earlier study of *ressentiment*. Chastened and penitent himself, Scheler was in quest of the spirit for all of Europe, a pacific quest in keeping with spiritual ideals. He reiterated and expanded these themes in several essays published during the remaining years of the war. With the aim of facilitating a larger catharsis than he had undergone, he also wrote on features of German life that had brought the nation to its present crisis. The maladies afflicting Germany, he said, were caused by antithetical impulses embedded in the German character: one was a wild grasping for power, the other a love for the highest planes of culture. The first was blind, the second weak. Only when the two were connected, when the love of culture was infused with power, would power be tamed and culture be able to guide. To join these disparate impulses, he insisted, must be the paramount task of Germany in the years ahead.[28] Scheler's analysis was hardly the first along such lines, but was among the more poignant. For despite his antipathy to his own time, his alienation and restlessness, his metaphysical searching, Scheler was deeply and obviously identified with Germany and thus speaking of himself as well; this made his criticisms more acceptable to Germans and even welcomed by the many who were beginning to feel tremors of doubt and remorse themselves. In his writings on the German character Scheler touched on matters that he would more fully explore in his later work on the sociology of culture and again in the last phase of his work on the philosophy of man. He was on the rise again.

It is difficult for those of us who did not live through the period to appreciate the many senses of ending and beginning that were felt by the participants of the First World War and its aftermath. The sheer magnitude of the conflict—involving each nation in Europe but tiny Switzerland—brought to an end a hundred years of general peace and marked the beginning of an awareness, resisted of course by xeno-phobes of every national stripe, that the Continent itself was an entity and that no nation in Europe could henceforth stand alone, solitary and independent of the others. The new weapons of war, the guns, tanks, planes, and bombs, and not least, the psychological weapons of propaganda that Scheler himself took some part in wielding, meant that for the first time in the memory of Europeans vast civilian popu-lations were as vulnerable to the machinery of destruction as the actual combatants, and that the old, honorable distinction between warriors and innocents, not often fully observed but always believed in, was for all practical purposes at an end. The periods just preceding the war and immediately following, so often contrasted in novels, plays, and films as periods of innocence and awakening or of illusion and disillu-sion—Mann's *Magic Mountain,* Schnitzler's *Hands Around,* Hesse's *Demian,* Renoir's *Grand Illusion*—meant that the old view of things was dead and that a new view—whether from the Right or the Left— was about to be born.

Scheler's view of the path to be taken by Europeans—neither the materialistic egoism prominent up to now in the West, nor the me-chanical collectivism emerging in the East—was a third way, put in religious terms, yet with several affinities to the secular outlook of the new coalition government installed in Weimar in 1918. Scheler wanted the individual to be elevated to the highest rank and at the same time fully to recognize his responsibilities to his fellows. This meant, partic-ularly in Germany, that each person must become as broadly culti-vated as possible, not trained merely in a narrow technical specialty, as had been the practice for many decades, but educated in general intellectual culture as well. Through the promulgation of common cul-tural ideals, he believed, a spirit of unity would be fostered, and it was precisely a *spirit* of unity that was prerequisite to the realization of unity in other spheres. The men of Weimar, whose government was beset by grave economic, political, and social dilemmas and on shaky grounds from the outset, perhaps dreamed above all of establishing a republic of reason whose citizens would understand the complexities of the world and be able to rule themselves. The neologism "Republicans of Reason" (*Vernunftrepublikaner*), which quickly became the catchword for many of the supporters of the Weimar government, was a compound of the ancient Greek term for the state, famous since Plato, and the modern term for universality, enshrined in the German consciousness since Kant—a difficult catchword to resist for a philosopher. Scheler soon established friendships with several members of the new government—including Walther Rathenau, the foreign minister—and endeavored to impart to their moderately socialist and liberal views elements of spiritual understanding.

The efforts to rebuild Germany after the war did not mean exactly the same things in each part of the nation. In Cologne the large Catholic population looked askance at the state-run universities, secular and irreligious, at which the young were enrolling in such great numbers. To provide a suitable education for their sons several Catholic businessmen decided to finance the reopening of the city's ancient university, shut down since the Napoleonic Wars a century before. Max Scheler, a prodigal returned to the fold and thus loved more than any who had never strayed, eloquent spokesman for Germany, intellectual of the first rank and philosopher of eminence, was a natural choice for their faculty. He was invited in 1919 to join the Sociological Institute of the University of Cologne as one of its major professors. His immediate colleagues were Hugo Lindemann, an outspoken socialist, and Leopold von Wiese, an equally outspoken liberal. Scheler was promised the first chair in philosophy as soon as the faculty was developed. The earlier ban against him was forgotten, closed off by the war years and Scheler's subsequent rise to fame. After a hiatus of nine years, Scheler was on the academic platform again.

And he taught as never before. He established himself quickly as a popular teacher and become a favorite at the intellectual and artistic salons of the city's leading families. He traveled widely throughout Germany, lecturing to large university audiences on educational, religious, and social topics. The Catholic Intellectual Union sponsored Scheler's lecture tours in the belief that he would help close the gap between Catholic and non-Catholic scholars, grown so wide since the war years that Catholic scholars were in danger of being cut off from the larger intellectual community of which they desired to be a part.[29]

But Scheler's learning and credentials would raise the level of Catholic discussion and let him reach a much wider audience to present the Catholic views on the issues of the day. So the Union hoped and in this was for a time not disappointed.

One of the most heated issues concerned the prospects of socialism, whose various strands—Marxist, trade unionist, parliamentarian—were claiming the allegiance of ever greater numbers of people from each of the social classes in Germany as well as the other nations of Europe. The heat was generated by hostilities between Right and Left, literally murderous in intensity, and by bitter factional disputes within the Right and the Left no less murderous in effect. In January 1919 Rosa Luxemburg and Karl Liebknecht, leaders of the radical Communist group Spartacus, were murdered by government troops. In February of the same year Kurt Eisner, prime minister of Bavaria, was also murdered, his killer a student of aristocratic background. Violence, a general strike, and the proclaiming of the Bavarian Soviet Republic were the immediate response, crushed with unbridled ferocity in two months' time by government troops. Scheler's former friend Gustav Landauer, the pacifist writer, was a victim of the violence, beaten to death in a jail cell in May 1919 by government soldiers. Nor did the murdering end with the quelling of the rebellion; only after 1922, when Walther Rathenau was shot to death by a band of youthful right-wing assassins, did it begin to subside. For a few years thereafter political life was quieter. By the time the Nazis began to stir up new turbulence, Scheler himself was dead of natural causes.

Into the storm of 1919 Scheler let fly a burst of lectures, essays, and books that were both controversial and influential. The German bishops had declared in an episcopal letter early in the year that to be for socialism was to "oppose Christ." [30] Scheler believed the bourgeois epoch was practically moribund, and given the mood of postwar Europeans a socialism of some type would very likely take its place. But which type would it be? A socialism of the Marxist type, he warned again, would reduce the variety of Europeans to one and give to this one full possession of the "real factors" of social life, the economy, which up to now had driven it. But Marxist socialism would leave Europeans bereft of the "ideal factors" of social life, morality, which alone could be their guide. To take the route of Marxism, moreover, would be to continue the violence of which Europeans had had enough. Genuine harmony could be achieved, he implored, not by reducing but by synthesizing the diversity of European culture. Socialism as well as Christianity, the outlook of each class and each nation, must contribute to the whole, and from the joint perspective the values of cooperation and individuality alike would be upheld. A synthesis of European culture would require a socialism of an altogether different type from the Marxist, such as a prophetic socialism, led by exemplary men whose high moral attainments would serve both to inspire their followers and to express their deepest aspirations.[31]

Drawing upon his ethical studies, Scheler sketched a typology of exemplary leaders.[32] Each type represented a point on the eternal scale of values. Each pair in turn, the leader and the values he represented, was associated with a distinct form of social life. The saint gave expression to values of the holy and appeared in corporate, churchly societies. The sage gave expression to values of the intellect and appeared in differentiated, complex societies. The hero gave expression to values of vitality and appeared in tight-knit, organic communities. Finally, the connoisseur gave expression to values of pleasure and appeared in kinship or tribal groups.

Notwithstanding the enormous differences in viewpoint and idiom between, say, Greek philosopher and Indian guru, each personified intellectual values and was equally a sage. The guru was often more, for when he exemplified in word and deed the values of the holy he was also a saint (*homo religiosus*). Several orders of value could thus be embodied in one person. But the inverse was also true; several persons could embody the same order of value. For of heroes there could be many—military, athletic, professional, civic, and so on—each representing the chief vital value of his community. The more inclusive the value represented, the less bound was the leader to his origins and in his affect. Peasant *or* aristocrat could become saints for the entire society; the aristocrat alone could become a connoisseur for members of his class. In any group or class, Scheler believed, the *perfected* personality would hold all the orders of value within his own being, and as each was called forth the lower ones would give way, sacrificed to the demands of the higher.[33]

There were several points of resemblance between Scheler's conception of exemplary leadership and Weber's conception of charismatic leadership, but also marked differences. Charismatic as well as exemplary leaders professed values at the highest pitch. But the charismatic leader was a revolutionary who transformed the normative order and some part of the values of a society. His was a creative response to situations that had shaken the meaning of the concerns greatest to humankind—life, birth, suffering, evil, death—and his effort was to set the meaning aright by shifting the grounds on which it was understood. The role played by the Old Testament prophets in the history of the Jews provided Weber with a powerful, if partial, illustration of his thesis.[34] The exemplary leader, on the other hand, was often not a revolutionary at all. He served to sustain, to strengthen a moral order; rarely did he endeavor to change it. His too was a creative act, but one that brought to a pure focus and thus confirmed values that already existed. Whether the exemplary leader was responding to a situation, to the welling-up of his own gifts, or to the intervention of God remained obscure in Scheler's analysis, although he provided many telling but fleeting illustrations of his general thesis. Charismatic and exemplary leaders were thus essentially the opposite of one another in their affect. Indeed, Weber made very much the same distinction, but paid scant attention to the exemplary types in comparison to Scheler's more elaborate treatment.

Yet the language Scheler used in describing the desirable future, "prophetic socialism," evokes an Old Testament image. When the image was coupled to the transformative role the leader was to play—not merely to express, but to synthesize European culture—Scheler was speaking in Weber's accent, and the exemplary leader merged into the charismatic. For Scheler too dreamed of revolution as so many of his time did—in his case a bloodless one, but not less sweeping in its arc.

Scheler was, however, not sanguine about the prospects. Everything hinged on the right kinds of leaders, and there were no such leaders that he could see forthcoming. The need for leadership was particularly acute among the young, who were being attracted to new, "salvationary" groups—psychoanalytic sects, religious socialists, Communists, solidarists, Rudolph Steiner's Anthroposophists, Stefan George's circle (in which Simmel and Weber had an interest), among many others. But in Scheler's view, many of these groups were being led by "false prophets."[35] He was not alone in this view. From the sardonic cartoons of Georg Grosz to the pessimistic pronouncements of the more sober minds in Germany—Weber, Troeltsch, Meinecke, and Rathenau among them—the likelihood of responsible leadership seemed slender. Scheler agreed with Weber that scholars in their professional capacities must not yield to the demands for political leadership made of them from every side, but hold fast to their duties to investigate, to explore alternatives, to analyze, and to weigh. He was not speaking as a mere evangel of the church or of Catholic creed. He was a Christian, of course, and had preferences, but he was also a scholar, a German, and a European, and he welcomed anything—such as the League of Nations—that promised to foster the growth of a cosmopolitan spirit.[36] The theme of reconciling the warring tendencies of modern life continued to haunt Scheler to the end.

Of the books Scheler published in this period the most notable was a collection of essays on the philosophy of religion entitled *On the Eternal in Man,* which has remained a subject of commentary by religious thinkers to the present day.[37] He also taught a course on morality and politics at the Institute of Political Studies in Berlin, founded in the early years of the Weimar republic. The institute, at which Scheler was one of the first teachers, opened as an evening school with 120 students and quickly became popular. Among its faculty were Theodor Heuss, Arnold Wolfers, and Hans Simon in political science, Albert Salomon in sociology, Sigmund Neumann and Franz Neumann in journalism and law, and Hajo Holborn in history. Charles Beard, Nicholas Murray Butler, G. P. Gooch, and André Siegfried also lectured there. By 1932 the institute had two thousand students. It was taken over in 1933 by Joseph Goebbels.[38]

Given the shattered postwar times, Scheler was received well, admired perhaps as much for the courage and dedication with which he presented his ecumenical views as for the views themselves. But he had severe critics too. From the Left it was charged that Scheler was a mere utopian lost in the mists of his own fabrications. For the political and economic troubles of Europe he offered empty spiritual balm when a concrete plan of action and organization was needed.[39] More difficult to answer was the observation that the exemplary leaders of which he spoke were responsible only to their conscience, their nation, and God, and if their conscience failed, they could as well become demogogues as saints. Scheler was aware of the danger and warned of it often, but could provide no sure safeguards against its occurrence. As a republican of reason he could only call for responsible leadership, hardly guarantee it. As an academic he could help provide the knowledge and discipline required for responsible leadership but had little control over their use. His response resembled the morally rigorous view Weber presented in his famous speech of 1918, "Science as a Vocation," and greeted in much the same way: with approval from those in whom a similar moral chord was touched, with jeers from those who could be satisfied with nothing less than an absolute answer.[40]

Scheler's single-minded preoccupation with spiritual questions was not only an intellectual response to the dissolution he saw about him. He was caught at a point on the wheel that had already passed its apex and begun to descend, and he struggled to halt and if possible reverse its downward course. He had a good and loving, although childless, marriage. He had rapidly become an esteemed member of the university. He had established friendships with several of the citizens of Cologne. And not least, he had become a star in the Catholic intellectual community. But even in his first year in Cologne, in the flush of his newfound success, the old torments reappeared. At a social gathering in which he held forth with his usual brilliance and charm, his eye caught the rapt gaze of a beautiful dark-haired young woman, twenty-six years his junior. Her name was Maria Scheu; she was a student at the university. He soon began a flirtation with her so blatant that it shocked the other guests and outraged his hostess, who later warned him that his behavior was not only offensive but he risked a scandal that could ruin his marriage and career. He attempted to desist. He threw himself into his work. He increased his travels—a diversionary maneuver, no doubt, but also a possible opportunity for more discreet assignations. None of his efforts succeeded. The strain of trying to curb his impulses began to tell. From the sparkling conversationalist who enlivened many a gathering, he turned into an unpredictable guest, breaking into the flow of discussion with sudden monologues on obscure theological subjects, falling into depressed silences. He was sorely troubled and sought the counsel of intimate friends and a priest. He fought with himself for three years. His last efforts snapped with the death of his close friend Rathenau.[41]

Rathenau was in many respects a mirror image of Scheler. An emancipated intellectual and dandy of Jewish origin, a millionaire industrialist turned socialist, a republican of reason, Rathenau bore in his own person contradictions no less numerous and severe than Scheler's and probably of a similar kind.[42] Since his appointment as foreign minister, Rathenau had been subject to a mounting campaign of vicious anti-Semitic slander by right-wing student groups, which included the terrorists and rowdies who would form the backbone of the rising Nazi movement. They wanted to make Germany pure, restore the nation to its past Prussian and Lutheran glories, and unite the cleansed population into a single, agrarian community. "Shoot down that Walther Rathenau / That cursed, goddamned Jewish sow," they shouted in meeting places and taverns, and soon enough they did.[43] At the memorial service he held at the University of Cologne in 1922, Scheler extolled Rathenau as the man who exemplified the qualities of statesmanship, vision, and courage Germany most needed in its leaders.[44] Rathenau had been, in Scheler's belated estimate, the exemplary leader that only two years earlier he had despaired of ever seeing! A few months later Scheler separated from Maerit. In spring 1924 he married Maria outside the church; before the year was out he broke with the Catholic community and several of his friends forever.

In 1924 Scheler was fifty years old, an age when a great many men of his generation and class, even during the agitated Weimar years, had achieved a stability of station that gave greater strength and shape to their lives. This rootedness Scheler too had won but, in acts that were shocking and inexplicable to his contemporaries, seemed willfully to destroy. Not since his youth, when he renounced the family and religion into which he was born, had Scheler given up so much. But although mature and accomplished, with an extraordinary intellectual reputation—tarnished, of course, by the scandals of his personal life— he had little, least of all a new religion, to which he could turn. His third marriage faltered from the start; he missed Maerit, whom he still loved and continued to see. His relationship to the University of Cologne was strained; Catholic students were forbidden to take his courses in philosophy and ethics. He applied to the University of Berlin for the post vacated by Troeltsch's death but, his defection from the church notwithstanding, was rejected on the ground that his outlook was still too Catholic. There was no other academic position in Germany available to him. From this bottom he once again began to climb with a burst of creative energy that was to be his last.

Scheler took to the lecture trail again. His province soon extended beyond Germany to Switzerland, Austria, Holland, and France. Visibly troubled, he nevertheless had lost hardly any of his fire and continued to entrance his hearers as before. His views began to shift, becoming markedly existentialist and liberal. Before long he lent his voice to criticism of the church, declaring that body to be dogmatic and narrow, too antiquated to serve as a proper model on which to reorganize the West. He was tireless in his call for enlightened, responsible leadership and spoke before many groups on the subject, including a gathering of high-ranking military officers who received him with enthusiasm. He published studies on the national role of universities and evening schools, on sociology and the philosophy of life, on the value and limits of a sheerly pragmatic motive in knowing the world, on youth movements, on forms of knowledge and society, on equality as a destiny and a task, on feminine rights, on humanity and history, and at the very end, in an introduction to his projected philosophical anthropology, on humankind's place in the cosmos.[45] His aim, as always, was to plumb as deeply as possible the ethos of modern life and to chart the directions available to the West. Borne on the celebrity of his name, his new, more sociological writings soon reached a scholarly readership international in scope.

The realm of the spirit continued to be important to Scheler. Yet in this phase of his thinking he began to attribute to the spiritual realm and each of its contents—values in particular, consciousness, ideas— increasingly less efficacy in the affairs of humanity. In a volume of studies on the sociology of knowledge, *Die Wissenformen und die Gesellschaft* (Forms of knowledge and society, 1926), he declared human association always to be a confluence of two factors, material and spiritual.[46] But real efficacy, he insisted, lay in the realm of material conditions whose inner workings are fateful for humanity. Marx had discovered a truth: "It is not the consciousness of men that determines their existence, but their existence that determines their consciousness." Marx's chief error, however, was to limit the understanding of existence to economic factors, to conditions of production and reproduction. For human existence is also conditioned by geological and political factors, which are no less real, no less necessary than the economic. Each such factor develops independently out of its own immanent tendencies. Indeed, in the earliest stages of social life the conditions of "blood" and sex—kinship—exercised their hold over people with an intractable power. At a later stage, political rule, the domination of kings, held sway. Only in the modern era has the economic "substructure" gained the ascendancy, lessening but by no means extinguishing the effect of the other material factors. In casting economic factors as the predominant shaper of human history, Marx was, however pioneering his investigations, an unwitting ideologist of the modern period.

But although material conditions are necessary for human life, Scheler held, they are not utterly fatal; they may be modified. The elements of the spirit also develop independently out of their inner tendencies. The logical-rational development of law and the immanent logic of religious history are examples of this process. People may choose freely among these elements. Unless spiritual elements are attached to biological drives, however, they will come to nothing. Without sex there can be no family that will regulate sexual rights, without hunger no economy that will regulate production and consumption. And should spiritual goals exceed the limits of the possible, in contradiction to biological drives and the causal laws of matter, they will remain mere utopias that, as Scheler put it, "bite on granite" and disintegrate. A perfectly planned economy, a constitution for world politics, a planned legal eugenics and racial selection, he believed, are utopias of this kind. Material factors are, as it were, sluice gates that release spiritual elements or inhibit their entry into the stream of life. But once released, spiritual elements can grow further, draw energy from the material substrates, and influence their direction. Thus Luther's doctrines of solitary faith (*sola fides*) and inner spiritual sanctity (*spiritus sanctus internus*) affected the course of Western history only after they had captured the interest of dukes, cities, territorial lords

leaning toward particularism, and the rising bourgeoisie. All philosophies that endeavor to reduce human life merely to the laws of matter
or the unfolding of spirit are equally in error. In the interplay of the
two realms of matter and spirit, of the real and the ideal, Scheler asserted, human necessity and human freedom are both modified.

Scheler's formulation of the relation of ideal to real factors was not
only ontological, but also explicitly methodological. This was devised,
in part, as a contribution to the "dispute over methods" (*Methodenstreit*) in Germany that had begun with Kant's distinction between the
realm of freedom—morality—and the realm of determinism—nature—both of which, Kant argued, were inhabited by all human
beings. The issue that had been contested for well over a century was
how can our specifically *human* actions be best understood—through
the nomothetic principles of natural science, or the idiographic interpretations of our free moral-spiritual acts?[47] Many of Scheler's contemporaries—philosophers, sociologists, historians, and economists—were active participants in the dispute, Dilthey, Meyer,
Rickert, Weber, Simmel, Knies, Troeltsch, Windelband, Stammler,
Roscher, Husserl, Cassirer, and Lask, among others.[48] In arguing that
neither the objects of the cultural sciences—values, ideas, and the
like—nor those of the natural sciences—biological drives, productive
forces, and so forth—can be reduced to each other, but stand always
in a particular conjunction, Scheler extended his quasi-cybernetic notion of explanation and aligned himself more closely, though far from
completely, with Weber's methodological position.[49]

Comte was undoubtedly correct, Scheler agreed, in his view that
positive science has grown to dominate the outlook of the modern age.
But he was mistaken in his judgment that religion (Comte's actual term
was "primitive theology"[50]) and metaphysics, prevalent in earlier
ages, were merely less adequate stages of humanity's knowledge of nature that have been surpassed. The so-called "Law of the Three
Stages" is spurious not only because religion, metaphysics, and science
are different things, but because each is the product of a separate impulse that is a permanent feature of human life. At the heart of the
religious impulse is the concern with salvation of the person and the
community of which the person is a part. Faith in a holy power envisioned as the source of all things, into which the person and the community can be integrated and rescued, is the characteristic religious
attitude. At the heart of the metaphysical impulse is the concern with
grasping the essential structure of the world. Wonder at the riddle of
the world, that there is anything rather than nothing, is the characteristic metaphysical attitude. At the heart of the scientific impulse is the

concern with rearranging the world to meet practical interests. Control and power over things and people are the characteristics of the scientific attitude.

The source of Comte's error—an error shared by many thinkers such as Mill, Spencer, Mach, and Avenarius—was a narrow, European-centered vision. India and east Asia have taken a path opposite to the European in which metaphysics has risen high above religion and science. There is no notion in these cultures of an infinite progress of knowledge that would make technical control of the world possible. The metaphysical attitude has in the East turned inward and grown into a sustained directive to attain wisdom. Eastern practices like meditating upon exemplary texts or submitting to special psychological disciplines aim not to control nature but to attain higher states of consciousness for the enrichment of human life.

Religion and metaphysics do not progress in the same fashion as science. Religious needs are constant, the number of basic metaphysical viewpoints is few. Why then has science become so prominent in the West? To correct what he considered the faulty views on this question, Scheler drew upon several ethnological, philological, and historical studies. In their mythical origins, he argued, religion, metaphysics, and science were indistinguishably fused. This kind of thought is associated with the most primitive, unitary human associations. But with growth in the division of labor each attitude became differentiated, separated from its source and more closely linked to a distinct social stratum that has been its chief, but by no means its sole, carrier. From its early appearance, the Western religious attitude has been animated by the Jewish conception of the deity as Creator of the universe. Humanity is obliged in this conception to continue the work of the Creator, to subject the lower, inanimate creations to human will. The Christian assimilation of this view served to differentiate it further. The burden of practical activity and labor fell upon the lower social orders. But as the working classes grew in numbers and became concentrated in cities, they slowly joined with a higher social stratum, the urban European bourgeoisie. The interpenetration of the two classes, the one whose manipulation of things was facilitated by technological means, the other whose freedom and leisure permitted it to engage in abstract speculative thought, yielded a new outlook: the effort to order and interrelate phenomena in a mathematical symbolism. This outlook that emerged visibly in the Renaissance rested on the notion of a process that can be fulfilled only by a greater division of labor. Spurred by the Reformation, which promoted the individuation of its adherents, new centers of learning, new departments of knowledge, new observations and deductions, new specialists were spawned in a profusion that seemingly has no end. The reach of the scientific attitude, which seeks intellectual and practical mastery over the phenomena of the world, is boundless. The religious attitude has meanwhile faded, although science itself continues to bear vestiges of its religious origins.

The ceaseless dividing of labor into smaller, more refined units, characteristic of life in the West, has led to the leveling of social strata. The cultural outcome has been an enrichment of social life, Scheler argued (reversing his earlier views), a commingling of accomplishments and gifts formerly reserved to a few. Indeed, Scheler saw in the women's movement an opportunity to extend such enrichment further, not merely to gain greater equality for women, but also to feminize social life and thus foster an attitude of greater receptivity among men. However, Scheler warned, the very process that produced these cultural riches also harbors the danger of confining persons in narrow specialties.

Measures must be taken, Scheler urged, to bridge the growing barriers among persons. Perhaps a European university could be established to provide a meeting ground for students and faculty from the nations of Europe. But more than this, knowledge of a different kind from the scientific must also be cultivated, metaphysical and religious knowledge, which will reinvigorate European culture and deepen the common understanding of the essence and meaning of life. It is because such knowledge is lacking, but also sorely needed, Scheler believed, that certain social developments have begun to exercise a greater, indeed an ominous, appeal since the close of the First World War. He referred to the federated groups, the Nazi bunds, that had sprung up in Germany, to the Fascist and Communist dictatorships in other nations of Europe, each of which claimed to possess absolute truth yet was antirational, antiscientific to its core. The promise of strength that such social developments offer is an illusion that will end by robbing Europeans of their freedom and their science.

It was Scheler's hope that a renewed metaphysical stimulus will be engendered from three sources in the modern world: from the small nations of Europe—Denmark, Holland, Switzerland, Spain—in which science is less developed and a more contemplative culture flourishes; from America, in which the great diversity of peoples has become increasingly antipathetic to the Anglo-Puritan tradition and bonds with China and the Eastern cultures are rapidly being forged; and from Russia, in which the deeply ingrained religious-metaphysical culture will flow into the new technologies being imported from the

West. Should more thoughtful, warmer persons emerge from these influences, science would no longer sink into the mere technicism and positivism permeating the major nations of the West. The sociology of knowledge, he believed, is a new discipline that will help rid people of their local prejudices, whether national or historical, reveal to them certain of their deepest needs, and bring together the perspective of each nation in a better-adjusted community of persons that would span the world.

The realism and hope, cosmopolitanism, seriousness—and not least, perhaps, the utopianism—with which Scheler addressed questions of growing import to intellectuals around the world won for him, within a year of the publication of his book on the sociology of knowledge, invitations to visit China, Japan, the University of Chicago, and the Soviet Union. He looked forward to seeing these exotic places and began to plan the lectures he would give. But he was soon reluctantly forced to decline the invitations. His heart disease had become too severe to risk the strain of arduous travel.

Scheler had won far-reaching intellectual fame. His books and essays were translated into several languages. Yet he felt increasingly isolated, and a mood of deepening despair began to pervade his writings. In the last book he published before his death, *Man's Place in Nature,*[51] he said he had pursued an answer to the question, What is man? since the first awakening of his philosophical consciousness. But this question was not his alone, for man has become more of a problem to himself in the present age than at any other time in history. None of the old cultural idols can serve as guides in the twentieth century; unrest and disunity are found everywhere in the civilized world; true culture is difficult to attain. Scheler could offer no ready solutions to these dilemmas but continued to counsel the pursuit of metaphysical knowledge. However, the grounds that he gave for this counsel were strikingly different from what he had espoused a few years earlier.

The Deity does not exist high above and separate from us, he exclaimed. We are bound to the earth, driven by earthly desires, yet we reach beyond ourselves for spiritual things. This reaching will never be consummated. But in our development the ground of being is progressively realized and the deity itself develops, for we are a partial mode of the eternal spirit and drive. Absolute being cannot protect us or complement our weaknesses, however much we clamor for such protection, for God is unfinished. Metaphysics, in Scheler's view, was thus "not an insurance policy for those who are weak and in need of protection, [but] something for strong and courageous minds." In place of an attitude of dependence Scheler called for an act of personal commitment to God, a commitment that would move us in the direction of attaining values in history and also be the making of God. For this a faith is required that cannot be theoretically justified. In the end Scheler took up again certain of the threads he had held in his youth, and with the pantheism of Spinoza interwove the daring of Nietzsche and the mysticism of Bergson.

With this last short work Scheler founded the modern version of philosophical anthropology, the branch of philosophy concerned with understanding humanity's essential identity.[52] Martin Heidegger, Helmuth Plessner, and Arnold Gehlen were among those of Scheler's younger contemporaries also considered to be the modern founders of philosophical anthropology. More recently, some of the themes of philosophical anthropology have appeared in the work of Jürgen Habermas, Axel Honneth, and Hans Joas.[53]

In the fall of 1927 Scheler was called to a post on the sociology faculty of the University of Frankfurt, which he was to assume the following spring. He was eager to join the distinguished faculty of lively young scholars with whom he envisioned fruitful collaboration—Ernst Cassirer, Max Horkheimer, Theodor Adorno, Karl Mannheim, Gottfried Salomon, Richard Wilhelm, and Rudolph Otto. In December of the same year he had a heart attack. He recuperated well enough to begin his new duties in April 1928. A few weeks later, on May 19, he had another heart attack, this time fatal. He was given a Roman Catholic burial in Cologne.

From a distance certain patterns become visible that might be obscured by a focus on the details of Scheler's life. Scheler seemed impelled, again and again, symbolically to kill everything he loved and to inflict terrible wounds on himself in the process. At the root of all this, I suspect, lay Scheler's feeling that he had been an accomplice in his father's death. For in willingly accepting his mother's favoring of him as a child over the other members of his family, especially in the face of her constant denigration of her husband, Scheler in effect usurped his father's place. What then became available to him was forbidden. In converting to Catholicism shortly after his father died, he sought not only to acquit himself of his father's death, but to distance himself from his maternal accessory, to extirpate her and everything for which she stood from his life. A break of such magnitude from one's family on the part of an adolescent boy of fourteen years is not the product of ordinary youthful rebelliousness, as Scheler's uncle believed. The two founts of his guilt, the virtual patricide and the maternal trespass from which he fled, were inseparably linked. To be rid of his guilt Scheler would have had to acknowledge his part in the acts that gave it rise and be chastised. Only then could he escape the circle of transgression and remorse. And this, despite great efforts, he was unable fully to do. He found fresh places to reenact these events but, apart from his self-recriminations, not the unambiguous punishment he also pursued. The expulsions he experienced were either indirect, or he was too quickly forgiven. Soon he very nearly jettisoned his new source of sustenance by marrying his first wife outside the church. The guilt he suffered should not be depreciated, but it did not provide him with a sufficient check. Rudolph Eucken, who gave him a new creed to placate his conscience, who nourished him intellectually and launched him on a new career, was abandoned in the sexual scandal that ruined Scheler's marriage and career. His mentor's teachings continued to have an obvious influence on Scheler's thought for many years. Yet after leaving Jena, Scheler never again referred to Eucken save for a few scant footnotes. The memory of Eucken had seemingly been expunged from Scheler's consciousness just as had the memory of his parents. Although—more likely, because—Scheler respected Husserl, he attempted to woo Husserl's students away from their master, a dangerous and rash challenge to which Husserl was more than equal. Husserl and Scheler never again met after Scheler was expelled from the phenomenological stronghold in Göttingen. The two men apparently concurred in this arrangement. Nevertheless, in later years Scheler continued to refer positively to his meeting with Husserl as the decisive turning point in his intellectual life. Husserl had been the one man successfully to bar Scheler's attempted intrusion. As Husserl's position remained unimpaired by Scheler's encroachment, Scheler could allow himself to be guiltless and to remember him. By less obvious and more legitimate means, Scheler became a powerful phenomenologist in his own right. But no sooner did he achieve this status, and just as he was on the edge of succeeding in his earlier challenge to Husserl, his interests abruptly veered from phenomenology to concentrate on religion and politics—the "second phase" of his thinking, as commentators have noted. The shift was all the more remarkable in that Scheler had uncovered exceedingly rich materials that would have taken many lifetimes to explore. He followed the same route in all matters large or small, whether religious, philosophical, political, social, or personal, changing direction as soon as he had gained mastery and setting off upon another tack. All of his work reflected this constant shifting, as he was well aware, but he had few of the resources that would bring together its separate parts. For no nourishment, no haven, no authority was long permissible to him. Each place he alighted he would violate and flee—and thereby frustrate expectations he had built up in others. Indeed, the substance of his work, not only the shape, reflected the insufficiencies in his personal life too. None of the leaders whose types he illuminated held legitimate authority and ruled. However important in social life, they were passive exemplars, heeded only by the inner promptings of their followers, promptings whose nature Scheler also cast much light on, but of which he was in unsure possession himself. The resemblance between the precarious relations of followers to such leaders and Scheler's relation to his own passive father is striking. All of the love in the former relations is conceived to flow in one direction, as it were, from below; failing to receive such love, the exemplary leader would go unrecognized and the things for which he stood collapse. Did not Scheler thus tacitly condemn himself, his own failings, for his father's demise? How could he, so impoverished of spirit and undeserving, remain steadfast in a faith whose love was of the exact opposite kind, flowing from above, as he had characterized the Christian attitude? Finding a place in the bosom of a new community in Berlin and receiving its members' confidence, Scheler abandoned his friends in a needless, sudden act of betrayal for which he was never forgiven. The slight asperity of tone with which Buber spoke of Scheler in later writings is a measure of the pain and anger that even this loving and benevolent man must have felt.[54] Then, after having won in a few short years what most men labor half a lifetime to achieve—love, work, community, and religion—Scheler in one blow separated himself from it all. The compulsive, faceless sexuality for which he was notorious was as much geared to bringing punishment on himself and his partners as it was an expression of lust. He was only too frequently found out. Finally, just as a new academic home opened to him, his heart gave out. Time and again he had reached the promised land only willfully to turn away. It was forbidden to him. He was a transgressor entitled to nothing—this he proved many times.

Selections

The selections in this volume are grouped in three parts, Scheler's writings on the sociology of the emotions, the sociology of knowledge, and the sociology of values. A few words will be said of each.

Sociology of the Emotions

Like many sociologists of his and our generation—Weber, Durkheim, Tönnies, Simmel, Parsons, Habermas, and Bellah, among others—Scheler's primary concern was with clarifying processes that fostered or diminished solidary relations among persons. But with the exception of Durkheim, no other sociologist has charted as clearly how sentiments, both positive and negative, figure in such processes.[55] Scheler showed how various feelings—community of feeling, fellow feeling, vicarious feeling, emotional infection, emotional identification, suffering, *ressentiment,* love, and hate—are structured by the values toward which they point. His phenomenology uncovers an area of experience ignored by Alfred Schutz and his American students, who concentrate on the structure of social *cognitions*—the schemes used, for example, when working together or in interpreting the actions of predecessors, strangers, norms of gender, and the like.[56]

The recent Anglo-American interest in the sociology of emotions is also concerned with the relationship of emotions to community and value, although the approach taken is less direct than Scheler's. The American studies emphasize how feelings are manipulated so that persons believe genuine shared values and communal relations exist when in fact they are only semblances, products of gullibility and guile. We judge from the anger aroused when a norm is violated how important the norm is held to be. We gauge a group's normative expectations by observing how these expectations are consciously, artfully constructed.[57] The Anglo-American studies give us well-defined analyses of community structures and an inferred relation of sentiments to community *norms*—a structuring of feelings that Scheler left virtually unexplored. In these respects, they are an advance over Scheler's work. But the delineation of positive affect in these studies, and of the relation of such affect to values, is barely begun. Are values with different orders of objects differently constituted? How are such values related to each other? These are the sorts of questions to which Scheler's analysis of both emotions and values contributes useful insights.

Part I consists of six chapters. Chapters 1 through 4 have been drawn from *The Nature of Sympathy,* a translation of the fifth edition of Scheler's *Wesen und Formen der Sympathie.* Chapter 5 is my translation of "Vom Sinn des Leides" (The meaning of suffering) in *Schriften zur Soziologie und Weltanschauungslehre* (Contributions to sociology and the study of worldviews). Chapter 6 is selected from *Ressentiment.*

Sociology of Knowledge

The growth of natural science in the modern West has been made much of by sociologists from Comte to Habermas. With a few notable demurrers, the value of scientific knowledge is often passionately asserted. But this fact gives rise to the paradox that many who love scientific knowledge insist that to mix love with this knowledge is to contaminate it, to introduce a bias that will compromise the integrity of the claims of scientific knowledge to objectivity and truth. The knowledge of other kinds and places, for example, the metaphysical knowledge of China and India, or of an earlier period of Western history, is thus often dismissed as an inferior kind, distorted by affect and value.

In his comparative analysis of the different combinations of love, knowledge, and the value of the sacred in ancient Greece, India, and the early Christian and later modern West, Scheler clarified the limited, European character of Western positivist views of knowledge. The positivist view is a partisan ideological construction, he held, by those who have raised rational-scientific standards above all others. But although important, rational standards *alone* are insufficient to support communal values. And it is these values that are most wanting in the West.[58]

The aim of Scheler's sociology of knowledge is to diminish the growing gaps between individuals in the West and also to facilitate communication among the peoples of the world who are being drawn into closer contact. As was true of other sociologists of knowledge who came after him—for example, Mannheim, Geiger, Foucault[59]— he was mindful of the dangers of a "knowledge" that passes itself off as universal, such as the positivist, the Kantian, the Marxist, or the Spenglerian, but is in fact parochial. His sociology of knowledge was intended to incorporate and go beyond European localisms, whereas many other sociologies of knowledge have sought primarily to reveal the limits of a particular era or unmask the interests and values of a particular group. Scheler was eager to combat a total relativism of knowledge and values—which implies that even a partial reconciliation of different views is impossible—while at the same time permitting full recognition of differences within these domains.

Scheler did not believe "perfect" communication among vastly disparate persons and groups is achievable, however. From his point of view, this aim, although it correctly identifies some part of the modern dilemma,[60] is utopian and fails to appreciate the strength of sentimental attachments to family, religion, profession, and nation. He attempted to develop laws of the stages of social life and the dynamics of their transformation. He also tried to formulate principles of cultural development and to comprehend how these two domains, the drive impulses of social life and the ingredients of culture, are coordinated. The scheme he devised is an evolutionary one, somewhat like Durkheim's[61] This scheme, he believed, would make it possible to appreciate differences in the settings and histories of peoples and thus permit some understanding among them. He was acutely aware of the role of national cultural and institutional contexts in the production of different kinds of knowledge—an insight that has been rewon many times since he wrote, and no doubt will be won again.[62] Scheler's sociology of knowledge was part of a broader sociology of culture. His work can open the narrow confines of, and enrich, sociological analyses that merely equate knowledge with ideology that promotes group or class interests.[63] Often valuable, these studies also serve further to divide persons with conflicting interests and usually tacitly endeavor to elevate another set of restricted interests, those of the analyst, over the interests that have been analyzed.

Part II consists of Chapters 7 through 9. Chapter 7 is my translation, with the assistance of Peter Haley, of the essay "Liebe und Erkenntnis." Chapters 8 and 9 are my translations of two parts of "Probleme einer Soziologie des Wissens" (Problems of a sociology of knowledge) in *Die Wissenformen und die Gesellschaft*.

Sociology of Values

A cardinal insight of the social scientists of the nineteenth and early twentieth centuries, now a commonplace, is that the culture of a society—its values, worldview, norms, rules—is not made up of random elements but exhibits a distinctive and ordered pattern. However banal this insight may seem now, several of the issues implied in it continue to generate fruitful research. One such question may be put this way, What are the principles intrinsic to a given society by which its members order the things they value? Ruth Benedict gave an early, famous answer in *Patterns of Culture*.[64] She sharply contrasted the ceremonial, "Apollonian" style in which the Zuñi Pueblo Indians of New Mexico engaged in all their activities with that of the frenzied, "Dionysian" style of the Kwakiutls of Vancouver Island. These cultural configurations, in turn, differ markedly from the "paranoid-schizophrenic" style of the Dobus of Melanesia.

There is another, more difficult question, however, that can be put in two forms. The first is, Can sociological analysis devise principles of value ordering that are truly cross-cultural in scope? Durkheim's answer to this question was to identify two general principles, a conception of the sacred and a conception of the profane, which, although needing to be translated into the particular values of any given society, coordinate the moral life of all societies. Weber's answer was to group the legitimating principles of all societies and all historical epochs into three ideal types, the charismatic, the traditional, and the rational. Each of these principles is governed by a separate set of abstractly formulated values, and the three of them combine in different ways under different conditions to give particular direction to the institutions of a given epoch. Parsons's answer was to conceive of the normative structuring of *all* social action in terms of the four-function scheme, from the "lowest" values applying to adaptation, to the "higher" values concerning goal attainment and integration, to the "highest" values of pattern maintenance.[65] In these approaches, the ordering of value systems is treated as an *object* to be understood through the interpretive abstractions of the sociologist.

The second way of putting the question of the value ordering of society is, Are there essential principles *inherent* to each and every system of values that impart order from the least to the most important values? Dilthey's methodology of *erleben* and his concepts of ideal types were meant to clarify a variety of social and value experiences, and thus promised to address the question. But his concentration on civilizing values that he assumed uncritically to be "high"—for example, education, art, philosophy, statesmanship—left the question essentially unaddressed. Simmel in his notion of the essential forms of sociation attended to such ubiquitous experiences as superordination/subordination, exchange, prostitution, sociability, and conflict, among others. Yet he too did not deal with the question of the value ranking of these experiences. Only in Max Scheler's ethics was the *experience* of value *ranking* treated as an object of study and analysis.[66]

To look at value systems and their ordering as objects and to look at the experiences of value ordering as objects are not necessarily antagonistic pursuits. Indeed, in one important respect they are complementary. One concerns the "outer" aspect of ordering, the other, the "inner." If the two approaches can be integrated, a deeper and more general sociological understanding will be the result.

In scope, structure, and the kinds of topics it analyzes, Scheler's work is more nearly parallel to the efforts of Durkheim, Weber, and Parsons. Until recently, Scheler's *Formalism in Ethics and Non-formal Ethics of Values* has been inaccessible to English readers. But even in translation it has previously been aimed mainly to a philosophical rather than to a sociological audience, and thus remains virtually unknown to a professional group that might be productively stimulated by it. It is in hope of promoting sociological reflection that selections from this book are offered here.

Chapters 10 through 12 are drawn from *Formalism in Ethics and*

Non-formal Ethics of Values, translated by Manfred S. Frings and Roger L. Funk.

Notes

1. See the account by I. M. Bochenski, "A Note on the Author," trans. Donald Nicholl and Karl Aschenbrunner, in Max Scheler, *On the Eternal in Man,* trans. Bernard Noble (Hamden, Conn.: Shoe String Press, 1972), p. 471; José Ortega y Gasset is quoted as saying "The first man of genius, the Adam of the new Paradise . . . was Max Scheler," in Herbert Spiegelberg, *The Phenomenological Movement* (The Hague: Martinus Nijhoff, 1971), 1:227.

2. See Peter Gay, *Weimar Culture* (New York: Harper Torchbook, 1970), p. 39.

3. According to David Lachterman, the same situation obtains among Anglo-American philosophers. See "Translator's Introduction" in Max Scheler, *Selected Philosophical Essays* (Evanston, Ill.: Northwestern University Press, 1973), p. xiv n. 3.

4. Karl Mannheim, *Essays on the Sociology of Knowledge,* ed. Paul Keck-skemeti (London: Routledge & Kegan Paul, 1952), and *Ideology and Utopia: An Introduction to the Sociology of Knowledge* (New York: Harcourt Brace, 1936); Alfred Schutz, "Scheler's Theory of Intersubjectivity and the General Thesis of the Alter Ego," in *Collected Papers,* vol. 1, pp. 150–79, ed. Maurice Natanson (The Hague: Martinus Nijhoff, 1973), and "Max Scheler's Philosophy" and "Max Scheler's Epistemology and Ethics," in *Collected Papers,* vol. 3, pp. 133–78, ed. I. Schutz (The Hague: Martinus Nijhoff, 1970).

5. For information on Scheler's life I have relied a great deal upon the meticulous documentation in John Staude's study, *Max Scheler* (New York: Free Press, 1969). I have learned and drawn much from this estimable study but differ in my interpretation of Scheler. Also useful was the excellent history by Herbert Spiegelberg, *The Phenomenological Movement,* sec. 5.

6. After Scheler became famous, the details of his religious background were subject to much speculation and gossip among Jewish circles in Munich. See the comments by Gershom Scholem, *From Berlin to Jerusalem* (New York: Schocken Books, 1980), p. 136.

7. Ferdinand Tönnies, *Community and Society,* trans. C. P. Loomis (East Lansing: Michigan State University, 1957). The original was published as *Gemeinschaft und Gesellschaft* in 1887. The pessimistic assessment, even condemnation, of modernity by German writers has frequently been related to the influence of the Lutheran outlook. See, for example, Golo Mann, *The History of Germany since 1789* (New York: Praeger, 1968), pts. 1, 4, and 5. Mann also notes that Leibniz, Lessing, Hegel, and Nietzsche (among the severest critics of the nineteenth century) were of "Lutheran descent" (p. 10). See also Fritz Pappenheim, *The Alienation of Modern Man* (New York: Monthly Review Press, 1959), for a critique of modern life that links Marx and Tönnies.

The recent, excellent study by Harry Liebersohn, *Fate and Utopia in German Sociology, 1870–1923* (Cambridge, Mass.: MIT Press, 1988), explores these issues in greater depth.

8. Some of Eucken's books have been translated into English: *Life's Basis and Life's Ideal: The Fundamentals of a New Philosophy of Life,* trans. Alban A. Widgery (London: Black, 1909), and *The Meaning and Value of Life,* trans. Lucy Judge Gibson and W. R. Boyce Gibson (London: Black, 1916).

9. Scheler's dissertation was published as *Beiträge zur Feststellung der Beziehung zwischen den logischen und ethischen Prinzipien* (Jena: Vopelius, 1899); the book he wrote for his habilitation was entitled *Die transzendentale und die psychologische Methode: Eine grundsätzliche Erörterung zur philosophischen Methodik* (Jena: Durr, 1900). These are reprinted in *Gesammelte Werke,* vol. 1, *Frühe Schriften,* ed. Maria Scheler and Manfred S. Frings (Bern and Munich: Francke Verlag, 1971).

10. See Spiegelberg, *Phenomenological Movement,* p. 229.

11. Some of Husserl's early works that influenced Scheler have been translated into English by J. N. Findlay in *Logical Investigations,* 2 vols. (New York: Humanities Press, 1970).

12. See the essay "Versuche einer Philosophie des Lebens" in Scheler, *Gesammelte Werke,* vol. 3, pp. 311–39.

13. Something of the excitement generated by Scheler in these years was communicated to me by my teacher Fritz Kaufmann, who was then a student of Husserl's at Göttingen.

14. Husserl is reported to have characterized Scheler and Heidegger as his "two antipodes." See Spiegelberg, *Phenomenological Movement,* p. 230.

15. Max Scheler, *Ressentiment,* trans. William W. Holdheim, ed. and introduced by Lewis A. Coser (New York: Free Press, 1961).

16. This is Scheler's characterization of Nietzsche's charge. See *Ressentiment,* p. 43. Cf. Friedrich Nietzsche, *The Genealogy of Morals,* trans. Francis Golffing (New York: Doubleday, 1956), sec. 1.

17. Max Scheler, *The Nature of Sympathy,* trans. Peter Heath, introduced by Werner Stark (London: Routledge & Kegan Paul, 1954).

18. See, for example, the bibliography in A. R. Luther, *Persons in Love: A Study of Max Scheler's "Wesen und Formen der Sympathie"* (The Hague: Martinus Nijhoff, 1972).

19. Both parts of Scheler's *Ethics* were translated as *Formalism in Ethics and Non-Formal Ethics of Values* by Manfred S. Frings and Roger L. Funk (Evanston, Ill.: Northwestern University Press, 1973).

20. The well-known passage reads, "Specialists without spirit, sensualists without heart; this nullity believes it has attained a level of civilization never before achieved" (Max Weber, *The Protestant Ethic and the Spirit of Capitalism,* trans. Talcott Parsons [London: Butler & Tanner, 1930], p. 182).

21. Cf. Sigmund Freud, *The Ego and the Id,* trans. Joan Riviere (London: Hogarth Press, 1927); Émile Durkheim, *Moral Education,* trans. Everett K. Wilson and Herman Schnurrer (New York: Free Press of Glencoe, 1961); Max

Weber, "Author's Introduction," in *Protestant Ethic,* pp. 13–31, and "Confucianism and Puritanism," in *The Religion of China,* trans. Hans H. Gerth (Glencoe, Ill.: Free Press, 1951), ch. 8; Talcott Parsons, "The Point of View of the Author," in *The Social Theories of Talcott Parsons,* ed. Max Black (Englewood Cliffs, N.J.: Prentice Hall, 1961), pp. 311–63; and *Theories of Society,* ed. Talcott Parsons, Kaspar D. Naegele, and Jesse R. Pitts (Glencoe, Ill.: Free Press, 1961), 1:38, 2:978–79.

22. According to Max Brod's account. See Max Brod, *Streitbares Leben: Autobiographie* (Munich: Kindler, 1960), pp. 89–91. See Staude, *Max Scheler,* ch. 3, for a fuller discussion of this episode.

23. Max Scheler, *Der Genius des Krieges und der deutsche Krieg* (Leipzig: Weisse Bücher, 1915).

24. Staude, *Max Scheler;* Spiegelberg, *Phenomenological Movement.*

25. Staude, *Max Scheler,* pp. 88–90.

26. Max Scheler, *Krieg und Aufbau* (Leipzig: Weisse Bücher, 1916), reprinted in *Gesammelte Werke,* vol. 11.

27. See "Repentance and Rebirth," in Scheler, *On the Eternal in Man,* pp. 33–65. This essay was first published as "Zur Apologetic der Reue" in *Summa,* no. 1 (1917), and reprinted in *Vom Ewigen im Menschen: religiösen Erneurung* (Leipzig: Neue Geist Verlag, 1921).

28. "Von zwei deutschen Krankheiten," in *Der Leuchter: Jahrbuch der Schule der Weisheit* 6 (1919). This essay is reprinted in *Gesammelte Werke,* 6:204–20.

29. Many Catholic scholars had, in fact, remained isolated from contemporary developments in philosophy and the social sciences and hardly spoke the same language as their Protestant and liberal counterparts. See the excellent study by Harry Liebersohn, "Religion and Industrial Society: The Protestant Social Congress in Wilhelmine Germany," *Transactions of the American Philosophical Society* 76, *pt.* 6 (1986).

30. My information on this is drawn from Staude, *Max Scheler,* pp. 104–11.

31. Max Scheler, "Prophetischer oder marxistischer Sozialismus," *Hochland* 17 (January 1919), reprinted in *Gesammelte Werke,* 6:259–72.

32. Scheler, *Formalism in Ethics and Non-formal Ethics of Values,* pp. 86, 104–10, 265–78, 519–51, 572–95. An unpublished essay Scheler wrote in 1914 was devoted specifically to model persons as leaders, "Vorbilder und Führer" (Exemplars and leaders). It was brought out in a volume entitled *Zur Ethik und Erkenntnislehre,* vol. 1 of *Schriften aus dem Nachlass,* ed. Maria Scheler, (Berlin: Neue Geist Verlag, 1933). It has since been republished in Scheler, *Gesammelte Werke,* ed. Maria Scheler (Bern: Francke Verlag, 1957), vol. 10, pp. 255–354.

33. See Scheler, *On the Eternal in Man,* pp. 330–37.

34. Max Weber, *Ancient Judaism,* trans. and ed. Hans H. Gerth and Don Martindale (Glencoe, Ill.: Free Press, 1952), esp. chs. 4, 9, and 12.

35. Scheler, "Vorbilder und Führer"; Staude, *Max Scheler,* pp. 122–29.

36. Scheler, *On the Eternal in Man,* pp. 125–31, 401–18.

37. Cf. Karol Wojtyla (Pope John Paul II), *The Acting Person,* trans. Andrej Potocki (The Hague: Kluwer-Nijhoff, 1979).

38. See Gay, *Weimar Culture,* pp. 39–40; Staude, *Max Scheler,* pp. 129, 227–29.

39. An excellent account of this leftist criticism is given by Staude, *Max Scheler,* pp. 104–12.

40. Max Weber, "Science as a Vocation," in *From Max Weber: Essays in Sociology,* trans. Hans H. Gerth and C. Wright Mills (New York: Oxford University Press, 1946), ch. 5. Although in broad agreement with Weber's view of the political vocation, Scheler criticized Weber's analysis of the scientific vocation for lacking philosophical underpinnings. See Max Scheler, "Sociology and Formulation of Weltanschauung" and "Max Weber's Exclusion of Philosophy," trans. R. C. Speirs, in *Max Weber's "Science as a Vocation,"* ed. Peter Lassman and Irving Velody with Herminio Martins (London: Unwin Hyman, 1989) pp. 87–98.

41. Cf. Staude's account, *Max Scheler,* pp. 139ff.

42. Cf. the standard account, Harry Graf Kessler, *Walther Rathenau: His Life and Work,* trans. W. D. Robinson-Scott and Lawrence Hyde (New York: Harcourt Brace, 1930).

43. "Knallt ab den Walther Rathenau / Die gottverfluchte Judensau," quoted by Gay, *Weimar Culture,* p. 153.

44. Max Scheler, "Walther Rathenau: Eine Würdigung zu seinem Gedächtnis," in *Gesammelte Werke,* vol. 6, pp. 361–76, *Schriften zur Soziologie und Weltanschauungslehre.*

45. These essays have been collected in Scheler, *Gesammelte Werke,* vols. 3, 4, 6, 8, and 9.

46. Scheler, *Gesammelte Werke,* vol. 8, *Die Wissenformen und die Gesellschaft.* A part of this work has been translated into English by Manfred S. Frings, *Problems of a Sociology of Knowledge,* ed. and introduced by Kenneth W. Stikkers (London: Routledge & Kegan Paul, 1980). My own translation of two of Scheler's essays from volume 8 of his *Gesammelte Werke* is included in the present volume (chs. 8 and 9).

47. For an account of the history of these methodological disputes, see Ernst Cassirer, *The Problem of Knowledge,* trans. William H. Woglom and Charles W. Hendel (New Haven: Yale University Press, 1950). See also Harold J. Bershady, *Ideology and Social Knowledge* (New York: John Wiley & Sons, 1973), chs. 2 and 3.

48. Although concentrating on Max Weber's contributions to the *Methodenstreit,* an excellent account of the principal issues is given by Guy Oakes. See Max Weber, *Critique of Stammler,* trans. and introduced by Guy Oakes (New York: Free Press, 1977); and Max Weber, *Roscher and Knies: The Logical Problems of Historical Economics,* trans. and introduced by Guy Oakes (New York: Free Press, 1975); see also the introduction by Oakes to Heinrich Rickert, *The Limits of Concept Formation in Natural Science,* ed. and trans. Guy Oakes (New York: Cambridge University Press, 1986).

49. Reverberations of several of the arguments can still be heard among

German scholars, for example, in the work of Hans-Georg Gadamer, *Reason in the Age of Science,* trans. Frederick G. Lawrence (Cambridge, Mass.: MIT Press, 1981); Jürgen Habermas, *On the Logic of the Social Sciences,* trans. Shierry Weber Nicholsen and Jerry A. Stark, introduced by Thomas McCarthy (Cambridge, Mass.: MIT Press, 1988); and Axel Hanneth and Hans Joas, *Social Action and Human Nature,* trans. Raymond Meyer (Cambridge: Cambridge University Press, 1988). Although the Anglo-American version of the dispute began later than the German one, it has continued with little interruption for several decades. See, for example, the recent collection ed. Paul Rabinow and William Sullivan, *Interpretive Social Science: A Second Look* (Berkeley: University of California Press, 1989).

50. This is the English translation of the term *primitivement théologique* in *Auguste Comte and Positivism: The Essential Writings,* ed. and introduced by Gertrud Lenzer (New York: Harper Torchbook, 1975), p. 285.

51. Max Scheler, *Die Stellung des Menschen im Kosmos* (Darmstadt: Verlag Otto Reichl, 1927). This has been translated into English, with an introduction, by Hans Meyerhoff (New York: Noonday, 1961).

52. Cf. Herbert Schnädelbach, *Philosophy in Germany, 1831–1933,* trans. Eric Matthews (Cambridge: Cambridge University Press, 1984), ch. 8.

53. Cf. the discussion in Hanneth and Joas, *Social Action and Human Nature.* See also Arnold Gehlen, *Man: His Nature and Place in the World,* trans. Clare McMillan and Karl Pillemer, introduced by Karl-Siegbert Rehberg (New York: Columbia University Press, 1988); and Jürgen Habermas, *The Theory of Communicative Action,* trans. Thomas McCarthy (Boston: Beacon Press, 1984, 1987), vol. 1, ch. 1 and vol. 2, ch. 8.

54. Cf. Martin Buber, *Between Man and Man,* trans. Ronald Gregor Smith (Boston: Beacon Press, 1947), pp. 181–99.

55. See Durkheim, *Moral Education,* and *The Division of Labor in Society,* trans. W. D. Halls, introduced by Lewis A. Coser (New York: Free Press, 1984), bk. 1, chs. 2 and 6.

56. See Alfred Schutz, "Scheler's Theory," and *The Phenomenology of the Social World,* trans. George Walsh and Frederick Lehnert, introduced by George Walsh (Evanston, Ill.: Northwestern University Press, 1967); see also Harold Garfinkel, *Studies in Ethnomethodology* (Englewood Cliffs, N.J.: Prentice Hall, 1967); and Aaron V. Cicourel, *Cognitive Sociology* (New York: Free Press, 1974).

57. A subtle analysis of several of these processes was made by Erving Goffman in *Frame Analysis: An Essay on the Organization of Experience* (New York: Harper & Row, 1974). A recent study of the manipulation of feelings is by Arlie R. Hochschild, *The Managed Heart: Commercialization of Human Feeling* (Berkeley: University of California Press, 1983). A different, more benign analysis of the social nature of emotions from an interactionist perspective is by Norman K. Denzin, *Interpretive Interactionism: On Understanding Emotions* (San Francisco: Jossey-Bass, 1984). See also the collection *The Social Construction of Emotions,* ed. Rom Harre (New York: Blackwell, 1986).

58. Although the analysis by Robert Bellah and associates is made along somewhat different lines, the conclusion is similar. See Robert Bellah et al., *Habits of the Heart: Individualism and Commitment in American Life* (Berkeley: University of California Press, 1985).

59. Karl Mannheim, *Ideology and Utopia,* trans. Louis Wirth and Edward Shils, preface by Louis Wirth (New York: Harcourt Brace & Co., 1949); Theodor Geiger, *On Social Order and Mass Society,* trans. Robert E. Peck, ed. and introduced by Renate Mayntz (Chicago: University of Chicago Press, 1969); Michel Foucault, *The Order of Things* (New York: Vintage Books, 1973).

60. This is a general criticism, from Scheler's perspective, that can be made of the aim of Jürgen Habermas's project. See Habermas, *Theory of Communicative Action.*

61. Durkheim, *Division of Labor in Society;* see also Émile Durkheim, *The Evolution of Educational Thought,* trans. Peter Collins (London: Routledge & Kegan Paul, 1977).

62. See especially the great works of Joseph Needham, for example, *The Grand Titration: Science and Society in East and West* (Toronto: University of Toronto Press, 1969); cf. Joseph Ben-David and Awraham Zloczower, "Universities and Academic Systems in Modern Societies," in *Science and Society,* ed. Norman Kaplan (Chicago: Rand McNally & Co., 1965); see Harold J. Bershady, "Practice against Theory in American Sociology," in *Talcott Parsons and Contemporary Sociological Theory* ed. Roland Robertson and Bryan S. Turner (London: Sage, 1991), pp. 66–84.

63. Cf. George Lichtheim, *The Concept of Ideology and Other Essays* (New York: Vintage Books, 1967). A recent instance of this kind of analysis is by A. W. Gouldner, *The Coming Crisis of Western Sociology* (New York: Equinox Books, 1971), chs. 6 and 7. Through oversimplification of his work, Karl Mannheim's *Ideology and Utopia* has become the standard text in this canon. For a range of perspectives, many similar though not identical to Mannheim's more complex views, see *The Sociology of Knowledge: A Reader,* ed. James E. Curtis and John W. Petras (New York: Praeger Publishers, 1972).

64. Ruth Benedict, *Patterns of Culture* (New York: Houghton Mifflin, Co., 1934).

65. See Émile Durkheim, *The Elementary Forms of the Religious Life* trans. Joseph Ward Swain (Glencoe, Ill.: Free Press, 1947); Max Weber, *Economy and Society,* ed. Guenther Roth and Claus Wittich (Berkeley: University of California Press, 1978), 1:212–301; Talcott Parsons and Neil J. Smelser, *Economy and Society* (New York: Free Press, 1956), pp. 18–38.

66. See Wilhelm Dilthey, *Selected Works,* ed. and introduced by Rudolph A. Makkreel and Frithjof Rodi (Princeton, N.J.: Princeton University Press, 1989), vol. 1, bks. 6–8; *Georg Simmel on Individuality and Social Forms,* ed. and introduced by Donald N. Levine (Chicago: University of Chicago Press, 1971), pt. 2.

I

THE EMOTIONS AND SOCIAL LIFE

1

The Planes of Feeling

We must first distinguish from true fellow feeling all such attitudes as merely contribute to our *apprehending, understanding,* and, in general, *reproducing* (emotionally) the experience of others, including their states of feeling. . . .

But it should be clear (before we even begin to consider this class of acts), that any kind of rejoicing or pity *presupposes,* in principle, some sort of *knowledge* of the fact, nature, and quality of experience in other people, just as the possibility of such knowledge presupposes, as its condition, the existence of other conscious beings. It is not *through* pity in the first place that I learn of someone's being in pain, for the latter must already *be given* in some form, if I am to notice and then *share* it. One may look at the face of a yelling child as a merely physical object, or one may look at it (in the normal way) as an expression of pain, hunger, etc., though without therefore pitying the child; the two things are utterly different. Thus, experiences of pity and fellow feeling are always additional to an experience in the other which is already grasped and understood. The givenness of these experiences (and naturally, their value) is not based, in the first instance, on sympathy or fellow feeling—still less is the existence of other selves so established. . . . Nor does this apply merely to the knowledge given in the proposition: "X is in pain" (for I can also be informed of this), nor to the factual judgment "that X is suffering"—the other person's experience may also be completely realized in the peculiar form of "reproduced" experience *without* any sort of fellow feeling being entailed thereby. It is perfectly meaningful to say: "I can quite visualize your feelings, but I have no pity for you." Such "visualized" feeling remains within the cognitive sphere, and is not a morally relevant act. The historian of motives, the novelist, the exponent of the dramatic arts, must

Reprinted with permission from *The Nature of Sympathy,* trans. Peter Heath and introduced by Werner Stark (London: Routledge & Kegan Paul, 1954), pp. 8–12. This is a translation of the fifth edition of Scheler's *Wesen und Formen der Sympathie,* ed. Maria Scheler (Frankfurt-am-Main: Schulte-Bumke, 1948). The first, smaller edition of this work was entitled *Zur Phänomenologie und Theorie der Sympathiegefühle und von Liebe and Hass* (Halle: Niemeyer, 1913).

all possess in high degree the gift of visualizing the feelings of others, but there is not the slightest need for them to share the feelings of their subjects and personages.

The reproduction of feeling or experience must therefore be sharply distinguished from fellow feeling. It is indeed a case of feeling the other's feeling, not just knowing it, nor judging that the other has it; but it is not the same as going through the experience itself. In reproduced feeling we sense the *quality* of the other's feeling, without it being transmitted to us, or evoking a similar real emotion in us.[1] The other's feeling is given exactly like a landscape which we "see" subjectively in memory, or a melody which we "hear" in similar fashion—a state of affairs quite different from the fact that we remember the landscape or the melody (possibly with an accompanying recollection of the fact "that it was seen, or heard"). In the present case there is a real seeing and hearing, yet without the object seen or heard being perceived or accepted as really present; the past is simply "represented." Equally little does the reproduction of feeling or experience imply any sort of "participation" in the other's experience. Throughout our visualizing of the experience we can remain quite indifferent to whatever has evoked it.

. . . That we cannot be aware of an experience without being aware of a self . . . is directly based upon the intuitable intrinsic connection between individual and experience; there is no need of empathy on the part of the percipient. That is why we can also have it given to us that the other has an individual self distinct from our own, and that we can never fully comprehend this individual self, steeped as it is in its own psychic experience, but only our own view of it as an individual, conditioned as this is by our own individual nature. It is a corollary of this that the other person has—like ourselves—a sphere of absolute personal privacy, which can never be given to us. But that "experiences" occur there is given for us *in* expressive phenomena—again, not by inference, but directly, as a sort of primary "perception." It is *in* the blush that we perceive shame, *in* the laughter joy. To say that "our only initial datum is the body" is completely erroneous. This is true only for the doctor or the scientist, i.e., for man only as he abstracts *artificially* from the expressive phenomena, which have an altogether primary givenness. It is rather that the same basic sense-data which go to make up the body for outward expression, can also construe, for the act of insight, the expressive phenomena which then appear, so to speak, as the "outcome" of experiences within. For the relation here referred to is a *symbolic,* not a causal one.[2] We can thus have insight into others, insofar as we treat their bodies as a *field of expression* for their experiences. In the sight of clasped hands, for example, the "please" is given exactly as the physical object is—for the latter is assuredly *given* as an object (including the fact that it has a back and an inside), in the visual phenomenon. However, the qualities (i.e. the character) of expressive phenomena and those of experiences exhibit connections of a unique kind, which do not depend at all on previous experiences of our own, plus the other's expressive phenomena, such that a tendency to *imitate* the movements of the gesture seen would first have to reproduce our own earlier experiences. On the contrary, imitation, even as a mere "tendency," already presupposes some kind of acquaintance with the other's experience, and therefore cannot explain what it is here supposed to do. For instance, if we (involuntarily) imitate a gesture of fear or joy, the imitation is never called forth simply by the visual image of the gesture; the impulse to imitate only arises when we have already apprehended the gesture *as* an expression of fear or joy. If this apprehension itself were only made possible . . . by a tendency to imitate and by the *reproduction,* thus evoked, of a previously experienced joy or fear (*plus* an empathic projection of what is reproduced into the other person), we should obviously be moving in a circle. And this applies also to the "involuntary" imitation of gestures. It already presupposes an imitation of the inner intention of action, which could be realized by quite different bodily movements.[3]

We do not imitate the same or similar bodily movements in observed connections of the inorganic, e.g. in inanimate nature, where they cannot be phenomena expressive of psychic experience. . . . we can understand the experience of animals, though even in "tendency" we cannot imitate their manner of expression; for instance when a dog expresses its joy by barking and wagging its tail, or a bird by twittering. The relationships between expression and experience have a *fundamental* basis of connection, which is independent of our specifically human gestures of expression. We have here, as it were, a *universal grammar,* valid for all languages of expression, and the ultimate basis of understanding for all forms of mime and pantomime among living creatures. Only so are we able to perceive the contradiction between what the gesture expresses and what it is meant to express. But apart from all this, the imitation of another person's expressive gestures certainly cannot explain the act of *understanding* his inner life. The only way of explaining imitation, and the reproduction of a personal experience similar to that underlying a perceived expressive gesture, is that through this a genuine experience takes place in me, objectively *similar* to that which occurs in the other person whose expression I imitate.

For such objective similarity of experience, however, there need be no present consciousness of the similarity, still less an intentionally directed act of "understanding" or a reproduction of feeling or experience. For my having an experience *similar* to someone else's has nothing whatever to do with understanding him. Besides, such a reproduction in one's experience would require the "understanding" of another's experience to be preceded in the participant, by a similar *real* experience (however brief); i.e., in the case of feelings, a reproduction of feeling, which would always be itself an actual feeling. But one who "understands" the mortal terror of a drowning man has no need at all to *undergo* such terror, in a real, if weakened form. This theory therefore contradicts the observable fact that in the process of understanding the thing understood is in no way experienced as real.

It also seems clear that what this theory could explain for us is the very opposite of genuine "understanding." This opposite is that *infection* by others' emotions, which occurs in its most elementary form in the behavior of herds and crowds. Here there is actually a common making of expressive gestures in the first instance, which has the secondary effect of producing similar emotions, efforts, and purposes among the people or animals concerned; thus, for instance, a herd takes fright on seeing signs of alarm in its leader, and so too in human affairs. But it is characteristic of the situation that there is a complete lack of mutual "understanding." Indeed, the purer the case, inasmuch as a rudimentary act of understanding plays little or no part in it, the more clearly do its peculiar features emerge, namely that the participant takes the experience arising in him owing to his participation to be his *own* original experience, so that he is quite unconscious of the contagion to which he succumbs. This resembles those posthypnotically suggested acts of will which are carried out without awareness of suggestion (unlike the obeying of commands, where one remains consciously aware that the other's will is not one's own); such acts, indeed, are characteristically regarded by the agent as being his *own,* and so too the experiences arising through participation in a common gesture of expression are ascribed, not to others, but to *oneself.* For this reason, even in daily life, we distinguish between merely aping someone ("taking him off" for instance) and really understanding him, and point the contrast between them.

Thus neither "projective empathy" nor "imitation" is necessary in order to explain the primary components of fellow feeling, viz. understanding, and the vicarious reproduction of feeling or experience. Indeed so far as the first-mentioned acts come into it, it is not understanding they produce, but the possibility of *delusive* understanding.

... *fellow feeling,* ... is primarily based upon those constituents of "vicarious" understanding already dealt with. Here there are *four* quite different relationships to be distinguished. I call them:

1. Immediate community of feeling, e.g., of one and the same sorrow, "with someone."
2. Fellow feeling "about something"; rejoicing in his joy and commiseration with his sorrow.
3. Mere emotional infection.
4. True emotional identification.

Notes

1. We feel the quality of the other's sorrow without suffering with him, the quality of his joy without ourselves rejoicing with him. On this, cf. Edith Stein, "Neues zum Problem der Einfühlung," dissertation, Freiburg, 1917, in English *The Problem of Empathy,* trans. Waltraut Stein, The Hague, Martinus Nijhoff, 1964.

2. We might also say that it is not the mere relation of a "sign" to the presence of "something," whereby the latter is subsequently inferred; it refers to a genuine irreducible property of the sign itself.

3. On the distinction between imitation of action and imitation of movement, cf. K. Koffka, *The Growth of the Mind,* trans. R. M. Ogden, London, Kegan Paul, 1924.

2

Community of Feeling, Fellow Feeling, Vicarious Feeling, Emotional Infection

1. Community of Feeling

Two parents stand beside the dead body of a beloved child. They feel in common the "same" sorrow, the "same" anguish. It is not that A feels this sorrow and B feels it also, and moreover that they both know they are feeling it. No, it is a *feeling-in-common*. A's sorrow is in no way an "external" matter for B here, as it is, e.g., for their friend C, who joins them, and commiserates "with them" or "upon their sorrow." On the contrary, they feel it together, in the sense that they feel and experience in common, not only the self-same value situation, but also the same keenness of emotion in regard to it. The sorrow, as value content, and the grief, as characterizing the functional relation thereto, are here *one and identical*. It will be evident that we can only feel mental suffering in this fashion, not physical pain or sensory feelings. There is no such thing as a "common pain." Sensory types of feeling are . . . by nature not susceptible of this highest form of fellow feeling. They are inevitably "external" to us in some respect, inspiring only commiseration "with" and "upon" the suffering of pain by the other person. By the same token, there is certainly such a thing as rejoicing *at* another's sensory pleasure, but never mutual enjoyment of it (as a common feeling-sensation). It may, however, be the case that A first feels sorrow by himself and is then joined by B in a common feeling. But this, as will be seen, presupposes the higher emotion of love.

2. Fellow Feeling

The second case is quite different. Here also, the one person's sorrow is not simply the motivating cause of the other's. *All* fellow feeling involves *intentional reference* of the feeling of joy or sorrow to the other person's experience. It points this way simply *qua* feeling—there is no

Reprinted with permission from *The Nature of Sympathy*, pp. 12–18.

need of any prior judgment or intimation "that the other person is in trouble"; nor does it arise only upon sight of the other's grief, for it can also "envisage" such grief, and does so, indeed, in its very capacity *as* a feeling. But here A's suffering is first presented *as* A's in an act of understanding or "vicarious" feeling experienced as such, and it is to this material that B's primary commiseration is directed. That is, *my* commiseration and *his* suffering are phenomenologically *two different facts,* not *one* fact, as in the first case. While in the first case the functions of vicarious experience and feeling are so interwoven with the very fellow feeling itself as to be indistinguishable from it, in the second case the two functions are plainly distinguished even *while* experiencing them. Fellow feeling proper, actual "participation," presents itself in the very phenomenon as a *re-action* to the state and value of the other's feelings—as these are "visualized" in vicarious feeling. Thus in this case the two functions of *vicariously visualized* feeling, and *participation* in feeling are separately given and must be sharply distinguished. . . .

Nothing shows the fundamental diversity of the two functions more plainly, than the fact that the first of them can not only be given without the second, but is also present as a basis for the very *opposite* of an (associated) act of fellow feeling. This happens, for instance, where there is specific pleasure in cruelty, and to a lesser extent in brutality. The *cruel* man owes his awareness of the pain or sorrow he causes entirely to a capacity for visualizing feeling! His joy lies in "torturing" and in the agony of his victim. As he feels, vicariously, the increasing pain or suffering of his victim, so his own primary pleasure and enjoyment at the other's pain also increases. Cruelty consists not at all in the cruel man's being simply "insensitive" to other peoples' suffering. Such "insensitivity" is therefore a quite different defect in man to lack of fellow feeling. It is chiefly found in pathological cases[1] (e.g. in melancholia), where it arises as a result of the patient's exclusive preoccupation in his own feelings, which altogether prevents him from giving emotional acceptance to the experience of other people. In contrast to cruelty, "*brutality*" is merely a disregard of other people's experience, despite the apprehension of it in feeling. Thus, to regard a human being as a mere log of wood and to treat the object accordingly, is not to be "brutal" towards him. On the other hand, it is characteristic of brutality, that, given merely a sense of life, undifferentiated, as yet, into separate experiences, given even the fact of an enhanced appearance of life or a tendency toward it, any violent interruption of this tendency (as in vandalism toward plants and trees, to which one cannot be "cruel"), is enough to mark it as brutal.

3. Emotional Infection

Quite different again from these, is the case where there is no true appearance of fellow feeling at all, although it is very frequently confused with this. Such confusion has given rise to the mistaken theories of positivism concerning the evolution of fellow feeling (Herbert Spencer) and, moreover, to a quite false appreciation of values, particularly in connection with pity. I have in mind the case of mere *emotional infection*. We all know how the cheerful atmosphere in a "pub" or at a party may "infect" the newcomers, who may even have been depressed beforehand, so that they are "swept up" in the prevailing gaiety. Of course such people are equally remote from a rejoicing of either the first or the second type. It is the same when laughter proves "catching," as can happen especially with children, and to a still greater extent among girls, who have less sensitivity, but react more readily. The same thing occurs when a group is infected by the mournful tone of one of its members, as so often happens among old women, where one recounts her woes, while the others grow more and more tearful. Naturally, this has nothing whatever to do with pity. Here there is neither a *directing* of feeling toward the other's joy or suffering, nor any participation in her experience. On the contrary, it is characteristic of emotional infection that it occurs only as a transference of the *state* of feeling, and does *not* presuppose any sort of *knowledge* of the joy which others feel. Thus one may only notice afterwards that a mournful feeling, encountered in oneself, is traceable to infection from a group one has visited some hours before. There is nothing in the mournful feeling itself to point to this origin; only by inference from causal considerations does it become clear where it came from. For such contagion it is by no means necessary that any *emotional* experiences should have occurred in the other person. Even the *objective* aspects of such feelings, which attach to natural objects, or are discerned in an "atmosphere"—such as the serenity of a spring landscape, the melancholy of a rainy day, the wretchedness of a room—can work infectiously in this way on the state of our emotions.[2]

The process of infection is an involuntary one. Especially characteristic is its tendency to return to its point of departure, so that the feelings concerned *gather* momentum like an avalanche. The emotion caused by infection reproduces itself *again* by means of expression and imitation, so that the infectious emotion increases, again reproduces itself, and so on. In all mass-excitement, even in the formation of "public opinion," it is above all this *reciprocal effect* of a self-generating infection which leads to the uprush of a common surge of emotion, and to the characteristic feature of a crowd in action, that it is so easily carried beyond the intentions of every one of its members, and does things for which no one acknowledges either the will or the responsibility. It is, in fact, the infective process itself, which generates purposes beyond the designs of any single individual.[3] Although these processes of infection are not merely involuntary but operate "unconsciously" (however conspicuous they may be), in the sense that we "get into" these states without realizing that this is how it comes about, the process itself can again become an instrument of conscious volition. This occurs, for instance, in the search for "distraction," when we go into gay company, or attend a party, not because we are in a festive mood, but simply in order to find distraction; here we anticipate that we shall be infected and "caught up" in the prevailing gaiety. When someone says that he wants "to see cheerful faces around him," it is perfectly clear that he does not mean to rejoice with them, but is simply hoping for infection as a means to his *own* pleasure. Conversely, an awareness of possible infection can also create a peculiar *dread* of it, as is found wherever a person shuns melancholy places or avoids the *appearance* of suffering (not the suffering itself), by trying to banish this image from the field of his experience.

That this form of emotional infection also has nothing whatever to do with genuine fellow feeling should be too obvious for any need of emphasis. . . . Suffering itself does *not* become infectious through pity. Indeed, it is just where suffering is infectious that pity is completely excluded; for to that extent I no longer view it as the *other's* suffering, but as my *own*, which I try to get rid of, by putting the notion of suffering out of mind. Indeed it is just where infection *does* occur via suffering, that pity for the other person's sufferings, as being *his*, can stay the infection itself; just as the emotional reliving of an earlier painful experience, which still weighs heavy upon the present, can take this weight off one's mind.[4] Pity would be a "multiplier of misery" only if it were identical with emotional infection. For only the latter— as we have seen—can produce in others a real suffering, a state of feeling akin to the infectious one. But such real suffering does not occur, however, in *true* fellow feeling.

Notes

1. From the psychopathological side, Kurt Schneider's valuable work *Pathopsychologische Beiträge zur psychologischen Phänomenologie von Liebe und Hass* is in part a verification, in other respects an elaboration and extension, of the phenomenology of sympathetic experience set out in the text

(Cologne, dissertation, 1921). Also in *Zeitschrift für die ges. Neurol. u. Psychiatrie*, vol. 65, 1921.

2. This shows that the process of infection does *not* lie in the imitation of others' expressed experiences, even though these may actually bring it about, where it is a case of infection through experiences undergone by animals or other human beings.

3. I refrain here from describing the immense part which infection plays in the historical evolution of whole systems of morality, in the genesis of psychopathic group-movements (from *folie à deux* to the emergence of enduring pathological customs and usages on a national scale), in the onset of panics, and particularly within all revolutionary mass-movements. Cf. Gustave Le Bon, *The Crowd: A Study of the Popular Mind*, Unwin, 1896, the *L'Ame révolutionnaire;* see also Gabriel de Tarde, *Les Lois de l'imitation*, Paris, 1895; and Sigmund Freud, *Group Psychology and the Analysis of the Ego*, New York, W. W. Norton & Co., 1959, trans. James Strachey.

4. It is not the mere reconstitution of repressed memories, nor yet the abreaction from them, but this *reliving* of them, that underlies whatever therapeutic efficacy psycho-analysis may possess.

3

Emotional Identification

The true *sense of emotional unity,* the act of identifying one's own self
with that of another, is only a heightened form, a limiting case as it
were, of infection. It represents a limit in that here it is not only the
separate process of feeling in another that is unconsciously taken as
one's own, but his self (in all its basic attitudes), that is identified with
one's own self. Here too, the identification is as involuntary as it is
unconscious. Lipps has wrongly sought to construe this as a case of
aesthetic empathy. Thus, according to him, the absorbed spectator of
an acrobat in a circus turn identifies himself with the performer, whose
movements he reproduces within himself, in the character of an acrobat. Lipps believes that only the spectator's real self remains distinct
here, his conscious self having sunk itself completely in that of the acrobat. Edith Stein has interposed a just criticism on this point.[1] "I am
not" she says, " 'one with' the acrobat; I am only 'with' him. The correlated motor-impulses and tendencies are carried out here by a fictional 'I,' which remains recognizably distinct as a phenomenon from
my individual self; it is simply that my attention is passively fixed
throughout on the fictional 'I,' and by way of this, on the acrobat."

There are other cases, however, insufficiently recognized either by
Theodor Lipps or Edith Stein, in which such identification is undoubtedly complete; which do not merely exemplify a moment of true "ecstasy," but may be of long duration, and can even become habitual
throughout whole phases of life. They are of two opposite kinds: the
idiopathic and the *heteropathic.* Thus identification can come about in
one way through the total eclipse and absorption of another self by
one's own, it being thus, as it were, completely dispossessed and deprived of all rights in its conscious existence and character. It can also
come about the other way, where "I" (the formal subject) am so over-
whelmed and hypnotically bound and fettered by the other "I" (the
concrete individual), that my formal status as a subject is usurped by
the other's personality, with all *its* characteristic aspects; in such a case,

Reprinted with permission from *The Nature of Sympathy,* pp. 18–35.

I live, not in "myself," but entirely in "him," the other person—(in and through him, as it were).

Such paradigm cases of identification, either by way of an all-inclusive propensity to infect, or as a state of complete and total infection of the very roots of individuality, I find exemplified in very different kinds of experience—of which only a few main types can be indicated here:

a. One such case is to be found in the very peculiar and as yet little understood processes of identification in *primitive* thought, observation, and feeling among savages, such as Lévy-Bruhl has recently described in detail.[2] They include, for instance, the identification of each member of a totem with an individual member of the totem species. According to von den Steinen, the Boroso allege that they are really identical with red parrots (araras), each member of the totem with a particular red parrot. It is not just that the destiny (birth, sickness, death) of a member of the totem is mysteriously linked with that of his totem animal in a merely causal sense; this connection is really no more than a consequence of their actual *identity*. Such identification occurs even with (objectively) inanimate objects, for instance with particular stones (Foy calls them man-stones). The literal identification of a man with his ancestors is another case in point: he is not merely like his ancestor, or guided and ruled by him, but actually *is,* in his present life, at the same time one of his ancestors. This stage of historical identification between man and ancestor is prior to anything implied by the term "ancestor cult." This cult, and its emotional bond with the ancestor in the form of piety, ritual obligation, etc., already represents a first stage of *liberation* from the primitive identification of the descendant with his ancestor, and presupposes a recognition that the two are *distinct* individuals. It seems to me that this is the type of primitive identification which survives, as it were, into historic times, in the phenomenon of mass self-identification with the "Leader" (engendering through him a sense of identity among the members themselves); and that it is also the source of the worldwide belief in reincarnation, which is simply a rationalization of these original habits of identification.[3]

b. True identification of the heteropathic type occurs in the religious *mysteries of antiquity,*[4] in the course of which the adept, by inducing a state of ecstasy, becomes aware of his true identity in the being, life, and destiny of the god or goddess—becomes, in short, divine. Such identification does not merely relate to particular moments in the existence, character, and life of the god (who is represented by an animal, e.g., the bull in the Orphic-Dionysian mysteries, or by a man); it extends to a specific cycle of his destined career, of which the planes are reproduced in the ecstasy. It is only through the gradual decay of these mystery-rites that many peoples have developed the arts of the theatre and the drama.[5] Here at last, the ecstatic *identification* is reduced to the level of mere symbolic *empathy.*

c. Genuine identification is also present where the relationship between a hypnotist and his subject is not just a temporary one, in which particular acts and undertakings are suggested, but becomes a stable and permanent state, such that the hypnotic subject is continuously "wrapped up" in all the individual personal attitudes of the hypnotist, thinks only his thoughts, wills only with his will, esteems his values, loves with his love, and hates with his hate—but at the same time is convinced that this other self with all its attitudes and forms of action is really his own. But whereas in primitive identification we have a genuine identity of *existence,* in intensified suggestion through continuous hypnosis, involving not merely specific acts and performances, but an adoption of the whole concrete outlook of the hypnotist, we have only an identity of *character,* coupled with an awareness of separation in actual existence. The hypnotic trance[6] creates a mental attitude which is primitive only in an artificial sense, and thereby provides a new forcing ground for suggestion (which does not have to be voluntary). . . . Psychologically, however, we must regard it as a more general characteristic of the hypnotic, that in it the intellectual center of all cognitive activity is put out of action, whereas the organic reflex system is stirred into increased activity, and this in respect of its most ancient functions and modes of operation; the "seat" of the hypnotic subject's own intellectual activity is so *usurped* by that of the hypnotist that his organic and motor centers also come under the latter's intellectual authority, employment, and control. The judgment, will, and choice of the subject, his love and his hate, are then no longer his own but those of the hypnotist, whose intellect is mounted, so to speak, on the back of the subject's reflex system. There can be no doubt, however, that the degree to which the subject effaces his own *character* in that of the hypnotist is largely dependent on his personal make up, and that the phenomena of identification and emotional coalescence here referred to are intimately connected with all the rest.

The desire for positive *self-abasement* shown by the weak toward the strong, with its instinctive (unconscious) aim of participation in the latter's power, is a primitive impulse prior, in our opinion, to the aim of self-preservation and self-protection against a (feared) power: it is merely utilized, pressed into service as it were, by the will to self-preservation and defense. One indication of this is that the "submissive instinct" may become quite pointless, and can even lead to ends antagonistic to those of self-preservation. Schopenhauer recounts the following observation made by an English officer in the Indian jungle: A white squirrel, having met the gaze of a snake, hanging on a tree and showing every sign of a mighty appetite for its prey, is so terrified by this that it gradually moves toward instead of away from the snake, and finally throws itself into the open jaws. It is of no consequence whether this be a case of conscious suggestion alone (quite involuntary, of course, on the snake's part), or whether it may not also involve a hypnotic narcosis of the squirrel's otherwise active higher centers;— plainly the squirrel's instinct for self-preservation has succumbed to an ecstatic participation in the object of the snake's own appetitive nisus, namely "swallowing." The squirrel identifies in feeling with the snake, and thereupon spontaneously establishes corporeal "identity" with it, by disappearing down its throat.

Masochism, whether of the gross or refined type, resembles its opposite, *sadism,* in being simply a (twofold) manifestation of the erotic craving for power. (The two conditions often alternate periodically in the same individual, according to the balance of power between the partners.) Even for the masochist, the object of enjoyment is not pure passivity as such, but his self-identifying participation in the dominance of the partner, i.e., a *sympathetic attainment of power.* Both masochism and sadism are found far more frequently in children than in adults—e.g., in their alternation between cruelty to animals, or even things, and passionate identification with them, between stubborn self-will and limitless surrender; in the case of adults they probably represent simply a fixation at a primitive stage of development (infantilism). Both states easily become sources of idiopathic and heteropathic identification. . . .

d. The cases quoted by Freud in his book, *Group Psychology and the Analysis of the Ego* (in Section 7, which deals with identification), should probably also be taken as instances of genuine (pathological) identification. There is the illustration in which a school-girl receives a letter from someone she secretly loves; her jealousy is aroused, and she reacts with an attack of hysterics, by which some of her friends are psychically infected, so that they also "catch" the fit. Freud comments, "It would be wrong to suppose that they take on the symptom out of sympathy. On the contrary, the sympathy only arises out of the identification, and this is proved by the fact that infection or imitation of this kind takes place in circumstances where even less pre-existing sympathy is to be assumed than usually exists between friends in a girls' school." Freud's first observation is certainly just. I should only

Emotional Identification 63

question whether "sympathy" arises at all here. For sympathy presupposes just that awareness of distance between selves which is eliminated here by the identification.[7]

e. The mental life of *children*, which in so many respects differs, not in degree but in kind, from that of the adult,[8] also exhibits a type of identification analogous to these pathological cases. Thus, in the "make-believe" of children, and still more when they are taken to see a play or a puppet show, the situation is very different from the parallel cases in which the adult "play-acts" or indulges—as they say—in aesthetic "empathy." What is empathy in the adult is self-identification for the child. What is only "play" to the adult is "in earnest" to the child and at least for the time being "reality." Consider the charming example given by Leo Frobenius, of the child playing "Hansel, Gretel, and the witch" with three burnt matches.[9] Even Freud's case of the child and the dead kitten belongs more to child psychology than psychopathology. In the child's mind, individual self-awareness is still too unstable and incoherent to resist the childish capacity, which far exceeds the adult's, for ecstatic surrender to some eidetically projected personage. When the little girl plays at "mother" with her doll, the make-believe character of the play, the "Let's pretend that I'm Mother," is apparent only to the adult onlooker. In the act of playing the child feels herself (in the image of her own mother in relation to herself), completely identified with "mother" (which still stands for an individual here, and is not an expression of general reference); the doll she identifies with herself. Hence it also comes about that the child's reaction in a theatre may so easily be quite unlike the adult's.

f. Some particular cases of *divided consciousness* recorded by T. K. Oesterreich may also be regarded as instances of genuine identification, alternating, however, with awareness of self-identity; Oesterreich himself attributes them to identification, and the same applies, perhaps, to certain phenomena of "possession," of which he has also recently given us a valuable account.[10] The particularly enlightening thing about these examples of self-identification is that they do not come about progressively, through the imitative performance of individual utterances, gestures, or actions, but in a sudden leap, as it were; they thus betray the fact that (as in Flournoy's case of the woman who sometimes fancied she was Marie-Antoinette), it is the prior state of self-identification with the other person which, throughout a succession of external circumstances quite out of keeping for the historical Marie-Antoinette, is responsible for the wholly automatic reproduction of appropriate behavior in matters of detail.

g. I distinguish a further case of genuine identification, belonging

neither to the idiopathic type in which the one individual self despo-
tizes, as it were, over the other, nor to the heteropathic in which the
one self is entirely "lost" in the other; it is that type of identification
characterized by what I call the phenomenon of "mutual coalescence."
The most elementary form of this is certainly to be found in *truly
loving sexual intercourse* (i.e., the opposite of the sensual, utilitarian,
or purposive act), when the partners, in an impassioned suspension
of their spiritual personality (itself the seat of individual self-
awareness),[11] seem to relapse into a *single* life-stream in which nothing
of their individual selves remains any longer distinct, though it has
equally little resemblance to a consciousness of "us" founded on the
respective self-awareness of each.[12] This phenomenon was doubtless
the chief source of the primitive vitalistic metaphysics underlying the
Bacchic orgies and mysteries, which led their initiates to believe themselves plunged back again into the one primeval source of *natura naturans* (creative nature), with an ecstatic dissolution of all individuality.

h. But the phenomenon of identification through coalescence is certainly not confined to the erotic sphere. It also reappears in the psychic
life of the unorganized *group*, as Le Bon first described it. Here too
there is not only an identification of all members with the leader, the
despotic idiopath (who therefore cannot and must not merge himself
in the collective consciousness); there is also a *further* outcome (engendered by cumulative and reciprocal infection), in the mutual coalescence of the members into a *single* stream of instinct and feeling,
whose pulse thereafter governs the behavior of all its members, so that
ideas and schemes are driven wildly before it, like leaves before a
storm. The nature and activity of the collective consciousness certainly
displays a sixfold analogy with the consciousness found subliminally
in dreams, in hypnosis, in animals, primitive peoples, and children—
the mob is a "beast" and an "overgrown child"—and lastly in many
pathological states, especially the hysterical ones. But though Freud
considers the emergence of this group mind to be closely related to
erotic coalescence, the demonstrable links in his group psychology are
still too few for me. Freud defines the primary group as "a number of
individuals who have substituted one and the same object (the leader
and hero or an 'idea' derived from him) for their ego-ideal, and have
consequently identified themselves with one another (in their ego)."[13]
The binding force here is said to be "libido," insofar as it has already
been permanently diverted from sexual objectives and repressed into
the unconscious. This hypothesis, if true, would explain in terms of a

single notion a wide range of hitherto unconnected phenomena (e.g., hypnosis, which Freud describes as "a group formation with two members");[14] but it seems to me not yet ripe for judgment, so long as the basic problems of the Freudian theory of love and sexuality remain unclarified.[15]

i. A large number of earlier writers (among others von Hartmann and Bergson), have adopted the identification theory of love, i.e., the formula that "love" of another consists in assimilating the other's self into one's own by means of identification; the typical case of identification of character which either leads these authors directly to the theory or provides the best supporting evidence for it, is the bond between *mother and child*. . . . The facts themselves tell quite another tale. Even before birth the parental and nursing instincts are manifestly quite *distinct* from the impulse of self-preservation. The natural horror of abortion, for which the motives are naturally those of self-preservation, shows this plainly enough. Even before birth the mother regards herself and her child as *two* entities, the impulses appropriate to each being distinct even as phenomena. There is no sort of continuous development from self-preservation (and its impulses) into maternal love. The psychic continuity lies, rather, between the reproductive and parental instincts. The "self-sacrifice" of the mother for the preservation of her young, so often recorded even among animals, displays an independence, an antagonism of the two impulses which certainly does not arise in the first place as an outcome of gestation, being already present beforehand, and distinguishable in the phenomena themselves. So far from speaking of the mother-child relationship, with von Hartmann, as the mother's assimilation of the child into her own self (and will to survive), it would be more appropriate to describe it as a progressive approximation to an identification of the mother with her child in the shape of an ecstatic *self-devotion* to its individuality. The dreamy state of a woman absorbed in contemplation of her present and future role as a mother is just such a state of kinesthetic ecstasy, as it were, in which the presence of the child-to-be is disclosed to her. But even the continuity between the parental instincts and what we are first entitled to call mother *love* is not so complete as is often asserted. I would say, indeed, that instinct and love very often run counter to one another here. Instinct, the outcome of the female reproductive urge, is all the more obviously at work so long as the child is young and still lacks an independent personality of its own. The unremitting solicitude of those mothers who are most "motherly" in this respect is often a positive hindrance to any kind of independent devel-

opment of personality in the child, and frequently retards its mental
and spiritual growth the more, in seeking to promote its physical welfare. Such continual solicitude, fussing, and foolish fondness is proverbially attributed to hens.[16] Does it not seem as if the purely maternal
instinct—unmixed with love—were seeking to draw the child back, as
it were, into the protecting womb? It is maternal *love* which first
checks this tendency, directing itself upon the child as an independent
being, slowly making his way from the darkness of mere physical life
into the increasing light of consciousness. Like love generally, it conceives the child in its terminus ad quem, not, as instinct does, in its
terminus a quo. . . .

. . . all types of identification proper should exhibit several common
features in the way they come about:

1. Their occurrence is always automatic, never a matter of choice or
of mechanical association. In our terminology we describe this by saying that they are due to a specific "vital causality," different in kind
both from rational purposiveness and from (formal) mechanical efficacy. Among other essential features of this basic causal relation we
may notice its automatic, vectorial, and goal-seeking (not purposive)
character; it is a concrete causality *a tergo* of the past as a whole (as
distinct from immediately antecedent causes of the uniformly recurrent, qualitatively identical type).

2. They occur only when two spheres of man's consciousness which
are by nature always present concurrently in him, are almost or wholly
empty of particular content: the cognitive, spiritual, and rational
sphere (which is personal in form), *and* the sphere of physical and corporeal sensation and sensory feeling. Only inasmuch and insofar as the
acts and functions operative in these spheres are put out of action, does
man become disposed to identification and capable of achieving it.

To attain to identification, man must elevate himself "heroically"
above the body and all its concerns, while becoming *at the same time*
"forgetful," or at least unmindful, of his spiritual individuality; he
must abandon his spiritual dignity and allow his instinctive life to look
after itself. We might also put it by saying that he has to become something less than a human being having reason and dignity, yet something more than an animal of the kind which lives and has its being
only in its physical circumstances (and which would indeed come
closer to being a plant instead of an animal, the closer its approximation to this marginal type).

The point is that gregariousness in animals represents an advance
toward the human level, whereas man becomes more of an animal by

associating himself with the crowd, and more of a man by cultivating his spiritual independence.[17]

Notes

1. "Das Wissen von fremden Ichen," *Psychologische Untersuchungen,* vol. 1, no. 4, 1905.

2. Cf. Lévy-Bruhl, *How Natives Think,* trans. Lilian A. Clare, Allen & Unwin, 1926, particularly p. 70. Cf. also D. Westermann, "Tod und Leben bei den Kpelle in Liberia," in *Psychologische Forschung,* vol. 1, no. 1–2, Berlin, 1921.

3. Cf. the admirable examples given by Leo Frobenius in his *Paideuma: Umrisse einer Kultur und Seelenlehre,* 3rd ed., Frankfurt-am-Main, 1928, pp. 42–47, of the forms in which this identification is expressed among the Ethiopians.

4. Cf. Odo Casel, O.S.B., *Die Liturgie als Mysterienfeier,* Freiburg, 1922, a book which brings together a large number of examples of such identification from the mysteries of antiquity. Cf. further Erwin Rohde's classic work, *Psyche,* trans. W. P. Hillis, Kegan Paul, 1925.

5. Cf. similar material in Frobenius, *Paideuma.*

6. Cf. the details of recent research on this subject assembled by Paul Schilder in his notable work *Über das Wesen der Hypnose,* Halle, 1912, which also deals with the anatomical and physiological aspects.

7. Cf. the cases of self-identification quoted earlier from Freud's *Group Psychology.*

8. Cf. E. R. Jaensch, *Eidetic Imagery: Typological Methods of Investigation: Their Importance for the Psychology of Childhood,* trans. Oscar Oeser, Kegan Paul, 1924. In certain children there occurs as a primary experience what Jaensch calls "eidetic imagery," an intermediate form of awareness between "perceiving" and "imaging," out of which there develops, along diverging lines, the disparity in act and content between perception and imagination in the adult.

9. *Paideuma,* p. 59. [The child becomes so terrified by her own "eidetic image" of the witch, that she cries to her father, "Come and take the witch away. I daren't touch her."—Trans.]

10. T. K. Oesterreich, *Possession, Demoniacal and Other,* trans. D. Ibberson, Kegan Paul, 1930.

11. Cf. [*Formalism in Ethics and Non-formal Ethics of Values,* trans. Manfred S. Frings and Roger L. Funk, Evanston, Ill., Northwestern University Press, 1973, pp. 280ff.]

12. Cf. Wagner's descriptive tone-poem in *Tristan,* also Gerhart Hauptmann's *Heretic of Soana,* London, Martin Secker, 1923.

13. Freud, *Group Psychology,* p. 80. [The first parenthesis is an interpolation of Scheler's; the second restores a phrase omitted by him.—Trans.]

14. Freud, *Group Psychology,* p. 78.

15. On this question cf. also Schilder's already quoted book, *Über das Wesen der Hynose,* and our treatment of Freud's ontogenetic theory, pt. 2, ch. 6, sec. 5 *infra.*

16. [To monkeys, in the German.—Trans.]

17. Empirical evidence for this may be found, above all, in the modes of identification characteristic of those groups which are in process of disintegration (though still to some extent "organized" in practice).

4

Fellow Feeling, Benevolence, Forms and Kinds of Love

It is through fellow feeling, in both its mutual and its unreciprocated forms, that "other minds in general" (already given previously as a field) are brought home to us, in individual cases, as having a *reality equal to our own*. Such acceptance of a common status (and the judgments based on this) are a prior condition for the emergence of spontaneous benevolence, i.e., love of someone simply because he is human and has the semblance of a man. Vicarious feeling is not sufficient to confer this equality of reality status: it only conveys the quality of the other's condition, not its reality. Thus we can easily *reproduce* in ourselves the joys and sorrows of characters in fiction, or the persons in a play (Faust or Gretchen, say), as the actor presents them; but so long as we maintain a generally aesthetic attitude, and do not, like the novelette-reading teenager, take their part as if they were real, we cannot have genuine *fellow feeling* for them. For the latter emotion *essentially* involves the ascription of reality to the subject whose feelings we share. It therefore disappears when the supposedly real subject is replaced by one which is presented as figurative or fictitious. It is precisely *in the act* of fellow feeling that self-love, self-centered choice, solipsism, and egoism are first wholly overcome.

The emotional realization of the unity of mankind as a species must therefore have been already achieved in fellow feeling, if benevolence (or humanitarianism) in this particular sense is to be possible. The closeness of their connection is evident from the fact that neither general benevolence nor fellow feeling depend upon a previous discrimination between the positive or negative *values* of men, or the values of the emotions we share with them. A genuine love of humanity does not discriminate between fellow-countrymen and foreigners, the virtuous and the criminal, the racially superior and inferior, the cultured and the uncouth or between good and bad generally. Like fellow feeling, it embraces *all* men, simply because they are men, though marking

Reprinted with permission from *The Nature of Sympathy*, pp. 98–174.

them off distinctly from the lower animals and from God. This, however, does not alter the fact that fellow feeling (which can also be bestowed on animals) differs from love of humanity, since the latter, like
all forms of love, is associated with a positive evaluation, such that it
conceives the human as possessing a special value—as compared with
the animal, and also the divine. Its quite specific and peculiar note of
feeling is sounded in Goethe's, "For I was a man and that is to be a
fighter."

In fellow feeling this specific valuation of the human as such is not
yet present. Certainly, once benevolence has gained its impetus from
pure fellow feeling, it can, by its own activity, enlarge the scope of the
latter to an unlimited extent; for the experience gained in active well-
doing, which proceeds from *love* only, and not from the essential passivity of fellow feeling, has the effect of continually increasing the
range of objects accessible to fellow feeling. But this does not alter the
fact that fellow feeling in general, as a felt intentional act, is a necessary condition for the possible emergence of benevolence. . . .

. . . We light here upon an ambiguity in the concept of "fellow feeling" which profoundly affects our problem. One may rejoice at another's joy and also repine at it; grieve at his sorrow, and also gloat upon
it. Both require that the state of mind should be conveyed or understood. Normally one only speaks of "fellow feeling" in connection
with the first-mentioned alternatives in each case, where the state of
mind and the functional reaction to it both have the same polarity. But
Darwin's account would only hold good for a sense of "fellow feeling"
which included the second alternatives as well. Now this is a matter of
the highest importance for ethics. For it is surely obvious that fellow
feeling has *positive* moral value in the *first* sense only, and equally obvious that all attitudes where the polarities are reversed are *negative* in
value. But Darwin connects the mere fact of sociality and its increase
with the presence of fellow feelings of the positive kind only; whereas
he should have attributed it to the presence and development of *all* the
heteropathic feelings and qualities, including the negative ones. This
leads him to the fundamentally erroneous belief that "social development" as such is in some sense a condition of moral *progress* and a
source of *positive* moral energy, and finally to the proposition "Good
is to live in company: evil, to dwell alone"—a notion which deservedly
roused Nietzsche to violent protest.

This can also be applied, of course, to man and his history. The
growth of social relations among nations and infranational groups,
and the increased solidarity of their interests, have not accentuated the
heteropathic responses, as such, for all their effect upon our capacities

for understanding. But the enrichment of understanding due to the greater intimacy of human contact has provided these responses with far more varied material. They have become, in consequence, unusually *diversified,* though the diversity extends to the *negatively* valuable as well as to the *positive.* In the course of its history, civilization has given rise to quite new forms of cruelty, brutality, envy, malice, etc., which never previously existed. Closer contacts and increased solidarity of interest have brought new "vices" as well as new "virtues," in their train.

There is equally little foundation for the Darwinian assumption that the sympathetic emotions are merely epiphenomenal to the "social instinct," the latter being itself a consequence of the social mode of life. We may confine ourselves to remarking that, so far as concerns the mere capacity for perceiving the liveliness of other living things and assimilating their experience, this feature is certainly not a consequence of the social mode of life, but is in some form, however elementary, a *natural endowment of all living creatures.* Nor is it a consequence, but a *presupposition,* of the possibility of any kind of sociality; for this, as such, must always be more than a mere spatial proximity and purely causal efficacy of things upon each other. There is no such thing as a "society" of stones. Things are only "social" when they are in some sense present "for one another." Hence the sociality and capacity of living things to pursue a reciprocal existence of any sort lie outside the relation of cause and effect. The development of such capacities is not the empirical consequence of an outwardly social form of life. On the contrary, the governing relation is one of parallel coordination. . . .

. . . Genuine acts of fellow feeling have positive moral value, though this is by no means true of heteropathic emotions in general. The degree of such value is determined:

1. According to the level of the emotion, which may be a spiritual, mental, vital, or sensory type of sympathy.
2. According to whether the pity is of the first type ("pity with someone") as distinct from mere "pity for someone." The value of emotional infection is negative rather than positive, its only effect being that of increasing the total amount of suffering present.
3. According to whether the fellow feeling is directed upon the center of self-awareness and self-respect in the other's personality or merely toward his circumstances.
4. In addition, the total value of an act of fellow feeling varies according to the worth of the value situation which is the occasion of the other person's sorrow or joy. In other words, to sympathize with

joys and sorrows which are appropriate to their circumstances is preferable to sympathizing with those which are not. By the same token, it is better to have sympathy for a person of superior worth than for someone of lesser value.

Fellow feeling possesses this value in its own right; it is not occasioned by the acts of beneficence which come about through fellow feeling, and pity especially. For "A sorrow shared is a sorrow halved; joy shared is joy doubled" is one of the few proverbs which brook examination from the moral point of view. However, it *is* one of the marks of *genuineness* in pity, that it should lead to acts of beneficence. . . .

. . . love and hatred differ, *as* acts even, from all other acts and from each other; the point being that they do not first *become* what they are by virtue of either their exponents, their objects, or their possible effects and results. No other truth has been more grievously flouted by our current habits of thought. It is implied in the foregoing, firstly, that love and hatred are *in no sense relative* to the polar coordinates of "*myself*" and "*the other.*" In other words, love and hatred are *not intrinsically social dispositions,* as are the functions of fellow feeling, for example.[1] Thus, one can "love or hate oneself," but cannot have fellow feeling for oneself. For if it is said of someone that he "pities himself" or that he "rejoices to find himself so happy today" (statements which undoubtedly designate phenomena of a quite specific kind), a closer analysis invariably discloses the presence of an element of fantasy, in which the person concerned regards himself "*as if he were someone else*" and shares his own feelings in this (fictitious) capacity. Thus I can fancy myself in the position of taking part in my own funeral, etc. But even then the act of fellow feeling remains, phenomenologically, a social one. No such illusion is necessary in the case of self-love and self-hatred. Hence it is by no means a necessary condition for the occurrence of love and hatred, that the act should be directed on someone else, or that there should be any consciousness of human relationships. If acts that are addressed to others, as such, are described as "altruistic," then love and hatred are in no way intrinsically altruistic acts. For the primary orientation of love is toward values, and toward the objects discernible, through those values, as sustaining them; whence it is essentially a matter of indifference whether the values concerned belong to the self or to others. The basic contrast is therefore between love, whether of self or others, and hatred, of self or others likewise. Conversely, acts addressed to others, as such, are by no means necessarily loving. For envy, malice, and spite are so addressed. If by "altruism" be meant an orientation toward other men, a predominant tendency to aversion from the self and its subjective experience, there is nothing in such a "social" attitude to connect it, as such, with a "loving" or "kindly" one. Moreover, if love for others is based in this way upon an act of aversion, it must equally be founded upon a still more ultimate *hatred,* namely of *oneself.* Self-aversion, the *inability* to endure one's own company (of which the "clubman" is a typical example), has nothing to do with love.[2]

But if it be no essential part of love that it should address itself to others, there is equally little necessity for it to relate to the *group.* There is such a thing as love for a group, and that in a twofold sense, namely love for the group as a whole, and love for each of its members, as "belonging to the group." But this can also coexist with a quite independent love for the individual himself, considered without reference to a group of any kind, or, it may be, in actual opposition to one. (Love for the uniquely private self.) The group, in all its aspects, is thus only *one* object of love among others. If, by a "social outlook" one is taken to mean a special liability to preoccupation with social matters, this also has nothing whatever to do with *love.* Though it is certainly possible for love, of a kind, to be realized in a "social outlook." Thus one may wish to benefit an entire nation, profession, community, or race, "out of love for them" (but never a class, for this is an embodiment of interests and, as such, valueless); but in doing so it should be realized that this involves a total exclusion of love or goodwill toward *individuals.* For it is a commonplace of observation that one may hate a group while loving certain of its members—not because they are members of the group, but in their individual capacity. Hence anti-Semitism, Germanophobia, Gallophobia, etc., are quite consistent with love for individuals in any given case.

Self-love and self-hatred are therefore no less fundamental than love or hatred of others. Nor is *"egoism"* the same as "self-love."[3] For in "egoism" the given object of love is not my individual self, released from all social ties and thought of as merely a vessel for such supreme categories of value as those which find expression, for instance, in the concept of "salvation." Its object is simply myself, as one in competition with others, who thereupon simply "fails to observe" that others have any value. It is typical of egoism that it implies a *glance at other people* and their values and goods, and consists in just this *"failure to observe"* the claims engendered by these values (which is already a *positive* act, and not just a failure to perform one). Egoism does not consist in behaving "as if one were alone in the world"; on the contrary, it is taken for granted that the individual is a member of society. The egoist is a man so taken up with his "social self" that he loses sight

of his individual private self. It is not that he loves this social self; he is
merely "taken up" with it, i.e., *lives* in it. Nor is his concern for his
own values, as such (for it is only by chance that he finds them in himself); it is for *all* values, in things or in other people, but only *insofar*
as they are, or might come to be *his,* or have something to do with
him. All of which is the very *opposite* of self-love.

Positive Delineation of the Phenomena[4]

The ultimate essences of love and hatred, as inherent in acts, can only
be *exhibited;* they cannot be defined.

In the first place love and hatred cannot be radically distinguished
on the grounds that hatred is simply love for the nonexistence of a
thing. For hatred is really a *positive act,* involving a presentation of
disvalue no less immediate than the presentation of *positive* value in
the act of love. But love is a movement, passing from a lower value to
a higher one, in which the higher value of the object or person suddenly flashes upon us; whereas hatred moves in the opposite direction.
It can be seen from this that hatred looks to the possible existence of a
lower value (itself of negative value, on that account), and to the re-
moval of the very possibility of a higher value (which again has a negative value). Love, on the other hand, looks to the establishment of
higher possibilities of value (which itself has a positive value), and to
the maintenance of these, besides seeking to remove the possibility of
lower value (which itself has a positive moral value). Hate, therefore,
is by no means an utter repudiation of the whole realm of values generally; it involves, rather, a *positive* preoccupation with lower possibilities of value.

This "higher" or "lower" quality of values is something inherently
given, requiring no such comparison of value as is always involved in
"preference," for example. Preference is not choice, nor is it in any
sense a conative act, but an act of emotional cognition.[5] We can prefer
Beethoven to Brahms, for instance, without actually choosing anything. Choice always relates to volition—never to objects as such. But
preference always assumes the existence of two values A and B, of
which one is then preferred to the other. This is not the case in love
and hatred. For love is that *movement of intention* whereby, from a
given value A in an object, its higher value is visualized. Moreover, it
is just this *vision* of a higher value that is of the essence of love. In its
ultimate nature, therefore, love is not just a "reaction" to a value already felt, such as "happiness" or "grief," for example, nor is it a morally determinate function, such as "enjoyment," nor yet an attitude to

a pair of previously given values, such as "preference." Though all preference is based on love, inasmuch as it is only in love that the higher value flashes out and can thereafter be preferred. . . .

Of course there *is* an awareness, in love, of the positive value of the things loved, for instance, the beauty, the charm, and the goodness of a person; but we can also be aware of this without any love at all. Love only occurs when, upon the values already acknowledged as "real" there supervenes a *movement,* an intention, toward potential values still *"higher"* than those already given and presented. These additional values are *not* yet manifested as positive qualities, being merely envisaged concurrently as potential ingredients of a corporate structural pattern. In so doing, love invariably sets up, as it were, an *"idealized" paradigm of value* for the person actually present, albeit conceiving this at the same time as an embodiment of his "true" nature and "real" value, which only awaits confirmation in feeling. To be sure, this "paradigm" is *implicit* in the values already disclosed empirically in feeling—and only the fact that it is so implicit keeps it free from interpolation, empathic projection, etc., and hence from delusion. But, for all that, it is not empirically "latent" in them, save as an appointed goal, an objective ideal challenge to a better and more beautiful fulfillment of the whole.

It is essentially as a movement tending to the enhancement of value that love acquires its significance (already explicit in Plato), as a creative force. This is not to say that love first creates these values or itself enhances them. Certainly not. But in all feeling and finding of values, all preference even (in relation, that is, to the spheres of feeling and preference), it is love that within *these* spheres of experience brings utterly new and superior values into existence; as it also does for the whole field of will, choice, and action to which preference gives rise. Love, in short, is *creative* of "existence," relative to these spheres. Hatred, on the other hand, is in the strictest sense *destructive,* since it does in fact destroy the higher values (within these spheres), and has the *additional effect* of blunting and blinding our feeling for such values and power of discriminating them. It is only because of their destruction (within these spheres) by hatred, that they *become* indiscernible.[6]

. . . The lover's notorious propensity (particularly in the case of sexual love), to "over-value," exalt, and idealize the object of his love, is by no means always present where it is commonly alleged to be. It is usually only the "detached observer" who arrives at this conclusion, because he fails to recognize the particular *individual* values present in the object, but discernible only to the sharper eye of love. The "blindness" then, is all on the side of the "detached observer." Indeed, the essence of individuality in another person, which cannot be described or expressed in conceptual terms (*Individuum ineffable*), is *only* revealed in its full purity by love or by virtue of the insight it provides. When love is absent the "individual" is immediately replaced by the "social personality," the mere focus of a set of relationships (being an aunt or an uncle, for instance), or the exponent of a particular social function (profession), etc. In this case it is the lover who actually sees *more* of what is present than the others, and it is *he* and not "others," who therefore sees what is objective and real. Only a falsely subjective devaluation of the real and objective to a mere "universality of application" or "general validity," . . . could necessarily lead to any other conclusion. In many cases, admittedly, this tendency toward "idealization" really does exist. But so far as it is present, it is not properly attributable to *love* for the other person, but to the obstacles which love encounters in the besetting tastes, interests, ideas, and ideals of the lover himself. But that is simply due to partial "egoism," to a failure to transcend oneself and the mental processes colored by one's own physical sensations and instincts, so as to make contact with the object and the values it contains. . . .

. . . *love is that movement wherein every concrete individual object that possesses value achieves the highest value compatible with its nature and ideal vocation; or wherein it attains the ideal state of value intrinsic to its nature.* (Hatred, on the other hand, is a movement in the opposite direction.) We are not concerned here with whether the love in question refers to oneself or to others, or with any other distinctions which might be drawn in this connection. . . .

What we have hitherto treated as the acts of love and hatred, are merely the *bare essentials* of identity in those acts which remain the same throughout all the differences they may exhibit. But we can now characterize these differences by means of a three-dimensional classification, into what I shall describe as the *forms, modes,* and *kinds* of love and hatred.

Corresponding to the basic division of all acts into vital acts of the body, purely mental acts of the self, and spiritual acts of the person, we also find love and hatred existing in three *forms:* spiritual love of the person, mental love of the individual self, and vital or passionate love. Although vital, mental, and spiritual acts are intrinsically different in themselves, and are felt as different, without prior reference to their source, they do have an essential affinity with these sources, namely the body, the self, and the person. At the same time, these emotional act-forms also have an essential reference to particular kinds of *value* as their noematic counterparts; vital acts to the values of the "noble" and the "mean" or "base"; mental acts to the value of knowledge and beauty (cultural values); and spiritual acts to the values of the "holy" and the "profane." The highest form of love is accordingly that which relates to objects (or persons), having the intrinsic value of holiness; mental love in that which relates to the "noble." Objects whose value is simply that of being "pleasant," engender neither love nor hatred. There is just a feeling of pleasantness (including reflexive modes of this, such as "enjoyment"), together with an "interest" in things that are pleasant, or indirectly pleasing, and so "useful"; but there is no love for them.[7] For although we may speak, colloquially, of "loving" a food, the expression is quite unsuited to the phenomenon it describes. Merely "pleasant" things cannot be suitable for love, seeing that they are incapable of an enhancement of value in the sense implicit in the nature of love. Hence there is no such thing as "sensual love," so far as the word "sensual" in this expression is taken to denote a particular kind of love, and not just a way of saying that love, in this instance, is accompanied and interspersed with sensual feeling and emotion. A purely "sensual" attitude to a person, for example, is at the same time an absolutely cold and *loveless* attitude. It necessarily treats the other as merely subservient to one's own sensual feelings, needs, and, at best, enjoyment. But this is an attitude wholly incompatible with any sort of intentional love for the other, as such. Such an attitude is quite justified, from the ethical point of view, in relation to objects having no other value in themselves than that of being pleasant, which means, in effect, to things that are, and appear to be, "dead." But if it relates to an object which is manifestly susceptible of other and higher values than that of being pleasant to the senses—be it only the smallest and most trifling instance of vital value in plant or animal; and if it is present, moreover, *by itself* and not as a mere concomitant of other emotional intentions, such an attitude is "evil," or "wicked" (and most evil of all when it concerns a person). This naturally applies also to any attitude of this kind in relation to oneself.[8] There is, of course, no self-love present in such a case, but a debasement of body and spiritual personality precisely similar to that which is involved in the corresponding attitude to others.

The profound differences between these three forms of love are clearly brought out by a variety of circumstances. Firstly, by the fact that the same person can be the object of hatred *and* love, in each of their three forms, on all these levels of existence and value *at the same time* (while sensual attraction may take yet another course of its own). Thus we can love a person deeply, for instance, without his inspiring a "passionate attachment" in us, indeed while finding his whole bodily aspect extremely repellent. It is equally possible to be fired with a violent passion for someone—not just a sensual attraction—without thereby finding anything to love in his mentality, the case of his emotions, his intellectual interests, or the nature of his spiritual makeup. It is a type the poets have often depicted, the man who combines a passionate love for another with hatred of their soul, while despising himself that he needs must love what, at higher levels of being and value, he cannot but abhor. On the other hand, even the deepest hatred embracing all levels save that of the person itself, may still retain a loving concern for the other's "regeneration." Hatred which extends even to this highest level of existence, is "diabolical"; where it attaches to the mental, it is "evil," while vital hatred is merely "wicked." People who display such an evident disparity and *conflict* in their love and hatred are usually described as "maladjusted" characters. But this very fact that there can be such a variety of "maladjustments" here, suggests that these functions of love are essentially *separable,* and continue to be so even when they actually work together in harmony and have but *one* object. A "well-adjusted" character is to that extent a special gift of fortune. If it be objected that such maladjusted characters are so uncommon that one cannot use them to establish the separability of these forms of love as a general law, we may reply that a character perfectly adjusted in this respect is certainly no less uncommon. If Goethe, for instance, is an embodiment of the one type, there are other great men, such as Schopenhauer, Luther, and Saint Augustine, who are equally representative of the other. Again, the oft-mentioned *ambiguities* in the use of the word "love" are traceable to these three forms. Thus in the first place we speak of "love" in that highest sense of the word implied, e.g., in Buddha's discourses or in the Gospel's injunction to "Love God before all things, and thy neighbor as thyself." In trying to visualize such a love we have a conspectus of all that is finest and holiest in man's history. Secondly, we use the word in contexts such as those of friendship, marriage, and the family, in which it is always love for the other as an individual soul that is implied. Lastly, we use the word "love" without qualification to denote the amorous passion of a man and a woman. But language itself marks the contrast of this and all other forms of love from ties of a purely sensual kind.

From these "forms" of love, let us now distinguish its "*kinds.*" They relate to those differences which make themselves felt to us as particular qualities of the emotion *itself,* without needing to consider the various *objects,* or common characteristics of these, to which such emotions refer. Thus we maintain that e.g., maternal and filial love, the love of home and country, and love in the implied sense of "sexual love," are already distinct from one another as actual emotions, and not merely by the fact of being exercised in different fields, like a love for art, for the state, etc. If we consider what these words denote, we find that the very *stirrings* of love in such cases already evince *separate and distinct qualities,* and that at a stage of development where they still lack objects, or at least where the empirical aspect, the character of the object, has hardly yet been given. The (German) language frequently marks this difference by combining the name of the object with the word "*liebe*" (love) in one and the same verbal unit, the object word being placed first.[9] Thus we cannot speak of *Staatenliebe* (love of the state), on the analogy of *Heimatliebe* (love of home) and *Vaterlandsliebe* (love of country), but only of *Liebe zum Staate;* there is *Gottesliebe* (love of God) but no *Kunstliebe* (love of art). Again, we do not have a *Vaterliebe* (father-love) corresponding to *Mutterliebe* (mother-love); the word "father-love" actually leaves us in doubt as to whether the father is the loving or the loved one, whereas "mother-love" is absolutely definite in referring to the mother's love for her child. The authenticity of the various kinds of love is warranted by their being recognizable as stirrings, *without* a semblance of the object to which they are directed having been given in any way. They are genuine *qualities of the acts themselves.* Thus a person having neither home nor country can still experience the characteristic stirrings of love for these things, even when they lack an object and persist therefore as yearnings without fulfillment. Again, when abroad for instance, one may be suddenly overtaken by a feeling of nostalgia, though without having any "thought" or "idea" of home in mind. Here we experience a powerful and peculiar hankering for somewhere far away and are overcome with tenderness for something which commends itself to us as fond and familiar. Perhaps we may endure this unsatisfied longing for a considerable time, without realizing that it is our home that we are yearning for. *Mother-love,* however, provides a particularly clear instance of a genuine *kind* of love in this sense. The occurrence of this affection (like that of the instinct associated with it), is quite unconnected with any form of experience with children on the part of the woman concerned. The presence of this specifically "motherly" disposition is not contingent upon the woman in question having children of her own, nor would the affection disappear, as such, if she had never seen children, or had absolutely no conception of the process of child-bearing. It is only these genuine kinds of love therefore, that are capable of true "*fulfillment*" in a given object. Those, on the other hand, which can only be distinguished according to their objects, are incapable of "fulfillment." Hence there is no "father-love" corresponding to "mother-love." And hence, too, a man's love for his child is much more powerfully affected by his love for the child's mother than is the mother's love for her child by her love for the child's father; just as it also depends to a far greater extent on the appearance and character of the child itself. His love for the child is also conditioned, of course, by the fact that it is "his own" child, but this only comes about by means of an act of judgment, and not in the immediate fashion characteristic of mother-love. This immediate feeling for the child as "hers," like the original longing for fulfillment of a love already evinced beforehand, is an intrinsic feature of the feminine consciousness as such, and has no analogy in the masculine frame of mind. Correspondingly, it is only in woman that the procreative urge has the form of an innate *instinct,* whereas in man this urge has merely the character of a wish, and not that of an instinct or drive; in other words, it is always based on grounds of some kind.[10] This can also be seen in the fact that in most cases the first awakening of the father's love for the child occurs at a more advanced stage of the child's development than the mother's, for it only begins when the mental and spiritual personality of the child has begun to assert itself more plainly.

Lastly, we distinguish the kinds of love from the mere *modes* thereof, which consist in nothing more than *conjunctions* of acts of love, notably with social dispositions and feelings of sympathy. These too have left their mark on language in such expressions as "kindness," "goodwill," "liking," "fondness," "grace and favor," "amiability" (whose colloquial meaning is not that of "worthiness to be loved," but implies an active attitude), "affection," "courtesy," "friendliness," "devotion," "attachment," "loyalty," "intimacy," "gratitude," "filial regard," and so on. A proportion of these terms denote attributes which are not part of the basic fabric of human nature, but only exist in the context of a given framework of historical development. Kindness, goodwill, gratitude, and affection, for example, are assuredly modes of love which are common to *all* men, and do not depend for their emergence on the level of historical development. But it is otherwise with amiability, courtesy, filial regard, etc. There are modes of hatred corresponding to these modes of love, but I shall not enter into their details here. Finally, we may distinguish these modes from mere emotional complexes in which love and hatred are simply ingredients, and do not thereby impart an underlying flavor to the whole. Such, for instance, are fidelity and humility (in regard to love), and envy, jealousy, and suspicion (in regard to hate).

Notes

1. Other examples of intrinsically social acts are those of promising, obeying, commanding, pledging oneself, etc. Cf. the penetrating analysis of "psycho-social" acts in H. L. Stoltenberg, *Soziopsychologie,* Berlin, 1914.

2. In my essay "Das Ressentiment in Aufbau der Moralen" [*Ressentiment,* trans. William W. Holdheim, ed. and introduced by Lewis A. Coser, New York, Free Press, 1961] I have exposed the limitless confusions inherent in the positivist equation of love and "altruism." Conversely, many of Nietzsche's arguments against love, in the chapter on "Love of one's neighbor" in *Also sprach Zarathustra* are applicable only to this positivist misrepresentation of love as altruism.

3. Compare Aristotle's penetrating discussion in the chapter on "Self-love" in the *Nicomachean Ethics.* How vastly superor he is, on this point, to all who advocate a "sociological" explanation for love and hatred!

4. Karl Jaspers's treatment in the chapter on "Die enthusaistische Einstellung in die Liebe" of his *Psychologie der Weltanschauungen* (Berlin, 1919) is in agreement on all fundamental points with the analysis presented in this chapter. On the problem itself, cf. Alexander Pfänder, "Zur Psychologie der Gesinnungen," in *Jahrbuch für Philosophie und phänomenologische Forschung,* vol. 3, Halle, 1916.

5. Cf. on this *Der Formalismus in der Ethik,* pp. 63 seq., pp. 260 seq. [*Formalism in Ethics and Non-formal Ethics of Values,* pp. 89ff. Some of this material is in ch. 10 of this volume.—Ed.]

6. As Jaspers pertinently remarks: "In love we do not discover values, we discover that everything is more valuable," "Die enthusiastische Einstellung."

7. As Malebranche rightly saw, in the *Recherche de la vérité.*

8. As Kant rightly points out in reference to onanism: cf. *Metaphysische Anfangsgründe der Tugendlehre,* translated in T. K. Abbott, *Kant's Theory of Ethics,* 6th ed., 1909.

9. [There is, unfortunately, no way of reproducing this argument convincingly in English.—Trans.]

10. To a man, conception and gestation are essentially no more than a "consequence" of the sexual act, and do not appear to be due to a genuine procreative instinct, as has also been justly observed by the gynecologist Hugo Sellheim, in *Das Rätsel des Ewig-Weiblichen.*

5

The Meaning of Suffering

An essential part of the teachings and directives of the great religious and philosophical thinkers the world over has been on *the meaning of pain and suffering*. Based on these teachings, invitations and instructions were issued to encounter suffering correctly—to suffer properly (or to move suffering to another plane).

Neither the interpretation of suffering nor the way of responding to it would be meaningful if the life of the emotions were exclusively restless, mute, and blind. If emotions were produced solely according to the principle of causality, they would operate merely as conditions that control us. However, our emotional life does not work in this way. Our emotions are organized into a highly differentiated system of natural disclosures and signs. By means of these signs we are made aware of ourselves. A given emotion occurs in experience already as something with a "meaning," a "sense." This emotion presents objective evaluations of states of affairs, of an activity or certain fate that may befall us, or of an anticipated value of such an event. In these anticipations, the emotions urge us to do something or caution us to stop. In the feeling of fatigue there is a warning that may be expressed in the language of common sense as "stop working" or "go to sleep." The vertigo we experience when we stand before an abyss urges us to "step back." The warning in this feeling seeks to save us from a fall by presenting the image of the fall in advance of its possible actuality. A dread announces to us a possible damage to life as a "danger" before such a thing occurs. Because of this dread, we are better able to cope with this possibility.[1] A hope drives us to act and promises us some good before we possess it. A shame preserves intact, and in public, one's affection for the body and mind of a person deemed worthy of

This essay was originally published in *Gesammelte Werke,* vol. 6, "Vom Sinn des Leides," *Schriften zur Soziologie und Weltanschauungslehre,* ed. Maria Scheler, (Bern and Munich: Francke Verlag, 1963), pp. 36–72. A literal translation of this essay into English by Daniel Liderbach appeared in *Max Scheler (1874–1928): Centennial Essays,* ed. Manfred S. Frings (The Hague: Martinus Nijhoff, 1974), pp. 121–63. Although helpful at several points, I found this translation to be rough and have retranslated Scheler's essay entirely.

this, as well as commitment to that person.[2] An appetite or a loathing clarifies for us emotionally the use or harm of a food. A repentance relieves us of our past and frees us for a new good because it purges the past, perhaps in a painful manner, and discards what was a burden.[3] All these examples show that emotions can have, in our experience of them, an inherent meaning. This meaning distinguishes itself clearly from its causal origin and purely objective purposefulness in daily life. Indeed, this meaning may relate to many kinds of pain apparently lacking in meaning.

Just as feeling is not devoid of meaning and sense, so is feeling not merely a state. Emotions can also be expressed in a variety of ways:[4] pain and suffering, not simply the stimulus that causes them, can be felt differently in functionally distinct levels. The stimuli that cause physical pain to which the emotions react are constant in history. But the capacity for enduring and tolerating pain, which is different from its stimuli, has varied in the history of civilization. The same is true for the capacity to be joyful. The capacity to be joyful is greater as the sensation of pleasure is smaller and more fleeting. The emotional function of "enjoying oneself" puts this sensation into play. Also, the emotional-functional acceptance of the same feeling can vary in the following ways: we can "give ourselves up" to suffering or pit ourselves against it; we can "endure" suffering, "tolerate" it, or simply "suffer"; we can even "enjoy" suffering (algophilia). These phrases signify *styles* of feeling and of willing based on feeling, which are clearly not determined by the mere state of feeling.

One level *above* these "functions of feeling" consists of acts of our *spiritual personality*. These acts, in which the whole of our life is integrated into the world, give an entirely different character to the size, place, meaning, and fruitfulness of our feelings. Here one can find differences of several kinds: of attentiveness, e.g., in being sensitive and insensitive to emotions; of mental movements, in which pain and suffering are sought or efforts made to escape them (for pain and suffering can actually be "overcome" only by being "suppressed" into the subconscious); of evaluation, in which suffering is seen as a penalty or atonement, a means of purification or correction, etc.; and finally, of religious and metaphysical *interpretation,* by means of which our emotions are integrated, beyond their immediate meanings, as a part is connected to the totality of the world and to its divine ground. Every philosophical doctrine of suffering thus conveys a special symbol of our palpitations of heart and attributes meaningful or meaningless powers to guide us in interpreting the play of our emotions.

The purely sensational and objective aspect of pain and suffering are equally factual for every living person, and this is the inescapable destiny of all. Nevertheless, in spite of this blind reality, there is a sphere of meaning and a sphere of freedom in which the great doctrines of salvation are rooted.

All suffering and pains of creatures have at least an objective *meaning*. As Aristotle already recognized, pleasure of any kind, and its opposite, express either that *life is enhanced or inhibited*. This statement remains correct in principle in spite of apparent exceptions. We can certainly drink a mouthful of ice water, which quenches our thirst pleasurably, although, in a flushed state, we run the risk of dying; there are painful operations, which save the life of the body; there are sweet, tasty poisons and bitter medicines in the literal and figurative senses. The degree of harm to life and pain appear only slightly to mirror one another: the tearing out of a fingernail causes great pain, although it is irrelevant to one's continued living, whereas the destruction of a part of the cerebral cortex, which is fatal, is painless. These and similar objections can be overcome by introducing three other truths along with Aristotle's principle:

1. Meaningful feelings of warning and attraction are directed only toward damaging or enhancing influences *typical* for the species of an organism as these influences are encountered in nature. If a part of the organism is normally protected from intrusions, as the cortex is protected by the skull, then pain is not alarming. Pain is the normal medium of communication between every organ and the brain concerning threats to the organ (the organ doesn't wait until damage has already occurred to warn the brain). But nature cannot take into consideration changing stimuli and combinations of stimuli caused by civilization and history. Nor can nature consider rare, artificial operations on the organism.

2. Pleasure and displeasure are symptoms *and* psychic reflections of the enhancement or inhibition of life. However, not all feelings may be taken as involving the *entire* life of the organism. Feelings mostly pertain only to the life activity of that part of the organism and its immediate state in direct contact with the stimuli. The lower, peripheral emotions, principally the sensations, do not err concerning the value they find in the stimuli. But they are completely *particularized* witnesses and, at the same time, generally shortsighted, i.e., the drink of water does enhance briefly the life activity of the immediately stimulated organ in spite of the terminal harmfulness to the whole organism by the stimulus in the long run.

3. The teaching of Aristotle is more solidly supported if combined

with the doctrine of *deep levels of feeling,* as I have developed this in another writing.[5] I referred to the following levels:

a. *Sensations,* which are localized throughout the organism—pain, sensual pleasure, itching, and tickling.

b. *Vital feelings,* which are restricted to the whole of the organism and its particular life center—weakness, vigor, weak and strong life feeling, restfulness and tension, fear, sense of health, sense of sickness. These feelings are not experienced as a kind of grief, sadness, or joy. They are not qualities of the spiritual "self" "possessing" a body, but are spread diffusely throughout the whole of the lived body. These feelings are self-relating because of the self-relatedness of the whole body.

c. *Psychic feelings,* which are immediately self-relating and, at the same time, relate functionally to prominent fantasy items, to persons of the environment, and to external or personal things. These relations are mediated primarily by one's imagination. On this level, emotion is "intentional" and values are grasped cognitively. One is able to feel the same thing again that was once felt. One can also respond to others sympathetically or compassionately. The sensations and vital feelings, in contrast, remain "static" because it is of their essence to be always merely "topical" and to belong only to the subject that feels them; they are not communicable as are the deeper feelings. Indeed, sensations are not communicable at all; vital feelings are communicable only to a limited extent. However, spiritual feelings are "static" in a different sense. In the changing feelings of the lived body, the higher feelings shift only slightly since they draw their meaning from processes represented independently of the body whose value they simultaneously lay hold of.

d. *Purely spiritual, religious-metaphysical feelings,* the "feelings of salvation," which relate to the core of the spiritual person as to an indivisible whole—happiness, despair, security, pangs of conscience, peace, etc. One who carefully studies both the levels of feeling and the many rich and lawful ways in which feelings are interrelated will soon learn that the experiences of "enhancement" and "inhibition," grasped either in the opposition between pleasure and displeasure or as something objectively announced, do not always refer in man to the "same thing" at each level. The life of the whole organism is experienced as enhanced or inhibited *only* in vital feelings. Actually, the organism experiences its life in vital feelings as being "hindered" or "helped." The particular, near sighted sensations must first be processed in the spiritual life center—the drive center. They must be "perceived" and "appreciated" in the interplay of feelings by the higher

synthetic functions, so that the sensations become biologically meaningful for the felt vitality of the whole organism. Spiritual and intellectual feelings, however, do not chiefly announce the enhancement and
inhibition of the "life" that we humans share essentially with the
higher animals. Rather, these feelings are intended to make known to
us the perfection and depreciation of our intellectual-spiritual *person*
whose moral destiny and individual direction are largely independent
of our animal life. This orientation to our spiritual person is true especially for the religious-metaphysical and moral feelings—for example, in each feeling of conscience.

The most formal, general concept under which *all* suffering may be
subsumed, from sensations of pain to religious-metaphysical despair,
appears to me to be the idea of *sacrifice*. Death, in the objective meaning of the word, is "sacrifice." It is a sacrifice the organic individual
has to endure for the procreation of the species. In addition, the origin
of death is closely linked with procreation and its related loss of substance and vitality. Nevertheless, death's natural approach and the
length of life of the species are dependent upon procreation. Death is,
morphologically, a sacrifice for the sake of a certain type of organization and differentiation (Minot), which appears for the first time in the
world of the Metazoa. All suffering and pain are, according to a metaphysical and most formal meaning, a sacrifice of the *part* for the *whole*
and of relatively *lower* values for *higher* ones.

However true Aristotle's basic thought is concerning pleasure and
displeasure as signs of the enhancement and constraint of life, the soul,
and the person, nevertheless this idea cannot make understandable the
meaning of the existence of suffering and pain in the world. What Aristotle explains is simply the meaningful and purposeful relation of
pleasure and pain to stimuli and reactions of the organism when stimuli augment or moderate life. These relations are meaningful and purposeful as a system of signs, of attractions and warnings, for a definite
behavior of the organism. All kinds of "training" of animals and humans, insofar as they use nonmoral rewards and punishments, merely
make use of these natural relations of feelings to specific life processes.
Thus, "self-training" is the proper name for one's own experiences of
learning, which the organism undergoes on the basis of success and
failure of originally merely arbitrary movements—such as reflexes or
play. On the other hand, any training that is artificial and externally
imposed uses only the natural system of rewards and punishments of
the organic life of feeling for situations, deeds, and goals not typical of
the natural way of life of the organism. However, the question must be
raised, if there is indeed a signal system of warnings and attractions

for life-enhancing and life-damaging behavior, why does this system take pain and suffering exclusively as signs? Why not other kinds of signals? Why not signals that do *not* hurt—as pain does? Why did the divine cause of the world, since he is so reasonable and wise, not use a less barbaric and intense remedy to provide for his creatures a system of natural signals to warn or attract them concerning what should be avoided or done for their self-preservation and self-help? And why were goodness and love, which higher religions assign exclusively to the Cause of the world, so little in keeping with his judgment that he chose pain and suffering to warn his creatures of a danger to life? The Aristotelian idea, which has often been used in a theodicy, is theologically insufficient. I proclaim boldly; if I had wanted to come to the idea of the existence of God by means of a cause-effect connection starting from nature and the existence of the world as known to me empirically, and not from an original, personal, and experiential contact of the core of my personality with a divine goodness and wisdom as found in a religious act,[6] then, even if the rest of the world shines in peace, bliss, and harmony, the existence of a single sensation of pain in a worm would completely suffice to destroy my belief in an "infinitely good" and almighty creator of the world.

Only when one sees pain and suffering in light of the idea of *sacrifice* is it, perhaps, possible to come closer to a more profound theodicy of suffering. This was the understanding of suffering early Christianity took originally with the powerful idea of the sacrificial suffering of God who, in Christ, was born out of love and died as a representative for humankind.

The ambiguous idea of "sacrifice" must first be clarified. One can only speak of an objective sacrifice when the attainment of a good of comparatively "higher value" appears to be necessarily related to destruction or lessening of a good of comparatively lower value—assuming there is an evil or a misery in such a lower value. This objective sense is distinct from freely sacrificing oneself or sacrificing something of which only free and wise persons are capable. When one admits merely positive and negative values and different quantities of each, but does not also acknowledge objective scales of value, one can speak only of costs but not of sacrifice. Whoever prefers a greater pleasure to a lesser one, or a longer-lasting future pleasure to a passing present one of the same kind, or lesser suffering to greater ones, does not thereby make a "sacrifice." He is only carefully estimating the "costs." The notion of sacrifice encompasses much more: not only a calculus of pleasure and displeasure, or an estimate of goods and miseries, but an irrevocable elimination of goods and pleasure that cannot reappear in other forms. Furthermore, sacrifice embraces a final establishment of misery and pain. Each sacrifice is, subjectively and objectively, always also necessarily a sacrifice *for something*. Mere positing of a misery or a suffering by itself as an objective event is meaningless. If suffering is freely pursued and intended it is absurd, pathological, as in algophilia, the passion for the gruesome, the negativity of purely destroying one-self and others. However, sacrificing "for" always implies a positive value of a higher level or the avoidance of an evil of a higher level—higher, that is, than the level on which the sacrificed good is found. "Sacrifice" is necessary when conformity among things and events that carry value inexorably links the realization of a higher positive value, or the avoidance of an evil of a higher range, to the establish-ment and realization of an evil of a lower range.

From the point of view of this formal notion of sacrifice, I assert that each kind of pain and suffering, regardless of how the person who suffers behaves toward any of them, is the subjective reflection in the psyche of sacrifice. Each suffering is correlated to objective events of sacrifice in which a good of a lower order is surrendered for a good of a higher order.

The fundamental ontological relationship here is between part and whole. However, the whole is not artificial. It does not exist only by the grace of our comprehensive understanding. It is real. And it is more than the sum of its parts. The whole in which suffering occurs is one whose being, effect, and value are independent of the being, effect, and value of its parts. Only when this whole, this totality, works and lives in its parts, while the parts are not only in but also work "for" the whole, can there be talk of sacrifice of a part for the whole. And only then does the possibility of any kind of suffering persist. In such cases the parts of the whole are also called its "members" in which the rela-tion between whole and part is a "connection in solidarity." Here the whole rules, leads, and guides "for" the parts, and the parts specifi-cally serve, are led by, and are guided "for" the whole. In a purely mechanical world there could be no possibility of pain and suffering. The same would be true in an absolutely "teleological" world, as theism thinks the world to be. Even if we assume a world whose parts are not independent substances equipped with dynamic properties, but only found exclusively in the existence and essence of the whole—as "dependent" parts, "modes," subjectively modeled profiles, or "per-spectives" of the whole—the minimum condition for the possible ex-istence of suffering and pain would be lacking. Neither the common, rational cause-effect kind of theism, nor the mechanistic materialist theory of association in the psyche, nor even the abstract pantheistic monism of Spinoza and Hegel is able to make intelligible the existence of suffering and pain. The condition for suffering is always the conflict of autonomous, independent parts with their functional position in a whole in which part and whole are related in solidarity. This conflict is always the most *general ontological* basis for the *possibility* of suffering and pain in the world. The special secondary causes that may appear to create suffering and pain in this or that form among earthly creatures are insignificant. We generally call displeasure only the way in which a member part of a whole, as defined, "has" or "experiences" the conflict with the whole against its own activity. Such conflict presumes spontaneous, though not arbitrary, activity of the whole as well as the part. If it were possible to eliminate each kind of opposition of the whole to the part wherever the part is not meaningfully working for the whole (we return later to the technique of "enduring" suffering), then the most general condition for possible pain of each kind would be eliminated. Pain would also be eliminated if the part accommodated completely to the dynamic working of the whole and expressed no opposition to it.

In the widest sense, each thing that presents itself as a unity of many parts may be considered to consist of relations of "part" to "whole." In our human world, we can find this unity in shallow, nonmetaphysical experience, i.e., in all life units—cells, organisms, sociobiological totalities. Furthermore, this unity is found in all persons, in their partial acts, and, without compromise to their individual dignity, in the collective personalities of which they are members—nation, state, church, civilization. If the *world* itself were such a complex whole—we certainly don't know that it is—we would have to credit the "world" too with a kind of suffering.

Natural death determines its goal and meaning at the time of its appearance. Death demands a natural self-sacrifice of the individual for the procreation and advancement of the species. This is the "sacrifice" that surrenders one life for more and automatically higher life. The idea of death is the most grief-filled thought possible for humans as creatures, insofar as death is considered from the point of view of one's own individual drive to live. In this view, death is separated from the goals immanent in the evolution of life as well as the objectives and fate of one's spiritual personality. Pain viewed in a similarly narrow way is like a death in miniature, a sign of death, a sacrifice of part of the organism for the preservation of the whole. Pain reminds us that death is ahead. We call "pain" that experience of subservience, limitation, and constraint a life unit (cell, tissue, organ, organ system) must undergo for the organization and integrity of the whole.

Pain and death are also similar to one another in that the condition of their appearance in the whole of nature became much more probable, indeed inescapable, as the organism grew qualitatively distinct and more complex. The unison of such internally differentiated organisms was maintained through hierarchization of functions and specialization of parts. But only this sort of unison created the conditions of pain. Among the distinct, complex, organized living creatures an evident morphological manifestation of death also began, namely the corpse. Here too the first evident, painful sensation was likely to have occurred. For the "struggle of the parts" (Roux) in the organism and their solidarity in the common, hierarchic service around the whole are the pure conditions of forming a vital unison. On the other hand, all "growth pains," including growing pains, are inhibitions in growing parts due to resistance of a stronger and more rigid environment; these have the same meaning in miniature that an individual death has for procreation of the species. Procreation has been called growth of the individual beyond itself. Growth too, insofar as it is more than growth in size, rests on the procreative division of the individual cells from which an organ develops. Death is thus comparable to a growth pain of the life of the individual beyond itself, whereas a growth pain is comparable to a death of the self-dividing cells and organs as though this were a path for further procreation. In both cases, the idea of sacrifice closely unites death and pain.

Everything we call "suffering," as opposed to "doing" and "working" (though not to pleasure), is of two kinds. The resistance of the whole against one of its parts is perceived by the part as being greater the less the part is able to offer counterresistance and preserve itself. Pain, as the inner perception of *this* "suffering," is the pain of being powerless, of need, of poverty, of the deterioration of strength, of old age. However, "suffering" does not grow less if the process is reversed, namely, if in its *efforts* to grow in power and size the part pits itself against the rigidity and organization of the whole. This is a contrary type of pain, the pain of growth, of becoming, of the "pangs of birth." The latter is a symptom of an increase in life and tends to be the more noble pain; the former is a sign of death and more common. Nevertheless, both are instances of "sacrifice."

Vital love is the drive to procreate among the more highly organized, bisexual beings. It is thus joined to death, for death is the basic response to the loss of substance and power in procreation for the whole. Death and pain are related just as integrally, for their formation is a result of the constructive, erotic powers of life units. Love and pain are, therefore, necessarily also intimately joined. As the motive force of each new unison in space and of all propagation in time, love establishes the necessary conditions of sacrifice, which are pain and death. The obscure urge of living beings to rise above themselves to more and higher life, generally expressed in the formation of unisons and in procreation, founds the necessary ontological conditions of pain. In this twofold sense, pain and death stem from love.

Love, death, pain, formation of unison, and *rising to higher organization* by means of differentiation and integration—these are inseparably established in the entire sphere of pure vital existence as an equivalent group of processes and states. This may be difficult to imagine, but we must endeavor to grasp, in a simple intuition, the whole, intimate, imperative unity of this basic manifestation of life. The life of organized plants, animals, and men is only a random example of the congruity of these vital processes. The elevation of life in this intuition issues in a lofty perspective in which the destiny of each living thing is seen as being allotted the same fundamental events as the life of all other living things, primitive or complex.

The principle that gives us the first insight into such coherences and their necessity is this: one cannot have the sweetness, unison, and community of love, nor the higher development and growth of life, without sacrifice, death, and pain. This insight can be grasped in its entirety not only with the mind but with the heart. In so doing we will be reconciled much more profoundly to the existence of pain and death than merely by intellectually understanding the truth of the purposefulness of pain. If we were to ask ourselves whether we were seriously prepared to renounce love and the higher development of life in order to be rid of pain and death, certainly only a few would answer with a simple yes. But if death and pain are the necessary channels through which the preservation and growth of life must go, we could only with difficulty say no to them. We may escape these channels partially and fight the pains of want, but not those of growth.

A second insight is tied to the first: sacrifice is Janus-faced, laughing and weeping at the same time. Sacrifice embraces both the joys of love and the pain of giving up life for what one loves. Sacrifice is, in a sense, prior to joys and pain, which are only its expressions and its children. In sacrifice, pleasure and pain are tightly bound into one "bouquet," as it were, in a simple human act. For life, whose every movement in seeking a new, higher state involves sacrifice, greets the new in this bouquet and departs from the old. This is clear in the highest form of sacrifice, in the free, conscious, spiritual sacrifice of love, in which one experiences in a single act the happiness of love and the pain of loss of the good surrendered in loving. From this purest and highest experi-

ence of a free spirit, a flame also illuminates even all nonspiritual suffering. The method of hedonism, which seeks quantitatively to balance
pleasure and pain in human life, such that greater pleasure yields optimism and greater pain pessimism, appears absurd in light of the
above. Both pleasure and pain are equally and originally rooted in sacrifice and sacrificial love. To deny pleasure or pain, or both, would be
to deny life itself. The concentration and synthesis of pleasure and
pain, their highest integration in the purest sacrifice of love, is the climax of life. In sacrifice, losing and gaining are identical.

Only in the lowest, most peripheral states of our sensible existence
are pain and pleasure distinct. The deeper we probe into ourselves, the
more we concentrate on the actual core of our person, the less are
pleasure and pain distinguishable. The pessimism of Schopenhauer,
for example, which held only pain to be positive and pleasure, as the
"calm" from tensions of life, need, and striving, to be negative, failed
to notice either the positive pleasure that occurs in the midst of vitality
or the greatest pleasure found in spiritual "creating." This pessimism
was oblivious to the suffering and pain that arise not from want or
need, but form an increment of vitality, from growth. In this view, life
never progresses except through the compelling drive of avoiding displeasure and tension, as John Locke had incorrectly taught and Schopenhauer repeated. The existence of "play" among men and the higher
animals, even the "random movements" of lower animals and one-
celled creatures, proves that life is pleasurably active out of the abundance of its forces. The useful effects of these motions, which memory
ascertains and associates with more precisely determined combinations of stimuli, are secondary to this primitive, pleasurable activity.
Only through becoming habituated to the benefits and "successes" of
such purposeless playful activity do so-called needs arise. The most
sublime creations of the human spirit are as little an exception to this
rule as is the strongest pleasure of the senses, the act of procreation.
Aesthetic enjoyment, "free of volition," does not signify, as Schopenhauer claimed, the greatest happiness. The gratification an artist or
scholar has in his own finished work is incomparably greater than the
enjoyment of those who admire it. Moreover, the pleasure the genera-
tor takes *in the process of creating* is greater than the pleasure others
find in his product, for he will take his work as "finished" only when
the joy inherent in creating begins to diminish for him. God alone
never tires of creating, as only his work is infinite. Nature has joined
the most exciting, sensuous pleasure of life to the procreation of life by
life. In this "brand" of sensual pleasure nature has shown the creation
of life by a living creature to be of incomparably greater distinction

than the pleasures that accompany simple maintenance of life, such as in satisfying hunger and thirst. The act of procreating, which occurred first among the Metazoa, was originally coincident with death as the evil of evils. This act separated itself from death more and more sharply, yet always remains the first origin of death.[7] Nature has found procreation worthy to be the most profound pleasure in comparison to which even the triumph of the will to power remains inferior.

The notion of the higher, so-called historical, evolutionary stages of humankind obscures these simple lawful states of affairs but does not eliminate them. Factors determined by suffering and pleasure are joined together naturally in human evolution but have no equivalent in descriptions based purely on biological laws. But biology is never determiend solely by logical ideas. When animated by spiritual love, our biological ideas encounter a new world of pains and joys.

Accordingly, a final principle may be formulated. The more extensively communities are organized, the greater will be the intimate interdependence of humans through the increase in differentiation and integration of civilization, intellectual culture, work, and life. Each stage in the evolution of human communities thus inevitably places a greater burden upon people in degrees as well as kinds of suffering and pain. For according to Minot,[8] death and the capacity for pain appear like a sacrifice of life for the greater development of the species. All observers agree that the constant, uniform serenity found among primitive peoples—who are seldom disquieted by the elemental suffering conferred on the species—has no equivalent in civilized societies. The *fear* of death is one of the most terrifying sources of suffering in humans as distinct from animals. In animals, this fear is bound only to their present, as a momentary anxiety in a particular situation. But among primitives fear of death is largely absent due to widely found beliefs in the afterlife of the dead, or of the invisible body and soul, or in reincarnation in new bodies that are the real identities of grandchildren and grandparents. The capacity among primitives to *suffer the same* feelings of pain as civilized people is undoubtedly less. Although primitive people are much more exposed to injuries, accidents, and the dangerous powers of nature, their fear of nature and alienation from it are nevertheless far less than those of civilized people. These emotions, of fear and alienation, were awakened by perceiving nature and its dangers as objects, and by the increasing struggle of technical civilization against nature. Among primitive people, individual self-consciousness is totally embedded in community, collective ideas, and emotions, and the conscious life of an entire living generation is set in the traditions, practices, and customs of the past. In the maternal arms of nature, community, and tradition, which are the factual conditions of primitive life, the individual person and the whole generation sleep and dream, as it were, without having a unique and distinct consciousness of the boundaries of *their own feelings*. In this lies the cause for the lack of every deeper suffering that arises only among civilized people. Civilized people are *alienated* from the protection of community, tradition, and nature. Each civilized person, alone, bears responsibility for himself and his behavior. Worry and anxiety are the inevitable counterparts of this isolation and insecurity.

The same principle holds true of the culture of historical civilizations. A sense of the dangers of the world, of the history of human activity and the prodigious accomplishments of civilization, culture, and the state, the great increase in human population, refinement of the senses and of customs, division of labor in the economy, and the specialization of knowledge—these and other specific characteristics of Western peoples have certainly *not led to their growing happiness*. China, Japan, and India would have remained happier had European civilization not been forced upon them. Within Western history suffering has advanced even faster than happiness. Rousseau and Kant were right on this point, that civilization creates more, even deeper, suffering by its successful struggle against the causes of suffering. The new sources of pleasure and enjoyment created in the West are considerable, but they pertain only to the more superficial feelings. The deeper emotions touching on the substance of humanity, such as peace of conscience or joys of love, are only slightly changeable over time. In these deeper emotions the organization of our senses is already so set that the intensity of pain is greater than that of pleasure. The increase in pain produced by new, growing pain stimuli is considerably more accelerated than the increase of pleasure in the equally new and growing pleasure stimuli.[9] We more easily accustom ourselves to an advancing standard of living, to inventions, new machines, and tools, than to miserable situations. Pain is more stable, less weakened by adaptation and habituation, and less relative than pleasure.[10] Talleyrand's observation that those who live after 1789 do not know the joys of life is not simply the view of a single man, or the prejudice of a man of the upper class, or valid only for the sudden changes introduced by the French Revolution. Could one not say the same thing, with far more reason, for the year 1914? Few dreams were so cruelly ruined by events as the nineteenth-century dream of increasing human happiness through the course of history. The technical and organizational means developed to produce this happiness had so deeply entangled the activities and minds of human beings that the goal for which all these activities had been undertaken dropped entirely from view. Basically, man has suffered *more* from the autonomy, accidents, and uncontrollable nature of technology than from the evils technology was to remedy.

Since Jean-Jacques Rousseau this condition has produced in thinking and feeling a dubious inclination toward cultural *pessimism*. Rousseau, Kant, Hegel, Schopenhauer, Eduard von Hartmann, Nietzsche, Tolstoy, Baudelaire, Balzac, and the Slavophiles Dostoyevsky and Strindberg are completely united at least in their negative evaluation of the quest of modern civilization and culture for happiness (eudaemonism). Western history before the nineteenth century entirely lacked such an exalted, unbroken orientation of the eudaemonic indictment of culture. In any case, this indictment is an index of the actual spirit of the times, whatever may be lacking in the justification of its theses.[11] The counsel and comfort we receive from these thinkers are certainly of very different kinds.

Not being familiar with the inescapable imperative of having to live in civilization, Rousseau, together with his whole century, counseled us naïvely to "go back to nature" as though it were an idyllic state. Kant declared one may not measure the worth and dignity of the human condition in the good fortune or painlessness of life. In the old, heroic Prussian spirit he proclaimed worth and dignity to be "in spite of all that!" The establishment "of a reign of consistent purposes in a lawful cosmopolitan community" is the highest earthly good, he believed, even if people under this reign were to suffer more. Happiness and the reward for virtue were relegated by Kant to the hereafter. For Fichte too, our duty is in rationally forming nature. He held the appeasement of our conscience in doing our duty should give us comfort in the face of our multiplying pains. Hegel solemnly explained that human history was not the "ground of happiness." In his fertile portrayal, humans are taken beyond their mute, individual suffering by the self-creation of god from the vortex of history. This god himself suffered in history, but his state of eternal "self-contradiction" eliminated all suffering through new deeds and creations. For Hegel, we are merely soldiers in service to the self-liberating, divine "idea." We are loyal to this idea and at war with suffering, which, metaphysically, is only our helper in the course of the working out of divine necessity. Suffering should be forgotten, Hegel counseled; it is only something the divine spirit "cunningly" presents as real in order to harness its own historical activity. Schopenhauer urged us to adopt the exact opposite attitude, namely, to resign ourselves to suffering the blind will that is the abiding essence of this world. As we are the blind will's most highly organized, conscious manifestation, we must suffer most deeply. Our only recourse, Schopenhauer believed, is in resignation and escape, for which he recommended the (idle) contemplation of philosophy, art, and the practice of religious asceticism. Just to exist is a "guilt," in his view, and thus existence is *suffering*. Only by making reality unreal, by denying our will, can we gain surcease from pain and find peace, if not real happiness. Eduard von Hartmann united Hegel's teaching on evolution and history with Schopenhauer's metaphysical pessimism. In his systematic, analytically acute reflections, which aimed to be true to life, he tried to show that humanity's suffering is increasing as civilization and culture progress. But, according to Hartmann, in this great process of the actualization of self and world mankind is being redeemed by historical evolution. By redeeming himself man also redeems the suffering God from the blind acts of the "fiat" of creation that originally gave this world and man their existence. As a doctrine of value, eudaemonism, whether individual, social, or evolutionary, has in Hartmann its most profound and sharpest supporter and critic. Nietzsche sought the measure of life's value in the full arc of the feelings between pleasure and pain. Although he believed deeper pleasures and suffering would, in general, eventually be eliminated, he anticipated more suffering in the future.

I doubt these counsels and comforts do justice to the large question of the historical direction pleasure and suffering will take in our lives. From different angles, each has circled round the strange, bright, dark, sweet, pleasure/pain character of sacrifice. And each has touched here and there an element of its riches. But none has encompassed the meaning of sacrifice, or plumbed its depths.

Kant, Fichte, Hegel, and the other "heroes" of the all-too-heroic Prussian Germany clearly saw the suffering and *value* inherent in sacrifice. But they failed to see that man is as little able to renounce his claim to happiness as his claim to being. The self-affirmation intrinsic to each pleasure is too secure to be denied. The value of any form of pleasure does not need to be justified. Pleasure "is" and is valuable because it *is*. Pascal said it well in his "Essay on the Passions of Love": "Pleasure is good and suffering bad. Man needs no proof of this. The heart feels it."

Heroism, with its disdain for pleasure, is a doctrine that consumes itself as necessarily as Aristippus's affirmation of pleasure. *Both inevitably* end in pessimism. In Germany, the pure heroism of Kant, Hegel, and Fichte has also had this outcome. Heroism's demand for deeds, coupled to its contempt for happiness, has one limitation: the implicit idea of a world in which heroic deeds are, metaphysically, *no longer worthwhile*. "Pure" heroism is as absurd as "pure" hedonism.

A world that existed for the sake of heroes would require these heroic beings to be tortured into displaying their "heroism." The world's best would, a priori, also be its martyrs. But such a world, with its torturing God, would not deserve heroes. The hero is only meaningful as long as he is a happy person in a sphere that goes beyond his suffering. The "absolute" hero is a fool, or a sick man who suffers from algophilia. Schopenhauer, Hartmann, and the other well-known pessimists of the "historic deed" recognized this problem.

What follows from all this is that the increasing suffering of developing civilization is worthwhile only when sacrifice is performed with love. *Sacrificial love* releases feelings of hidden bliss that compensate for the increasing pain and raise the concern of the spirit above pain. It is the pleasure of love in the creative, cultural growth of the community, and sympathy for the historicity of life, that finally compensates for the pain inherent in growth. Mere heroism is blind to such love and its most noble pleasures. Love may be cheerful *or* sorrowful to provide functional pleasure. Eudaemonism is also blind to the meaning of the necessary growth of pain. Only "sacrifice" grows, and its necessity and growth are not limited either to pleasure or to pain. Nietzsche came closest to the truth: the whole of the curve of life activity between profound pleasure and profound pain occurs "prior" to pleasure and pain. These feelings are only the accidental terminal points reached by the pendulum of life in its full swing. But the "meaning" of this swing is "sacrifice." Nietzsche did not comprehend this meaning, as he was interested only in the multiplicity of life and the scope of its movement.

Let us now turn to the things humanity learned from arduous experience as to how one should conduct oneself in the face of pain and suffering. We will not learn too much because of the immensity and darkness of the problem and the ever mute, pure fact of pain. Nevertheless, each *technique* for enduring suffering has its root in a metaphysical or religious *ethic*.

I will first point out some *main types* of *doctrines of suffering*. There have been, in history, many ways of *encountering* suffering: suffering has objectified, resigned to, tolerated, escaped from, dulled to the point of apathy, heroically struggled against, justified as deserved punishment, and denied. There is, finally, the remarkably intricate Christian doctrine of suffering: to achieve redemption from suffering *through* suffering by the merciful love of God—the "royal way of the cross."

The first of these types, the objectification of suffering, is present in greater purity in the *teachings of Buddha* and is repeated in various forms up to Spinoza and Goethe. The later Brahman Upanishads were the first to teach of an endless wandering of souls in ever-new bodies whose suffering was understood as punishment for sins in an earlier life. Metaphysical pessimism appeared openly in the philosophies of Samkha and Yoga. These views secured suffering in the encompassing ground of *being*, which included the struggle and drives in things and humans. Buddha, the great teacher of death, fulfilled his soul's needs with sweet autumnal serenity on this ground. Buddha wanted to find a way of terminating the restless wandering between guilt and atonement. His method was continually to separate the superindividual self from every drive for individuality, that is, from the power co-extensive with suffering. His equation was this: desire = reality = suffering = individuality. The separation he sought occurs in *objectifying* suffering and desire, a process in which the presumed connection between suffering, desire, and reality turns into a pure image. The technique of consciously expelling desire, pain, and suffering from the center of the psyche achieves this objectification. Love, the "redemption of the heart"[12] (not the positive blessing of the heart, as among Christians), and sympathy are only meaningful as a vehicle of this technique. The goal of this process is neither the salvation of the person nor the liberation of a happy individual self from the dim confusion of the organic. The goal, rather, is to achieve a calmness of the soul in which all desire, individuality, and suffering are dissolved and extinguished. In this calm, individual and cosmos lose reality because both turn into a mere image. But the fact that one's own suffering is being enclosed within the great necessary suffering of the world simultaneously disposes one to a mild *resignation*.[13]

There are *two* entirely opposed ways of avoiding pain and suffering. One is in active struggle against objective natural or social causes of pain and suffering and in resolute resistance to evil as though evil were an objective quality of the world. This was the way taken by the heroic-active civilization of the West. The second way consists of the attempt to avoid suffering and all subjective responses to evil through the purposeful and rigorous halting of our automatic resistances to them. The Indian learned early that we reflexively resist pain stimulated by natural and social evils. But through the intellectual skill of *nonresistance to evil* by complete "toleration" of it from the center of life, suffering could be abolished. Moreover, since evil, according to this view, is not objectively real but only the shadow *our* suffering casts upon the world, evil itself is also indirectly abolished.

In its most radical, consequential, and sublime form, the second alternative was the way of Buddha. Far less consequentially it was also the way taken by the late Stoa of Epictetus and also by *Christianity*. It was again embraced recently by Leo Tolstoy, who placed it at the heart of his entire system of ethics. The theses of the Gospel, "Do not resist miseries" and "He who lives by the sword shall perish by the sword," are consistent with the rewards promised by the so-called passive virtues. Nevertheless, this manner of encountering pain, suffering, and misery is not as deeply meaningful for Christianity as for Buddhism. For not only are the sorts of techniques Buddha adopted and developed from the Yoga teachings missing in Christianity, but the personal example Jesus gave in his life and death is basically different from that of Buddha. Jesus often showed that he intended to resist misery and malice. He cleared the temple of the money changers, opposed the Pharisees in "holy wrath," and prayed to God that "this cup might pass him by." And in his last desperate cry on the cross, which expressed his own deep pain and the burden of the sins of humanity—sins he knew he suffered as a "substitute" and experienced in the depths of his heart with all the torment of sin inherent in humanity—he showed nothing of the quiet, estranged, cool composure with which Buddha lived and died in conversation with friends. Nevertheless, the Christian ideal has embraced the patiently heroic acceptance of the cross. This has been the tragic ideal of the Christian martyrs who *valued* passive endurance of suffering *over* active resistance. In most cases, this has become an essential ingredient of a universal Christian ideal.[14]

The eastern Christian church above all, especially the Russian Orthodox, has been influential in promulgating an ethic of nonresisting, passive acceptance of suffering and misery. This ethic has assisted Slavic peoples in adjusting to their own almost masochistic character and to the violence of czarist tyranny under which they lived. In almost all respects, passive acceptance has won out over active elimination of misery and malice. This can be seen in the resigned responses of the Russian farmer of the old order to the cold of winter, hunger, thirst, the invasion of war, the assault by his lords, the force of his own and others' passions, criminal deeds, and all of life's destinies. These attitudes are expressed in the poetical-prophetic writings of the great Russian poets and thinkers, not least, Tolstoy and Dostoyevsky,[15] which glorified humble, passive suffering.

Yet, in opposition to the Western ideal of active heroism which so fatefully shaped our culture, including Western monasticism, there lives in Indian and Buddhist thought the idea of a passive heroism able to conquer the human heart in sharp contrast to the usual methods of encountering suffering, misery, and evil. This passive-heroic ideal can be formulated briefly this way:

The Buddhist attitude is as little a *simple* acceptance and toleration of suffering as is Western heroism merely a fervor actively to eliminate the external causes of suffering through systematic hygiene, technology, therapy, and civilization. Rather, it is the ardent, active will totally and radically to dispose of even the smallest atom of suffering, coupled to the fanatical belief in the practical possibility of this goal, that *connects* the Buddhist attitude with Western *active* heroism. From the Greek myths of Prometheus and Heracles to the technological-capitalistic northern European philosophies of Francis Bacon, Karl Marx, and William James, nothing was known of the difference between noble suffering, which absolves, and servile suffering, which degrades.[16] Thus, in the Western view as in the Eastern, each and every suffering is equally bad and should be abolished. Buddha charted the *path* of the will exactly opposite that of the West and, with this, established his kind of heroic activity. Briefly expressed, the West situated the means of eliminating suffering in external, technical activity directed toward nature and the organization of the community; Indian Buddhism fixed elimination of suffering in the internal activity of the psyche directed toward the drives of the organism. The burning heat of the tropics is, for Buddha, symbolic of the whole of the life drives and their center. In Buddha's thought the drives are a kind of primary, preexistent "thirst" in relation to which even the objective world is relative. In place of the passive-heroic maxim, "Do not resist misery," Buddhism put a different metaphysical and epistemological imperative, which may be characterized as follows: "Through a highly focused mental act abolish *not* misery, but any instinctive, automatic, and involuntary resistance to misery that can *possibly* arise." Buddha counseled us to abjure our "thirsts," for they are the first cause of the illusion of the *self-sufficient* existence of the world, its forms and things. Thirst is the eternal condition of suffering, which comes from the world whose existence and essence is imposed upon us without our choice. And as our "thirst" ever recreates the self-sufficient world, the Buddhist maxim may be restated as, "Resist by all means! But not the world. Rather, resist your inner, spontaneous organic-psychic resistance against misery." Misery itself is not real but only a *shadow* of possible resistance that is, simultaneously, the *impulse of existence* in all things. Resistance is only a phantasm that deceives us that the autonomous world exists.

Buddhism does not have, as do other religious and metaphysical doctrines, a separate instruction on suffering as one of its constituents; Buddhism *is* an instruction on suffering. The four golden truths that are its oldest and firmest elements entirely concern these points:[17] (1) the essence of suffering, (2) the cause of suffering, (3) the condition for elimination of suffering, (4) the way to achieve this condition with the mind. Only the fourth point treats the ethics and technique of suffering; the other three, together with the famous rule of cause and effect, that "all creatures by their activities find themselves inescapably in the states they deserve," specify a metaphysics and epistemology of suffering.

Although the Buddhist technique for elimination of suffering is of primary interest to this essay, a few words must be said as to its metaphysical and epistemological presuppositions. I will not be concerned with historical exactness or with questions of historical and psychological origins. My interest is in a *worldview* that sees Buddhism as the most towering example of a specific, possible, ideal attitude toward suffering.

Buddha's teachings on the *origin* and *meaning* of suffering are difficult to grasp and have been subjected to vastly different interpretations. The central question here, I believe, is how Buddha came to identify the existence—not essence—of the world and humanity with *suffering*. Does this identity, which sounds to us almost totally baseless, depend on a simple oversight of the innumerable and genuine kinds of pleasure, happiness, serenity, and blessedness of this world? Is the identity a generalization of Buddha's personal experiences or the experiences of the history of his people? Is his strange teaching a result of the burning, exhausting climate in which he lived, and the torments exacted upon the people there? Is the peace, quiet, and quenching of "thirst" Buddha sought only his elevation to a spiritual principle of the "cool of the shade" seldom bestowed upon the Indian people? Is his teaching a compulsive world denial, an expression of the death drive of a superannuated, sinking race denying a priori all positive feeling for active struggle against the world that a vital, soaring race would have?[18] Such an aging race would expect salvation in an attitude of gentle and quiet superconsciousness, and attempt completely to flatten and eliminate all forms of consciousness and existence. Does Buddha's teaching derive from a *notion* of fortune, happiness, and the highest good so elevated over people because of the intense longings of their hearts that in comparison *all* actual existence must appear as "suffering"? Is his teaching rooted in a deviant, compulsive fixation on the phenomena of birth, age, illness, and death, which were characterized in the first of the golden truths as the most striking witnesses for the fact that each existence and life is suffering? These phenomena played a great role in the well-known, although mythical, history of Buddha's conversion. Finally, is his teaching and its acceptance by Indian people less an expression of fragile, gently evolving lives whose active racial drives have already been deeply broken, than a witness to and, indirectly, an intellectual product of powerful and passionate characters? Are such characters so absolutely fascinated, charmed, even intoxicated by all the phenomena that can excite our human passions that they are incapable of moderation and must, to maintain themselves, *completely abstain* from the dangerous exhilarations of pleasure? Is the psychological technique of *withdrawing the self* from the causal connections of action and existence (a point to which I will return later)—the "I am not part of this," "this is not me," "this is not my property"—perhaps only a mental antidote against an overdeveloped drive to be chained ecstatically and irrevocably to any beloved phenomenon? Is such a drive so powerful that only by *systematically nipping it in the bud* will the passions be hindered from destroying the *whole* of life?

I do not believe there is much value in discussing these and other historical, racial, climatic, or psychological hypotheses before the objective *meaning* of Buddha's teaching is completely understood. And there is a long way to go before such understanding is achieved. Perhaps the hypotheses suggested above are more germane to other issues than the ones I am raising. They may better help answer the question of the conditions Western people must achieve, with their general psychological makeup, before they can turn themselves toward Buddhist teaching.

Therefore, back to the question, What does the presupposition in the first of the golden truths mean? "Existence is suffering, beginning and ending, change and variation—whether their essence is pleasure or pain—these are suffering." As long as I take Buddha to be one of the most profound minds of humanity and not a quack and plain pessimist of anger à la Schopenhauer, I will never equate the core of his thinking on suffering with his experience of suffering. One must concede that things stimulating fear, displeasure, pain, suffering, and horror were cited as witnesses to and examples of the world's "suffering"—namely, sickness, poverty, death, loss of loved ones, and so on. But the *core* of Buddha's thinking on suffering is far more formal; it goes beyond the inner experience of humans to embrace more than displeasure and pain. Buddha's thought embraces each *external* thing that impinges upon man with irresistible force, each infliction, each thing that, etymologically, is an "affect"; it embraces any "assault" on man by independently existing things and being that possess their own causal connections and conditions. The attitude taken toward "suffering" expresses an opposition more to "activity" and "work" than to pleasure.

Three things are clear: first, no personal experiences of suffering drove Buddha to his teaching that the existence of the world is suffering. Is it not true that in the myth of his life Buddha is presented to us before his conversion in the most glorious of circumstances; is it not also true that we know of his conversion only through compassion with, or a representative *intuition* of, the essential pattern of suffering of the world, which caused his conversion? Second, what one can call only with great caution Buddhist "pessimism" does not carry with it an anger toward, or indictment or accusation of, the world or the creator of the world. Anger does not exist in Buddha's worldview. Indeed, for Buddha, the *idea* that the world could possess another nature, be a "better" world, is never raised. Schopenhauer's view that in its essence this is the "worst of all possible worlds" is as distant from Buddhism as Leibniz's dictum that this is the "best of all possible worlds." Generally, it is not the essence of the world, but the *autonomy of its existence* uncontrolled by our *mental acts,* its apparently total independence from our intellects, that constitutes for Buddha the essential and final root of suffering. Suffering is the resistance of the world's autonomous parts to us. Third, all notions of *balancing suffering with pleasure,* such as are advocated in the metaphysically pessimistic views of Schopenhauer and Eduard von Hartmann, are completely missing in Buddha's thought. The culminating point in the ascending steps of salvation, the simultaneous salvation of self and world, no longer contains the pure pleasure of serenity, quiet, and peace as in the preceding meditative steps. Pleasure is not rejected because it is pleasure, but because it is as much an *affect* as suffering and pain. Pleasure inflames and nourishes the thirst for attachment to things and, necessarily correlated to this, the fascination with the illusion of the independent existence of the contents of the world. Only for pedagogical reasons, therefore, and to guide the soul is pleasure rejected more than pain. On the other hand, the intuitive representation of the pain of death, loss of loved ones, illness or age, even if not actually suffered, is immensely valuable in gradually exhausting the constant, automatic, and instinctive enticement to posit existence, and this aids us in eradicating the common source of all affects.[19] Pleasure is "worse" than pain only because it tempts us to believe the existence of things is independent of our desires when in fact the existence of all things is totally dependent on mental control over our desires. Pain brings the existence or nonexistence of things factually under control of our mental powers. Pain is good not because it is pain, but because it can free us to a higher degree than pleasure from the intellectual deception of *autonomously* existing objects, from the illusion of a world that forces itself upon us without asking our permission. Observed rather than actually endured suffering, for example, of *one* dead or sick person, provides a clear instance of misery and demonstrates to us that *the autonomous existence of the world is a lie*. Positively expressed, this has the value of bringing the existence or nonexistence of the world under *control* of our *intellectual activity,* which is unwittingly wrested from us by our desires.

The primary insight of Buddha is to *integrate completely the teachings on knowledge with the teachings on salvation*. The intimate connection of the two yields the *technique* of suffering. His theory of knowledge is wholly a *realism* concerning the existence of the world, his theory of salvation an *idealism* concerning our norm and task in life. Fundamentally, the world *is* a reality that *should* be idealized, *become* an image through the activity of the mind. Novalis's profound words, "The world is no dream, but should become a dream," are far removed from the idealism of Kant and Schopenhauer, who offer as a theoretical insight what for Novalis was the content and goal of an interior act and a history of cultural formation relying on such acts. However, the doctrine of Buddha is still much farther removed from this late Western idealism. The primary phenomenon of Buddha's discovery consists in evaluating the quiet addressing of things to us: "we are," things say, "we are such and such without relying on your consent, we are independent of any possible knowledge you have." Buddha discovered this discourse, directed to naïve consciousness, is basically a "lie." It is an apparition, samsara, the product of unyielding desires that spring either from our individual attachments, *our* "*thirsts,*" or the "thirsts" of our ancestors implanted in us by procreation. In any case, this lie derives from an involuntary human activity that has become automatic but can be reversed in principle by a saint. The answer of the world to this involuntary human *activity* is resistance. Thus resistance equals reality—the reality of the world. The teaching that each existence is a product of actions is the premise for the doctrine that productive actions can be *canceled* by "stepping out" of the self, and therefore out of causal connections, by a "holy indifference." By ridding oneself of wretched "causality" one attains the "solitude" and isolation that belong to the most profound core of the self. The development of Buddhist thought consists only of rational structures added to the original intuition of the certitude of salvation, namely, that from the deepest *recesses of his spirit* man has the power to dispel the illusion of infinite causal connections. "Only that which depends on action can be changed or eliminated through action." This axiom expresses the entire teaching of Buddha.

"Elimination of suffering" in Buddhist thought means no more than to unmask, by means of spontaneously obtained knowledge, the chimera of objects existing independently of us. This means locating the void of "nothing"—in the sense that things no longer resist us—at exactly the point where the things previously appeared in their separate existence with all their prominence, freshness, and splendor. As seen with *complete* knowledge, the world and nothing, nirvana, are strictly parallel correlates. For Buddha, knowledge is not "participation," "image," "designation," "order," or "form," but an *emptying of the contents* of the world from our apprehension by severing the chain of desire that binds us to these contents and makes their existence possible. Knowledge is thus a stopping of the conflict as to whether world contents exist or do not exist in our immediate present; in this respect, knowledge is primarily an abolishing of all affirmations or denials of existence.

There is clear opposition in Buddhist thought to *Western* pessimism. In the West, pessimism is a mere reaction to optimism. Schopenhauer's and Hartmann's denial of the world, because of their insight into the irrational character of its existence, became a doctrine of salvation. Buddha did not teach this. He stood beyond reflecting on existence and nonexistence, beyond affirming and denying the world. His holy *indifference* to the world was a result of his insight into the superfluous contrast between pure knowledge and its correlate, between nonexisting and "not-nonexisting," that is, nirvana. This indifference is for Buddha the goal of salvation; it appears subjectively as "extinction."

A part of the Buddhist technique removed from the Indian context with its underlying current of pessimism as to existence is at the base of an optimistic notion of existence in *Spinoza*[20] and *Goethe*. According to their thinking, affect persists only in "confused, unclear presentations and thoughts," that is, in a deficiency of reasoning. The inference is that affect may be completely removed by a more informed, sharper view, just as the hazy heavens seen by the naked eye rearrange themselves into a mosaic of stars when seen through a telescope. This inference is certainly not without basis in our psychological experience. The degree to which we suffer seems to decrease as we look directly and steadily into the face of suffering and its object. Suffering also decreases if it is located outside ourselves and simultaneously inhibited by encircling and isolating it in order to add color to our lives. Heightened attention too allows feeling to dissipate. But this route does not take us far; moreover, its theoretical foundation is false. Emotions are not "confused thoughts." There is a depth and intensity to suffering such that to strike at the objects of suffering rather than the actual experience produces the opposite effect—suppresses and condenses suffering into an objectless lump that floats in the psyche. One may indeed ask whether the growing pessimism of the Indian mind was not at first produced by some century-long development of the technique of enduring suffering. Above all, one may ask, Whence comes the *power* to step outside oneself if a deeper, preexisting happiness does not grant that power? Each conquering of suffering is an effect, not a cause, of a more profoundly located happiness.

Since everything in this world is suffering, what of bitter or mildly serene *resignations* such as *Schopenhauer,* following the Indians, liked to recommend? Such "solace" is dubious. In any case, that soul is nobler, indeed experiences *joy,* who is content to suffer alone rather than burden a growing community with its suffering.

Is the hedonist escape from suffering any better? The hedonist attempts by sheer will to accumulate a surplus of pleasure. But already earliest Greek thought did not support this teaching. Not Aristippus, or the pessimist Hegesias, who urged his students to commit suicide (peisithanatos), or Epicurus, who, in place of the positive, sensual maxim to have pleasure in the present, which Aristippus taught was the highest good, preferred mere lack of pain and equanimity (ataraxia), was able convincingly to justify hedonism. The historical reversal of the hedonist system into the most bleak pessimism is only one concrete example of an interior *law* of the spirit, "There are things that do not occur when consciously sought," and its corollary, "There are things more likely to occur the more a person strives to avoid them." Happiness and suffering are such things. Happiness always flees to greater distances from one who seeks it. Suffering approaches the fugitive more quickly the more rapidly he flees. This is especially true for "deeper" feelings. *Aristippus* began his teaching by claiming he did not aspire after riches, horses, or women but only his *pleasure* in them. He taught that only a fool strives for things and goods, the wise man for his pleasure in things and goods. Thus, Aristippus transformed the abundance of the world and the value of its contents into a poor, bare scaffolding for the pleasures of his flesh. He did not acknowledge that, in forming and contemplating this world with love, happiness would bloom, as it were, as a blessed by-product and reaction. He never asked whether his cherished lover loved him in return; nor, when he ate a fish, whether he was tasty to the fish, but only whether the fish was tasty to him! However, Aristippus was the "fool." Without intending to, he removed the ground on which the bloom of happiness grows by *withdrawing* any free, loving, and active submission to the world or to the loved one. He did not see that pleasure, especially of the greater kind, is found only if a person does not actively seek pleasure, but seeks its content and inner value. He also did not see that the core of happiness in love can be found only by turning away from oneself and surrendering to a subject who responds in love to the love given. He did not grasp the firm law of life that the practical effort to win happiness steadily lessens the permanence and depth of happiness if will and action are geared solely to achieving it, for strictly speaking only sensual pleasure can be practically realized.[21] He did not notice that pain is intentionally avoidable only to the extent it is near the peripheral zone of the senses. And he did not recognize that the suffering involved in continually avoiding pain inevitably becomes more dreadful as a result of one's heightened sensitivity to pain. He did not see the basic fact that the emotions should be sources, symptoms, and gifts, rather than objects, of willing. Thus, his technique of feeling suffering ends inevitably in a longing for death.

The three further ways of *encountering* suffering—dulling it to the point of apathy, *struggling heroically* against it, and *suppressing* it to the point of finding evidence that suffering is an illusion—are all found at their peak at one time or another in antiquity, from the teachings of the *Cynics* to their later descendants in the *Stoical* school. The direction of development went from the pole of heroic struggle, as in the saga of Heracles, the hero revered by the school of Cynics founded by Antisthenes, to the pole of self-suggestion that interpreted suffering as illusion, advocated in the later methods of the Stoics.

The *heroic attitude* of a warrior against suffering sent by the gods and Moira is the ancient attitude *par excellence*. It is quite different from the hedonistic escape from suffering or from Christian love and acceptance of suffering as the divine, friendly physician of salvation of the soul, and even more radically different from Buddhist teaching. The ancient champion of suffering sought to overcome suffering as he would a valiant enemy, through perseverance and struggle. He sought the fame of being a *master* of suffering, and of success in his power. In this way, he took the measure of his value and insured that the world would be aware of him. This almost athletic *self-evaluation*, which only secondarily considered any beneficial consequences for the community, is at the heart of ancient heroism and asceticism of suffering. The demeanor of peace, composure, and constancy generally associated with the gestures of the declaiming orator, and with which the ancient hero of suffering tends happily to die (the death of Socrates did not entirely lack these characteristics), was repeatedly imitated up to the time of Frederick the Great, whose letters are strongly colored with this stoic spirit.

The *efficacy* of this heroic attitude is limited, however. It is insufficient before the more profound suffering of the soul, the suffering that escapes control of the aggressive will. Too often the heroic attitude buries the fame of victory over external suffering in the deeper suffering of an embittered and hardened heart. Because heroic pride cannot acknowledge a point where the will's control cannot go, heroism drives suffering into the *depths* of the soul. Above all, the heroic attitude is completely dependent on the reflected image of itself it creates in others. Augustine, in *The City of God,* judged the heroic suicide of the assaulted Lucretia profoundly and correctly: "The act committed on her without her consent filled her with shame. Being a Roman with a passion for praise, she was afraid that, if she lived, men might think she did willingly what she had endured by violence. Hence, as witness of her intention, she decided to put that punishment before the eyes of men who could not read her conscience."

The *asceticism of becoming less sensitive* to suffering appears where the active heroic will breaks down. In this asceticism the ancient "slave" morality resided, just as in heroism the ancient "master" morality was found. Epictetus and the Stoics of the imperial age are representative of the ascetic attitude. To the extent it is successful, however, the action of becoming less sensitive not only tears out from the psyche the roots of every higher and lower joy. This intellectually proud ideal of apathy is a specter that, when embodied, would immediately break down one who had assimilated it, for one would then lack all power of direction and all order that the play of emotions gives to life. This ideal is "the ghost that walks over graves." A few years ago a patient at the Charcot Clinic was described in the following way: as an aftereffect of an illness, she experienced loss of a great number of organic sensations and deeper emotions. She had no sense of time or duration, no feeling of hunger, no sympathy for her children. She had to look at the clock to distinguish five minutes from two hours. She could eat only according to the clock, since neither hunger nor appetite guided her. She even had to go to sleep according to the clock, and so on. Although she felt indifferent to her children, she could manage the *judgment* these were her children, and this enabled her to act dutifully toward them. Her consciousness of existing was shrunk almost to the level of "Cogito, ergo sum." Deprived of every emotional spontaneity, her awareness of herself was filled with horror, for it was as though she consisted only of "foreign objects." This unfortunate creature, who had to apply all of her mind to the simplest pursuits, may be taken as representing an approximation of what the ideal stoic person would look like—if there were such a person.

Another method of encountering suffering was also introduced by the Stoic school. This method aimed to achieve not insensitivity to suffering but its *denial*. At times, the consequence of denial is a kind of so-called metaphysical justification of the evil of the world, at other times a kind of self-suggestion. The first of these came strongly to the fore again in the metaphysical optimism of *Spinoza*'s ethics and *Leibniz*'s theodicy in the seventeenth and eighteenth centuries. The second occurred again in the oddly successful *Christian Science movement* in America.

The metaphysical version of denial holds that, because our *view* of the world is too egocentric and particular, the very idea of misery causes us to suffer. According to this teaching, we see misery because we stand too close to the world—just as the viewer of a painting who stands too close sees only spots of color where there is actually meaning and harmony. This kind of metaphysics constructs an invisible order of realities such that each affliction is seen as merely apparent and converted into a good. But given this view, miseries come to be so great and widely distributed that no degree of constructing and fantasizing would succeed in ordering them into an invisible context! This metaphysics is truly "reckless" (Schopenhauer), since it saps all internal as well as external energy in the struggle with misery.

The second consequence of denial of suffering introduced by the Stoa, that of self-suggestion, is expressed in the dictum that suffering exists only "in and because of our imagination," not because of things themselves. Suffering would cease, the Stoics held, if the imagination were suppressed or modified by energetic thinking. Based on the maxim that "pain is not evil," a growing, systematically drilled technique of *repression and illusion* was inserted into later antiquity. This technique caught on as the world feeling of the late ancient world became more negative. By late antiquity the earnest attempt was made, just as with the believers in Christian Science, simply to expel evil, suffering, and pain from this world. This was the last effort of Laocoön—the profound symbol of antiquity's great suffering—to defend himself against the serpents attacking him. After that, the Christian teaching on the meaning of suffering and the proper way to encounter it entered the world.

With great cogency, the *Old Testament* attributed a sense of justification to suffering. Each suffering had to be, finally, a *penalty,* an earthly realization of divine justice and reprisal. This penalty was for the sins of the individual, the parents, the whole fallen race. However, a voice of the sufferers raised itself mightily in the late Psalms, most movingly in the Book of Job, and again in Ecclesiastes against this dreadful interpretation. For to the misery of "innocent" suffering was added misery for a sin committed who knows when—the penalty of suffering for an unknown sin.[22] A harsh thought that tends to appear among us today is that God chastises even those he loves, not to punish them but to purify their essences from involvement with worldly goods so that they may be religiously faithful. To the unfortunate Job this would perhaps have sounded like a warm, mild voice of salvation. It was not only this thought that developed in full force in the Christian world, however, but the flashing fire of the messianic hope that preceded it and brought forth the heroic suffering of the Jewish people, which proved itself so well in Jewish history.

When one considers the interpretations, techniques, and narcoses by which the spirit of old wanted to empty the ocean of suffering, the *Christian teaching on suffering* seems a complete *reversal* of attitude. First, Christianity simply and naïvely *acknowledges* suffering. This offers a powerful release of tension, which in itself must have had a redemptive effect. In Christianity, there is none of the ancient arrogance toward suffering, none of the self-praise of the sufferer who measures the degree of his suffering against his own powers to which others bear witness. There is also in Christianity no stern pride by which one hides oneself and others in the appearance of equanimity and the rhetoric of a suffering and dying "sage." The long suppressed cry of the suffering creature resounds everywhere in Christianity freely and harshly. Jesus gave voice openly on the cross to the most profound suffering, the feeling of being separated from God: "Why have you forsaken me?" And in this there are no *re*interpretations: pain is pain, it is misery; pleasure is pleasure, it is positive *bliss,* not mere "tranquility" or "redemption of the heart" which Buddha considered the good of goods. In Christianity, there is no diminution of sensitivity, but a mellowing of the soul in totally *enduring* suffering either alone or with others. However, an entirely new source of power emerges that sustains suffering, a power that flows out of a blessedly intuited higher order of things as revealed through love, insight, and action. The endurance of suffering has a new meaning—it is a *purification* by God's compassionate love, which has sent suffering as a friend of the soul. Only through these two thoughts together did Christianity, without reinterpretation, apparently succeed in integrating the full gravity and misery of suffering as an essential factor with the order of the world and its redemption. In spite of its torment, Christianity succeeded in making suffering a welcome friend of the soul, not an enemy to be resisted. Suffering is purification, not punishment or correction. The great paradox of Judaism, "suffering righteousness," vanishes as a drop in the ocean in the paragon of the innocent man who freely receives suffering for others' debts—the man who is at the same time God himself and invites everyone to follow him on his way to the cross. Suffering *may* again be innocent yet also acquires, through the divine quality of the suffering person, a wonderful, new nobility.

But what does "purification" mean? It does not mean that only suffering permits one to grow morally or religiously—as a false pathological mania for suffering has often proclaimed. Nor does it mean that an ascetic, voluntary self-affliction of pain and suffering makes one more spiritual and brings one closer to God. Purification means that the pain and suffering of life fix our spiritual vision on the *central,* spiritual goods of life and salvation—the goods offered to us, before all else, according to the faith of the Christian in grace and redemption of Christ. Purification does not mean the creation of a moral or religious quality, but the discrimination of genuine from baser qualities, a gradual sloughing off of lower characteristics from higher ones in the center of our souls. The interpretation that suffering *in itself* brings men nearer to God is far more Greek and Neoplatonic than Christian. It was only in the third century that the *Greek Orthodox* church brought this interpretation into Christianity.[23] The Russian mania for suffering and the isolated asceticism of Russian monasticism have their origin in this interpretation. This distinction becomes still clearer when one grasps the innermost *union of suffering and love* in Christian doctrine. The invitation to *suffer* with and in Christ in the community of the cross is rooted in the more decisive invitation to *love* like and in Christ. The community of love is not rooted in the community of the cross; rather, the community of the cross is rooted in the community of *love.* Christian asceticism does not have a normative meaning as though it were a self-sufficient way to God; it is only a technique to learn to sacrifice goods and happiness for an end, to learn to be able to offer these sacrifices when love demands it. This asceticism does not diverge from the path to community, but returns to it. The ascetic attitude is not taken in order to ready one for an ecstatic contemplation of God, but for the *labor of love* in whose achievement the believer knows himself to be most deeply in God and in Christ. Within Christian asceticism the so-called passive virtues of submission, patience, and the humble reception of suffering remain *subordinated* to the active virtue of love.[24]

However, the Christian doctrine of suffering receives its deepest meaning through an insight that also confirms the secular psychology of our present age. This is the insight into the *character of grace,* the ease and poise yielded by any profound emotion of happiness. Lawful conformities exist between deep levels of emotions, their effects and fulfillment.[25] The Christian doctrine of suffering asks for *more* than a patient tolerance of suffering. It asks for—better put, points to—a *blessed suffering.* At its core, the Christian attitude toward suffering is based on a belief that only the person who is blessed and depends upon God can tolerate pain and suffering correctly, can love and, where necessary, seek suffering out. In Letters to the Corinthians, Paul allows the soul to sing a hymn of rising joy while envisioning the ongoing ruin of its body and earthly goods. Paul permits the soul to attract to itself the suffering of the world that it will become even more blessedly aware of the centrality of its salvation and deliverance in God. What was experienced and preached by Paul was described as lived in the deeds of the martyrs. It was not the glowing *prospect* of a happy afterlife, but the experienced *happiness* of being in a state of grace of God while in throes of agony that released the wonderful powers in the martyrs.

When Luther's little daughter Magdalene died, Luther said, "I am indeed merry in the spirit, but sad in the flesh. It is a marvel to know that she is certainly in peace and better off and yet to be so sad." In this is expressed the outstanding *opposition to eudaemonism!* Eudaemonism does not know that in different levels of our psyche we can be, simultaneously, emotionally negative and positive—as Luther so vividly described it. From the extensive emotions of the senses, related to the flesh (pain, lust, etc.) to the happiness and despair of our most profound self, there are *levels* of emotion in which qualities of pleasure and displeasure are equally possible. We can suffer pain happily and drink the froth of wine unhappily. However our attention may shift between the levels at which we experience emotions, the pattern and coherence of emotion at one level remain unaffected by the order and sequence of emotion at another. Emotions are so far removed from the control and intention of the will that the more profound and central they are the more they bestow the *character of grace* upon their experience. The emotions function typically as *sources* of willing and acting among these levels. Only dissatisfaction at a more central level, basically *unhappiness in one's innermost heart,* produces in the *will* a tendency to seek pleasure in the outermost sphere of the senses as a *surrogate* for lack of inner happiness. One can tolerate pain of the senses and suffer more easily and happily, the more satisfied one is at the core, that is, the "happier" and more dependent one is on God. Hedonism is, thus, already a sign of despair. The experience of purification, the traversal of suffering from peripheral levels in order to enter the deeper "castles of the soul" and remain there for the reception of a higher world of spiritual powers—this can lead to a meaningful, non-algophiliac love of suffering. Suffering can be *loved* as though it were the gracious strokes of the hammer the divine sculptor uses upon us to bring out the ideal self from the material of an existence originally lost in the confusion of the senses and of selfishness. The eudaemonist knows none of this.

The eudaemonist seeks pleasure, but finds tears. The follower of Christ possesses happiness. He seeks pain so that his happiness, which outlasts the fluctuations of peripheral feelings, may become more profoundly and clearly known. For the man of antiquity, who was fundamentally a eudaemonist, the external world was happy and joyous, but the world's *core* was deeply sad and dark. Behind the cheerful surface of the world of so-called merry antiquity there loomed "fate" and "chance." For the Christian, the external world is dark and full of suffering, but its core is nothing other than pure bliss and delight. The Christian attitude toward suffering, in sum, took the following course. Initially, suffering was renounced and the hedonist attitude adopted. The failure of hedonism was followed by seeking to overcome suffering, either through heroism or stoic defiance. But these too failed. Finally, in the midst of suffering the attitude was taken of opening one's soul, through Christ, to the power of God, of commending and giving oneself over to God's mercy. Central happiness thus entered the Christian through the *grace* that allowed him to carry each suffering happily as a symbol of the cross. However, since he received suffering as a friend, knowing that it was given with merciful love as a means of purification, the Christian became even more *certain* of the happiness that allowed him to bear his suffering. Each suffering lodges the "place" of this happiness still deeper in the Christian's being. The same love in which the Christian follows God and Christ, the "omnia amare in Deo," and that leads him to suffering and sacrifice, is also the source of the beatitude that allows him to endure suffering happily. This happiness is always more profound and grand than the sacrificial suffering to which love leads. In the words of Thomas à Kempis, "When you come to the point that affliction and grief become sweet and taste good for the sake of Christ, then you can be sure that all is well with you. Then you have found the garden of paradise on earth. As long as suffering is difficult for you and you seek to flee it, as if you wanted to escape it, just so long goes it woefully and badly for you and the flood of affliction pursues you."

Notes

1. The analogy with the paramecium has already been established by Jennings.

2. Shame impels the blood of the sexual organs into the veins of the head, thus diminishing sexual excitement. But consciousness is thereby unified, and the merely libidinous arousal, which radiates in all directions, is subjected to *love*. Shame is the "conscience of eros" and is, therefore, stimulating. But this is not a sense stimulation as is, e.g., flirtation.

3. A detailed analysis of the act of repentance is in my book, *On the Eternal in Man,* Hamden, Conn., 1972; see especially ch. 15, "Repentance and Rebirth." See also my book *The Nature of Sympathy,* London, 1954.

4. If the perception of feeling is wanting, or is considerably weakened, then a situation of depersonalization arises, as Loewy and Schilder have pointed out. The mentally sick certainly experience feelings but, because they lack a unified function of feeling, as something separate from the ego, unconnected to the ego's whole thrust. Cf. Paul Schilder, *Selbstbewusstsein und Personlichkeitsbewusstsein,* Berlin, 1914, p. 60.

5. Cf. *Formalism in Ethics and Non-formal Ethics of Values,* pt. 2, ch. 5, sec. 8.

6. Concerning the only justification of this last approach, cf. "Problems of Religion," in *On the Eternal in Man.*

7. Notable objections to the above statement were first made by Goethe; a significant development of Goethe's ideas is in the work of Herbert Doms, "Über Altern, Tod, und Verjüngung," in *Ergebnisse der Anatomie und Entwicklungsgeschichte,* vol. 23, Munich, 1921. Unfortunately, this work could not be evaluated.

8. Cf. C. S. Minot, *The Problem of Age, Growth, and Death,* New York, 1908, and *Moderne Probleme der Biologie,* Jena, 1913.

9. Cf. A. Kowalesky, "Studien zur Psychologie des Pessimismus," in Loewenfeld, *Grenzfragen des Nerven und Seelenlebens,* Wiesbaden, 1904.

10. People and races have similar feelings of pain more often than similar feelings of pleasure. It is easier to feel suffering with another than to rejoice with him.

11. Cf. the essay in the fourth volume of this work, "Recent Attempts toward a Philosophy of the History of Decadence." [This was apparently a projected study that was not published.—Ed.]

12. According to R. Pischel's translation, this is the recurring epithet of love in Buddha's sermons.

13. There is a whole series of related and mutually supporting psychic techniques that should lead to an understanding and release of suffering. One

may learn this best in the marvelous translation of the conversations of Buddha that K. E. Neumann has given us. Cf. *Die Reden Gotamo Buddhas,* Munich, 1921; cf. also Fr. Heiler, *Die buddhistische Versenkung,* 2nd ed., Munich, 1922, and L. Ziegler, *Der ewige Buddha,* Darmstadt, 1922.

14. This ideal is also expressed in the Christian theory of the state in which every active revolution against authority is rejected even when authority commands something contradictory to natural law.

15. Maxim Gorky, in his *Die Zerstörung der Persönlichkeit* (German translation), Dresden, 1922, strongly objected to the attitude of Dostoyevsky and Tolstoy that it unconsciously served the interests of the middle class and thus postponed the revolution. This economic-Marxist interpretation is so spurious it is unworthy of serious refutation.

16. On this, some good insights and observations are in Max Brod, *Heidentum, Christentum, Judentum,* Munich, 1922. It is curious that Brod accused me of being ignorant of this distinction. In any case, in my *Formalism in Ethics,* sec. V8, I discuss the point that the practical management of emotions is inversely related to the depth at which they are experienced.

17. Cf. for the following, Herman Oldenberg, *Buddha: Sein Leben, seine Lehre, seine Gemeinde,* 6th ed., pp. 235–51.

18. A "death drive" for the individual was first shown by Metchnikoff. He imagined himself to be on the point of "natural" as well as abnormal and pathological death. But a death drive is altogether different from willing or wishing death. Is there a "death drive" for whole races? I doubt it.

19. All languages have the same root equating suffering with passivity and displeasure. This is understandable, as suffering is more clearly reflected in pain than pleasure.

20. Cf. pts. 2 and 3 of the *Ethics,* on affections and freedom.

21. Cf. my explanation in *Formalism in Ethics,* secs. V8 and 9.

22. The "Fall of man" is only the limit concept of this dialectic of suffering.

23. Cf. my essay "Über östliches und westliches Christentum," in *Gesammelte Werke,* vol. 6, ed. Manfred S. Frings (Bern and Munich: Francke Verlag, 1971).

24. This is what divides Christian from Buddhist teaching on suffering. In Buddhism, love is "the redemption of the heart" whose renunciation can be valued as self-sacrifice and self-denial.

25. The concept of depth levels of emotions is more precisely developed in my book *Formalism in Ethics,* sec. V8.

6

Negative Feelings and the Destruction of Values: *Ressentiment*

Among the scanty discoveries which have been made in recent times about the origin of moral judgments, Friedrich Nietzsche's discovery that *ressentiment* can be the source of such value judgments is most profound. This remains true even if his specific characterization of Christian love as the most delicate "flower of *ressentiment*" should turn out to be mistaken.

> But *this* is the event: out of the stem of that tree of revenge and hatred, of Jewish hatred—the most profound and sublime of all, the hatred which creates ideals and transforms values and which has never had its like on earth—there grew something equally incomparable, a *new love,* the most profound and sublime kind of love:—and indeed from what other stem could it have grown? . . . But let us not think that it grew as the negation of that thirst for revenge, as the antithesis of Jewish hatred! No, the reverse is true! This love grew from it as its crown, as the triumphant crown unfolding ever more broadly in the purest brightness and solar plenitude. In the lofty realm of light, so to speak, it aimed at the goals of that hatred, at victory, booty, seduction—with the same urge which made the roots of that hatred dig more and more thoroughly and covetously into whatever had depth and was evil. This Jesus of Nazareth, as the living Gospel of Love, this "Saviour" who brought bliss and victory to the poor, the sick, the sinners—did he not represent seduction in its most sinister and most irresistible form, seduction and a detour to precisely those *Jewish* values and innovations of the ideal? Is it not true that Israel has reached the final aim of its sublime vindictiveness through this "Saviour," this seeming adversary and destroyer of Israel? (*Genealogy of Morals,* Part I, Section 8).

Reprinted with permission from *Ressentiment,* trans. William W. Holdheim, ed. and introduced by Lewis A. Coser (New York: Free Press, 1961), pp. 43–78. The earliest version of this work was entitled "Über Ressentiment und moralisches Werturteil" (On *ressentiment* and moral value judgment), published in *Zeitschrift für Pathopsychologie* 1, no. 2/3 (1912). A final, expanded version was published as "Das Ressentiment in Aufbau der Moralen" (*Ressentiment* in moral systems), in *Abhandlungen und Aufsätze* (Essays and Articles) (Leipzig: Weisse Bücher, 1915), vol. 1. "M.S." means the bracketed note was written by Maria Scheler, the German editor.

The slave revolt in morality begins when *ressentiment* itself becomes creative and produces values: the *ressentiment* of beings to whom the real reaction, that of the deed, is denied, who can only indulge in imaginary revenge. Whereas every noble morality springs from a triumphant accept-ance and affirmation of oneself, slave morality is in its very essence a nega-tion of everything "outside" and "different," of whatever is "not oneself": and *this* negation is its creative deed. This reversal of the perspective of valuation—this necessary determination by the outside rather than by one-self—is typical of *ressentiment:* in order to arise, slave morality always needs a hostile external world. Physiologically speaking, it needs external stimuli in order to act at all,—its action is fundamentally a reaction. (Part I, Section 10)

—I see nothing, I hear all the more. It is a cautious, a gentle and insidi-ous muttering and whispering in all nooks and corners. It seems to me that they are lying; a sugary mildness sticks to every sound. Weakness is to be made a *merit,* there can be no doubt—it is as you said—

—Go on!

—and impotence, inability to retaliate, is to become "goodness"; timo-rous lowliness becomes "humility"; submission to those whom one hates is "obedience" (obedience toward one of whom they say that he decrees this submission,—they call him God). The inoffensiveness of the weak, even the cowardice in which he is rich, his unavoidable obligation to wait at the door acquires a good name, as "patience," it is also called virtue; the inability to avenge oneself is supposed to be a voluntary renunciation of revenge, sometimes it is even called forgiveness ("for *they* know not what they do—we alone know what *they* do"!). They also speak of "love for one's enemies,"—and they sweat while doing so. (Part I, Section 14)

These are the chief passages in which Friedrich Nietzsche develops his remarkable thesis. For the moment, let us ignore the relation of *ressentiment* to Christian values in order to penetrate more deeply into the *unit of experience* designated by the term.

Instead of defining the word, let us briefly characterize or describe the phenomenon. *Ressentiment* is a self-poisoning of the mind which has quite definite causes and consequences. It is a lasting mental atti-tude, caused by the systematic repression of certain emotions and af-fects which, as such, are normal components of human nature. Their repression leads to the constant tendency to indulge in certain kinds of value delusions and corresponding value judgments. The emotions and affects primarily concerned are revenge, hatred, malice, envy, the im-pulse to detract, and spite.[1]

Thirst for revenge is the most important source of *ressentiment*. As we have seen, the very term *"ressentiment"* indicates that we have to do with reactions which presuppose the previous apprehension of another person's state of mind. The desire for revenge—in contrast with all active and aggressive impulses, be they friendly or hostile—is also such a reactive impulse. It is always preceded by an attack or an injury. Yet it must be clearly distinguished from the impulse for reprisals or self-defense, even when this reaction is accompanied by anger, fury, or indignation. If an animal bites its attacker, this cannot be called "revenge." Nor does an immediate reprisal against a box on the ear fall under this heading. Revenge is distinguished by two essential characteristics. First of all, the immediate reactive impulse, with the accompanying emotions of anger and rage, is temporarily or at least momentarily checked and restrained, and the response is consequently postponed to a later time and to a more suitable occasion ("just wait till next time"). This blockage is caused by the reflection that an immediate reaction would lead to defeat, and by a concomitant pronounced feeling of "inability" and "impotence." Thus even revenge as such, based as it is upon an experience of impotence, is always primarily a matter of those who are "weak" in some respect. Furthermore, it is of the essence of revenge that it always contains the *consciousness* of "tit for tat," so that it is never a mere emotional reaction.[2]

These two characteristics make revenge the most suitable source for the formation of *ressentiment*. The nuances of language are precise. There is a progression of feeling which starts with revenge and runs via rancor, envy, and impulse to detract all the way to spite, coming close to *ressentiment*. Usually, revenge and envy still have specific objects. They do not arise without special reasons and are directed against definite objects, so that they do not outlast their motives. The desire for revenge disappears when vengeance has been taken, when the person against whom it was directed has been punished or has punished himself, or when one truly forgives him. In the same way, envy vanishes when the envied possession becomes ours. The impulse to detract, however, is not in the same sense tied to definite objects—it does not arise through specific causes with which it disappears. On the contrary, this affect *seeks* those objects, those aspects of men and things, from which it can draw gratification. It likes to disparage and to smash pedestals, to dwell on the negative aspects of excellent men and things, exulting in the fact that such faults are more perceptible through their contrast with the strongly positive qualities. Thus there is set a fixed pattern of experience which can accommodate the most diverse contents. This form or structure fashions each concrete experience of life and selects it from possible experiences. The impulse to detract, therefore, is no mere result of such an experience, and the experience will arise regardless of considerations whether its object could in any way, directly or indirectly, further or hamper the individual concerned. In "spite," this impulse has become even more profound and deep-seated—it is, as it were, always ready to burst forth and to betray itself in an unbridled gesture, a way of smiling, etc. An analogous road leads from simple *Schadenfreude* to "malice." The latter, more detached than the former from *definite* objects, tries to bring about ever new opportunities for *Schadenfreude*.

Yet all this is not *ressentiment*. There are only stages in the development of its sources. Revenge, envy, the impulse to detract, spite, *Schadenfreude,* and malice lead to *ressentiment* only if there occurs neither a moral self-conquest (such as *genuine* forgiveness in the case of revenge) nor an act or some other adequate expression of emotion (such as verbal abuse or shaking one's fist), and if this restraint is caused by a pronounced awareness of impotence. There will be no *ressentiment* if he who thirsts for revenge really acts and avenges himself, if he who is consumed by hatred harms his enemy, gives him "a piece of his mind," or even merely vents his spleen in the presence of others. Nor will the envious fall under the dominion of *ressentiment* if he seeks to acquire the envied possession by means of work, barter, crime, or violence. *Ressentiment* can only arise if these emotions are particularly powerful and yet must be suppressed because they are coupled with the feeling that one is unable to act them out—either because of weakness, physical or mental, or because of fear. Through its very origin, *ressentiment* is therefore chiefly confined to those who *serve* and are *dominated* at the moment, who fruitlessly resent the sting of authority. When it occurs elsewhere, it is either due to psychological contagion—and the spiritual venom of *ressentiment* is extremely contagious—or to the violent suppression of an impulse which subsequently revolts by "embittering" and "poisoning" the personality. If an ill-treated servant can vent his spleen in the antechamber, he will remain free from the inner venom of *ressentiment,* but it will engulf him if he must hide his feelings and keep his negative and hostile emotions to himself.

But let us examine the various sources of *ressentiment* more closely.

Impulses of revenge lead to *ressentiment* the more they change into actual *vindictiveness,* the more their direction shifts toward indeterminate groups of objects which need only share one common characteristic, and the less they are satisfied by vengeance taken on a specific object. If the desire for revenge remains permanently unsatisfied, and especially if the feeling of "being right" (lacking in an outburst of rage, but an integral part of revenge) is intensified into the idea of a "duty," the individual may actually wither away and die.[3] The vindictive person is instinctively and without a conscious act of volition drawn toward events which may give rise to vengefulness, or he tends to see injurious intentions in all kinds of perfectly innocent actions and remarks of others. Great touchiness is indeed frequently a symptom of a vengeful character. The vindictive person is always in search of objects, and in fact he attacks—in the belief that he is simply wreaking vengeance. This vengeance restores his damaged feeling of personal value, his injured "honor," or it brings "satisfaction" for the wrongs he has endured. When it is repressed, vindictiveness leads to *ressentiment,* a process which is intensified when the *imagination* of vengeance, too, is repressed—and finally the very emotion of revenge itself. Only then does this *state of mind* become associated with the tendency to detract from the other person's value, which brings an illusory easing of the tension.

The following factors contribute to strengthen these preconditions:

The desire for revenge, which is itself caused by a repression, has powerful repressive tendencies. This is expressed in the saying that "revenge is a dish which should be taken cold." Everything else being equal, it is therefore always the attitude of the weaker party. But at the same time, the injured person always places himself on the same level as his injurer.[4] A slave who has a slavish nature and accepts his status does not desire revenge when he is injured by his master; nor does a servile servant who is reprimanded or a child that is slapped. Conversely, feelings of revenge are favored by strong pretensions which remain concealed, or by great pride coupled with an inadequate social position. There follows the important sociological law that this psychological dynamite will spread with the *discrepancy* between the political, constitutional, or traditional status of a group and its *factual* power. It is the difference between these two factors which is decisive, not one of them alone. Social *ressentiment,* at least, would be slight in a democracy which is not only political, but also social and tends toward equality of property. But the same would be the case—and *was* the case—in a caste society such as that of India, or in a society with sharply divided classes. *Ressentiment* must therefore be strongest in a society like ours, where approximately equal rights (political and otherwise) or formal social equality, publicly recognized, go hand in hand with wide factual differences in power, property, and education. While each has the "right" to compare himself with everyone else, he cannot do so in fact. Quite independently of the characters and experiences of individuals, a potent charge of *ressentiment* is here accumulated by the very *structure of society.*

We must add the fact that revenge tends to be transformed into *res-*

sentiment the more it is directed against lasting situations which are felt to be "injurious" but beyond one's control—in other words, the more the injury is experienced as a destiny. This will be most pronounced when a person or group feels that the very fact and quality of its *existence* is a matter which calls for revenge. For an individual, a case in point would be a physical or other natural defect, especially one that is easily visible. The *ressentiment* of cripples or of people of subnormal intelligence is a well-known phenomenon. Jewish *ressentiment,* which Nietzsche rightly designates as enormous, finds double nourishment: first in the discrepancy between the colossal national pride of "the chosen people" and a contempt and discrimination which weighed on them for centuries like a destiny, and in modern times through the added discrepancy between formal constitutional equality and factual discrimination. Certainly the extremely powerful acquisitive instinct of this people is due—over and beyond natural propensities and other causes—to a deep-rooted disturbance of Jewish self-confidence. It is an overcompensation for the lack of a social acknowledgement which would satisfy the national self-esteem. In the development of the labor movement, the conviction that the very existence and fate of the proletariat "cries for revenge" also became a mighty dynamic factor. The more a permanent social pressure is felt to be a "fatality," the less it can free forces for the practical transformation of these conditions, and the more it will lead to indiscriminate *criticism* without any positive aims. This peculiar kind of "*ressentiment* criticism" is characterized by the fact that improvements in the conditions criticized cause no satisfaction—they merely cause discontent, for they destroy the growing pleasure afforded by invective and negation. Many modern political parties will be extremely annoyed by a partial satisfaction of their demands or by the constructive participation of their representatives in public life, for such participation mars the delight of oppositionism. It is peculiar to "*ressentiment* criticism" that it does not seriously desire that its demands be fulfilled. It does not want to cure the evil: the evil is merely a pretext for the criticism. We all know certain representatives in our parliaments whose criticism is absolute and uninhibited, precisely because they count on never being ministers. Only when this *aversion* from power (in contrast with the *will* to power) becomes a permanent trait, is criticism moved by *ressentiment.* Conversely, it is an old experience that the political criticism of a party loses its pungency when this party becomes positively associated with the authority of the state.[5]

Another source of *ressentiment* lies in *envy, jealousy,* and the *competitive urge.* "Envy," as the term is understood in everyday usage, is due to a feeling of impotence which we experience when another person owns a good we covet. But this tension between desire and nonfulfillment does not lead to envy until it flares up into hatred against the owner, until the latter is falsely considered to be the *cause* of our privation. Our factual inability to acquire a good is wrongly interpreted as a positive action *against* our desire[6]—a delusion which diminishes the original tension. Both the experience of impotence and the causal delusion are essential preconditions of true envy. If we are merely displeased that another person owns a good, this can be an incentive for acquiring it through work, purchase, violence, or robbery. *Envy* occurs when we fail in doing so and feel powerless. Therefore it is a great error to think that envy—along with covetousness, ambition, and vanity—is a motive force in the development of civilization. Envy does not strengthen the acquisitive urge, it weakens it. It leads to *ressentiment* when the coveted values are such as cannot be acquired and lie in the sphere in which we compare ourselves to others. The most powerless envy is also the most terrible. Therefore *existential envy,* which is directed against the other person's very *nature,* is the strongest source of *ressentiment.* It is as if it whispers continually: "I can forgive everything, but not that you *are*—that you are *what* you are—that I am not what you are—indeed that I am not *you.*" This form of envy strips the opponent of his very existence, for this existence as such is felt to be a "pressure," a "reproach," and an unbearable humiliation. In the lives of great men there are always critical periods of instability, in which they alternately envy and try to love those whose merits they cannot but esteem. Only gradually, one of these attitudes will predominate. Here lies the meaning of Goethe's reflection that "against another's great merits, there is no remedy but love." [7] In his *Torquato Tasso* (Act II, Scene 3) he suggests that Antonio's relations with Tasso are characterized by this kind of ambiguity. An analogous dynamic situation is seen between Marius and Sulla, Caesar and Brutus. Besides these cases of existential envy, which are rare, the innate characteristics of groups of individuals (beauty, racial excellence, hereditary character traits) are the chief causes of *ressentiment* envy. These types of envy are the only ones which entail that illusory devaluation of the envied values which will be discussed further down.

In all these cases, the origin of *ressentiment* is connected with a tendency to make comparisons between others and oneself. This attitude requires a brief examination. Each of us—noble or common, good or evil—continually compares his own value with that of others. If I choose a model, a "hero," I am somehow tied to such a comparison. All jealousy, all ambition, and even an ideal like the "imitation of

Christ" is full of such comparisons. We cannot agree with Georg Simmel, who says that the "noble man" refuses to compare himself to anyone. A man who refuses any comparison is not noble, but an "oddity" in the Goethean sense, a "unique buffoon," or perhaps a snob. Yet Simmel has the right thing in mind. A comparison can be conceived in different ways. The two terms of a relation may be apprehended separately, prior to and independently of any comparison or other relation (such as "similarity" or "identity"). Conversely, the perception of the terms may be the actualization of a previously apprehended but still indeterminate relation. It is a proven phenomenal fact that the relation between two terms (for example, colors, sounds, faces, etc.) can be contained in the perception of one of these terms alone. Thus we may be struck by the particular resemblance of one face to another which yet we cannot picture, but have to seek in our memory. The awareness of a relation here determines the conscious appearance of the second term. There is, indeed, phenomenal proof that there are pure experiences of relatedness, which select and actualize their terms only afterwards. The specific contents then come to occupy the still indeterminate places of a previously given relation. These distinctions are important here. The attitude which Simmel calls "nobility" is distinguished by the fact that the comparison of values, the "measuring" of my own value as against that of another person, is never the constitutive *precondition* for apprehending either. Moreover, the values are always apprehended in their entirety, not only in certain selected aspects. The "noble person" has a completely naïve and nonreflective awareness of his own value and of his fullness of being, an obscure conviction which enriches every conscious moment of his existence, as if he were autonomously rooted in the universe. This should not be mistaken for "pride." Quite on the contrary, pride results from an experienced *diminution* of this "naïve" self-confidence. It is a way of "holding on" to one's value, of seizing and "preserving" it deliberately.[8] The noble man's naïve self-confidence, which is as natural to him as tension is to the muscles, permits him calmly to assimilate the merits of others in all the fullness of their substance and configuration. He never "grudges" them their merits. On the contrary: he rejoices in their virtues and feels that they make the world more worthy of love. His naïve self-confidence is by no means "compounded" of a series of positive valuations based on specific qualities, talents, and virtues: it is originally directed at his very *essence* and *being*. Therefore he can afford to admit that another person has certain "qualities" superior to his own or is more "gifted" in some respects—indeed in all respects. Such a conclusion does not diminish his naïve awareness of his own value, which needs no justification or proof by achievements or abilities. Achievements merely serve to confirm it. On the other hand, the "common" man (in the exact acceptation of the term) can only experience his value and that of another if he relates the two, and he clearly perceives only those qualities which constitute possible differences. The noble man experiences value *prior* to any comparison, the common man *in* and *through* a comparison. For the latter, the relation is the selective precondition for apprehending *any* value. Every value is a relative thing, "higher" or "lower," "more" or "less" than his own. He arrives at value judgments by comparing himself to others and others to himself.

Two different human types share in this basic attitude, for it can go together with either strength or weakness, power or impotence. The energetic variety of the "common" man becomes an *arriviste,* the weak variety becomes the *man of ressentiment.*[9]

An *arriviste* is not a man who energetically and potently pursues power, property, honor, and other values. He does not deserve this name as long as he still thinks in terms of the intrinsic value of something which he actively furthers and represents by profession or calling. The ultimate goal of the *arriviste*'s aspirations is not to acquire a thing of value, but to be more highly esteemed than others. He merely uses the "thing" as an indifferent occasion for overcoming the oppressive feeling of inferiority which results from his constant comparisons.

If this type of value experience comes to dominate a whole society, then the "system of free competition" will become the soul of this society. This system is in its "purest" form when the comparison transcends such specific spheres as classes or "estates," with their fixed customs and ways of living. The medieval peasant prior to the thirteenth century does not compare himself to the feudal lord, nor does the artisan compare himself to the knight. The peasant may make comparisons with respect to the richer or more respected peasant, and in the same way everyone confines himself to his own sphere. Each group had its exclusive task in life, its objective unity of purpose. Thus every comparison took place within a strictly circumscribed frame of reference. At the most, these frames of reference could be compared in their totality. Therefore such periods are dominated by the idea that everyone has his "place" which has been assigned to him by God and nature and in which he has his personal duty to fulfill. His value consciousness and his aspirations never go beyond this sphere. From the king down to the hangman and the prostitute, everyone is "noble" in the sense that he considers himself as irreplaceable. In the "system of free competition," on the other hand, the notions on life's tasks and their value are not fundamental, they are but secondary derivations of the desire of all to surpass all the others. No "place" is more than a transitory point in this universal chase. The aspirations are intrinsically *boundless,* for they are no longer tied to any particular object or quality. The objects have become "commodities," destined for exchange and defined by their monetary value.[10] The progression of time is interpreted as "progress," and a specific "desire for progress" goes with this way of thinking. The "possession" or "enjoyment" of some unit of qualitative value used to be the end point of every economic motivation which forms a phenomenal unit of experience, great or small. Money, as a means of exchange, was only a transitional goal. Now, however, the final aim is a *quantity* of monetary value, and it is the quality of the commodity which has become a mere "transitional goal." The structure of the motivation, which used to be commodity—money—commodity, is now: money—commodity—money (Karl Marx). Of course we can still enjoy qualitative values, but our enjoyment—and indeed its very possibility—is now limited to those objects which are most immediately recognized as units of commodity value.

There is a parallel tendency in the evaluation of the different *phases of life* (childhood, youth, maturity, old age). Not one of these phases has retained its own particular value and its peculiar significance. We are only aware of the *surplus* value which one phase may have as compared to the other. The ideas of "progress" and "regression" are not drawn from an empirical observation of the phases of life as such—they are selective yardsticks which we apply to ourselves, to others, and to history. Jean-Jacques Rousseau was the first to protest against the pedagogical theories which consider childhood and youth as mere precursors of maturity. Leopold von Ranke rejected the childish liberal belief in historical progress in the following magnificent sentences: "Such a 'mediated' generation would have no significance of its own. It would only be important as a stepping-stone toward the next generation, and it would have no direct relation to the divine. However, I affirm that every epoch is directly related to God, and its value does not lie in what it engenders, but in its very existence, in its own self."[11] The desire for progress corresponds to the view rejected by Ranke, for it has no definite objective goals. It is activated by nothing but the wish to surpass a given phase, to set a "record," and the specific goals are only *secondary consequences* of this desire and indifferent "transitional points" in the movement of progress.

The case is different when the bent towards relative valuation is accompanied by *impotence.* Then the oppressive sense of inferiority which always goes with the "common" attitude cannot lead to active behavior. Yet the painful tension demands relief. This is afforded by the specific *value delusion of ressentiment*. To relieve the tension, the common man seeks a feeling of superiority or equality, and he attains his purpose by an illusory *devaluation* of the other man's qualities or by a specific "blindness" to these qualities. But secondly—and here lies the main achievement of *ressentiment*—he falsifies the *values themselves* which could bestow excellence on any possible objects of comparison.[12]

At this point, we must discuss one general aspect of the philosophical problem of value which is extremely important for an understanding of the *ressentiment* delusion. It is the question of the *fundamental relation between value consciousness and desire*. There is a theory, widespread ever since Spinoza, according to which the meaning of the terms which designate positive or negative value (such as "good" or "bad") is ultimately equivalent to the statement that something is the object of desire or aversion. Good, in Spinoza's view, means "to be desired," or when there happens to be no desire at the moment, "to be capable of inciting desire." According to this theory, aspiration and aversion are therefore not founded on any preceding value consciousness. On the contrary, this value consciousness is itself nothing but the realization that we desire the object or could desire it. I have refuted these theories in detail elsewhere.[13] What interests us here is the fact that the theory is itself a product and at the same time a description of *ressentiment*. In fact, every aspiration clearly contains a value consciousness on which it is founded. It appears in the way in which we "feel" the values in question, in the act of "preferring" etc. But when we feel unable to attain certain values, *value blindness* or *value delusion* may set in. Lowering all values to the level of one's own factual desire or ability (a procedure not to be confused with the conscious act of *resignation*), construing an illusory hierarchy of values in accordance with the structure of one's personal goals and wishes—that is by no means the way in which a normal and meaningful value consciousness is realized. It is, on the contrary, the chief source of value blindness, of value delusions and illusions. The act of resignation proves that a thing can be appreciated even when it lies beyond one's reach. If the awareness of our limitations begins to limit or to dim our *value* consciousness as well—as happens, for instance, in old age with regard to the values of youth—then we have already started the movement of devaluation which will end with the defamation of the world and all its values. Only a timely act of resignation can deliver us from this tendency toward self-delusion. Only this act, moreover, keeps us from grudging others what we can no longer desire. The *independence* of our value consciousness from our wishes and abilities is further proved by the fact that perversions of the desires (such as for food or sex—for example, masochism) do not necessarily taint the sense of values. According to Ribot and others, the feelings remain normal especially in the early stages of such perversions. Thus "loathsome" food still arouses loathing, despite the impulse to eat it. Only later "the feelings gradually follow the impulse" (Ribot), but even then the sense of values may remain unaffected. There are no "perversions of value feeling" which correspond to the perversions of desire, there are only *illusions and delusions* of value feeling. This is understandable, for "feeling" or "preferring" a value is essentially an act of cognition.

Therefore a man who "slanders" the unattainable values which oppress him is by no means completely unaware of their positive character. It is not as if they simply "did not exist" in his experience. In that case we could not speak of a "delusion." Nor can we say that he feels these values, but contradicts his own experience by false judgments— that would be a case of "error" or mendacity. The phenomenal peculiarity of the *ressentiment* delusion can be described as follows: the positive values are still felt as such, but they are *overcast* by the false values and can shine through only dimly. The *ressentiment* experience is always characterized by this "transparent" presence of the true and objective values behind the illusory ones—by that obscure awareness that one lives in a *sham world* which one is unable to penetrate.[14]

As we said before, the manner in which *ressentiment* originates in individuals or groups, and the intensity it reaches, is due primarily to hereditary factors and secondarily to social structure. Let us note, however, that the social structure itself is determined by the hereditary character and the value experience of the ruling human type. Since *ressentiment* can never emerge without the mediation of a particular form of impotence, it is always one of the phenomena of "declining life." But in addition to these general preconditions, there are some *types of ressentiment* which are grounded in certain typically recurrent "situations" and whose emergence is therefore largely independent of individual temperament. It would be foolish to assert that every individual in these "situations" is necessarily gripped by *ressentiment*. I do say, however, that by virtue of their *formal character* itself—and quite apart from the character of the individuals concerned—these "situations" are *charged* with the danger of *ressentiment*.

First of all, *woman* is generally in such a situation. She is the weaker and therefore the more vindictive sex. Besides, she is always forced to compete for man's favor, and this competition centers precisely on her personal and unchangeable qualities. It is no wonder that the most vengeful deities (such as the Eumenides, that sinister generation of vipers) have mostly grown under matriarchal rule. Aeschylus's *Eumenides* presents an extremely clear and plastic picture of a power which heals from *ressentiment*—that of Apollo and Athene, the deities of a new masculine civilization. We also note that the "witch" has no masculine counterpart. The strong feminine tendency to indulge in detractive gossip is further evidence; it is a form of self-cure. The danger of feminine *ressentiment* is extraordinarily intensified because both nature and custom impose upon woman a reactive and passive role in love, the domain of her vital interest. Feelings of revenge born from rejection in the erotic sphere are always particularly subject to repression, for communication and recriminations are barred by price and modesty. Besides, there is no tribunal which repairs such injuries, provided they violate no civil rights. It must be added that women are forced to great reserve by stronger barriers of convention and modesty. Therefore the "old maid," with her repressed cravings for tenderness, sex, and propagation, is rarely quite free of *ressentiment*. What we call "prudery," in contrast with true modesty, is but one of the numerous variants of sexual *ressentiment*. The habitual behavior of many old maids, who obsessively ferret out all sexually significant events in their surroundings in order to condemn them harshly, is nothing but sexual gratification transformed into *ressentiment* satisfaction.[15] Thus the criticism *accomplishes* the very thing it pretends to condemn. Anglo-American sexual morality is proverbially "prudish," and the reason lies in the fact that these countries have long been highly industrialized. Everything else being equal, the representative feminine groups of such countries will be increasingly recruited (probably even by hereditary selection) from those individuals who lack specially feminine charms. Their "calculations" and their active participation and rise in an essentially utilitarian society are relatively unhampered by the cares of love and motherhood. The purer feminine type tends to be pushed into prostitution if it has no inherited fortune.[16] *Ressentiment* imitates genuine modesty by means of prudery. Conversely, it depreciates true modesty, for the prostitute's criteria come to be representative of the prevailing morality. Genuine feminine modesty, which conceals what it secretly knows to be beautiful and valuable, is interpreted as a mere "fear" of revealing physical defects or faults in dress and makeup. For the prostitute, those qualities with which she herself is insufficiently blessed are nothing but "the result of education and custom." At the end of the eighteenth century, especially in France, the prostitute's *res-*

sentiment governs not only public opinion, but actually inspires the theories of moralists and philosophers.[17]

Another situation generally exposed to *ressentiment* danger is the older generation's relation with the younger. The process of aging can only be fruitful and satisfactory if the important transitions are accompanied by free *resignation,* by the renunciation of the values proper to the preceding stage of life. Those spiritual and intellectual values which remain untouched by the process of aging, together with the values of the next stage of life, must compensate for what has been lost. Only if this happens can we cheerfully relive the values of our past in memory, without envy for the young to whom they are still accessible. If we cannot compensate, we avoid and flee the "tormenting" recollection of youth, thus blocking our possibilities of understanding younger people. At the same time we tend to negate the specific values of earlier stages. No wonder that youth always has a hard fight to sustain against the *ressentiment* of the older generation.

Yet this source of *ressentiment* is also subject to an important historical variation. In the earliest stages of civilization, old age as such is so highly honored and respected for its experience that *ressentiment* has hardly any chance to develop. But education spreads through printing and other modern media and increasingly replaces the advantage of experience. Younger people displace the old from their positions and professions and push them into the defensive.[18] As the pace of "progress" increases in all fields, and as the changes of *fashion* tend to affect even the higher domains (such as art and science), the old can no longer keep up with their juniors. "Novelty" becomes an ever greater value. This is doubly true when the generation as such is seized by an intense lust for life, and when the generations compete with each other instead of cooperating for the creation of works which outlast them. "Every cathedral," Werner Sombart writes, "every monastery, every town hall, every castle of the Middle Ages bears testimony to the transcendence of the individual's span of life: its completion spans generations which thought that they lived for ever. Only when the individual cut himself loose from the community which outlasted him, did the duration of his personal life become his standard of happiness."[19] Therefore buildings are constructed ever more hastily—Sombart cites a number of examples. A corresponding phenomenon is the ever more rapid alternation of political regimes which goes hand in hand with the progression of the democratic movement.[20] But every change of government, every parliamentary change of party domination leaves a remnant of absolute opposition against the values of the new ruling group. This opposition is spent in *ressentiment* the more the losing group feels unable to return to power. The "retired official" with his followers is a typical *ressentiment* figure. Even a man like Bismarck did not entirely escape from this danger.

A further rich source of *ressentiment* lies in certain typical interfamily and intermarital relations. Above all there is the "mother-in-law," a tragic rather than ridiculous figure, especially the *son's* mother, in whose case matters are further complicated by the difference in sex. Her situation is one which the devil himself might have invented to test a hero. The child she loved since its birth and who loved her in return, the son for whom she has done everything, now turns to another woman who has done nothing for him and yet feels entitled to demand everything—and the mother is not only supposed to accept this event, but to welcome it, offer her congratulations, and receive the intruder with affection! It is truly no wonder that the songs, myths, and historical reminiscences of all nations represent the mother-in-law as an evil and insidious being. Other analogous situations are the younger children's relations with the firstborn son, the older wife's with the younger husband, etc.

There is usually no *ressentiment* just where a superficial view would look for it first: in the *criminal*. The criminal is essentially an active type. Instead of repressing hatred, revenge, envy, and greed, he releases them in crime. *Ressentiment* is a basic impulse only in the crimes of spite. These are crimes which require only a minimum of action and risk and from which the criminal draws no advantage, since they are inspired by nothing but the desire to do harm. The arsonist is the purest type in point, provided that he is not motivated by the pathological urge of watching fire (a rare case) or by the wish to collect insurance. Criminals of this type strangely resemble each other. Usually they are quiet, taciturn, shy, quite settled, and hostile to all alcoholic or other excesses. Their criminal act is nearly always a sudden outburst of impulses of revenge or envy which have been repressed for years. A typical cause would be the continual deflation of one's ego by the constant sight of the neighbor's rich and beautiful farm. Certain expressions of class *ressentiment,* which have lately been on the increase, also fall under this heading. I mention a crime committed near Berlin in 1912: in the darkness, the criminal stretched a wire between two trees across the road, so that the heads of passing automobilists would be shorn off. This is a typical case of *ressentiment,* for any car driver or passenger at all could be the victim, and there is no interested motive. Also in cases of slander and defamation of character, *ressentiment* often plays a major role.

Among the types of human activity which have always played a role in history, the *soldier* is least subject to *ressentiment*. Nietzsche is right in pointing out that the *priest* is most exposed to this danger, though the conclusions about religious morality which he draws from this insight are inadmissible. It is true that the very requirements of his profession, quite apart from his individual or national temperament, expose the priest more than any other human type to the creeping poison of *ressentiment*. In principle he is not supported by secular power, indeed he affirms the fundamental weakness of such power. Yet, as the representative of a concrete institution, he is to be sharply distinguished from the *homo religiosus*—he is placed in the middle of party struggle. More than any other man, he is condemned to control his emotions (revenge, wrath, hatred) at least outwardly, for he must always represent the image and principle of "peacefulness." The typical "priestly policy" of gaining victories through suffering rather than combat, or through the counterforces which the sight of the priest's suffering produces in men who believe that he unites them with God, is inspired by *ressentiment*. There is no trace of *ressentiment* in genuine martyrdom, only the false martyrdom of priestly policy is guided by it. This danger is completely avoided only when priest and *homo religiosus* coincide.[21]

In present-day society, *ressentiment* is by no means most active in the industrial proletariat (except when it is infected by the *ressentiment* of certain "leader" types), but rather in the disappearing class of artisans, in the petty bourgeoisie, and among small officials. The exact causes of this phenomenon cannot be examined here.

Two specifically "spiritual" varieties of *ressentiment* humanity are the "apostate" type and to a lesser degree the "romantic" state of mind, or at least one of its essential traits.

An "apostate" is not a man who once in his life radically changes his deepest religious, political, legal, or philosophical convictions—even when this change is not continuous, but involves a sudden rupture. Even after his conversion, the true "apostate" is not primarily committed to the positive contents of his new belief and to the realization of its aims. He is motivated by the struggle against the old belief and lives only for its negation. The apostate does not affirm his new convictions for their own sake, he is engaged in a continuous chain of acts of revenge against his own spiritual past. In reality he remains a captive of this past, and the new faith is merely a handy frame of reference for negating and rejecting the old. As a religious type, the apostate is therefore at the opposite pole from the "resurrected," whose life is transformed by a new faith which is full of intrinsic meaning and value. Tertullian (*De spectaculis*, 29ff.) asserts that the sight of Roman

governors burning in hell is one of the chief sources of heavenly beatitude. Nietzsche rightly cites this passage as an extreme example of
apostate *ressentiment*.[22] Tertullian's sentence "credible est, quia inep-
tum est, certum est, quia impossibile est—credo, quia absurdum" (*De
carne,* ctr. 5, praeser. 7) is also a typical expression of his apostate
ressentiment. It pungently sums up his method of defending Christianity, which is a continuous vengeance taken on the values of antiquity.[23]

To a lesser degree, a secret *ressentiment* underlies every way of
thinking which attributes creative power to mere *negation* and *criticism*. Thus modern philosophy is deeply penetrated by a whole type of
thinking which is nourished by *ressentiment*. I am referring to the view
that the "true" and the "given" is not that which is self-evident, but
rather that which is "indubitable" or "incontestable," which can be
maintained against doubt and criticism. Let us also mention the principle of the "dialectical method," which wants to produce not only
non-A, but even *B* through the negation of *A* (Spinoza: "omnis deter-
minatio est negatio"; Hegel).[24] All the seemingly positive valuations
and judgments of *ressentiment* are hidden devaluations and negations.
Whenever convictions are not arrived at by direct contact with the
world and the objects themselves, but indirectly through a critique of
the opinions of others, the processes of thinking are impregnated with
ressentiment. The establishment of "criteria" for testing the correct-
ness of opinions then becomes the most important task. Genuine and
fruitful criticism judges all opinions with reference to the *object itself*.
Ressentiment criticism, on the contrary, accepts no "object" that has
not stood the test of criticism.

In a different sense, *ressentiment* is always to some degree a determinant of the *romantic type of mind*. At least this is so when the romantic nostalgia for some past era (Hellas, the Middle Ages, etc.) is
not primarily based on the values of that period, but on the wish to
escape from the present. Then all praise of the "past" has the implied
purpose of downgrading present-day reality. Hölderlin's love for Hellas is primary and entirely positive, it springs from deep congeniality
with the Greek mind and character. On the other hand, Friedrich
Schlegel's nostalgia for the Middle Ages is strongly tinged with *ressentiment*.

The formal structure of *ressentiment* expression is always the same:
A is affirmed, valued, and praised not for its own intrinsic quality, but
with the unverbalized intention of denying, devaluating, and denigrat-
ing *B*. *A* is "played off" against *B*.

I said that there is a particularly violent tension when revenge, hatred, envy, and their effects are coupled with impotence.[25] Under the

impact of that tension, these affects assume the form of *ressentiment*. Not so when they are *discharged*. Therefore parliamentary institutions, even when they harm the public interest by hampering legislation and administration, are highly important as discharge mechanisms for mass and group emotions.[26] Similarly, criminal justice (which purges from revenge), the duel, and in some measure even the press—though it often spreads *ressentiment* instead of diminishing it by the public expression of opinions. If the affects are thus discharged, they are prevented from turning into that psychical dynamite which is called *ressentiment*. If the discharge is blocked, the consequence is a process which may best be designated as "repression." Nietzsche did not describe this process in detail, but he certainly had it in mind. The repressive forces are a feeling of impotence (a pronounced awareness of inability accompanied by intense depression), fear, anxiety, and intimidation. These physical forces become repressive especially when the steady and constant pressure of authority deprives them, as it were, of an object,—i.e., when the person himself does not know "of what" he is afraid or incapable. Thus *fear*, which always has specific objects, here plays a secondary role. Much more important is that deep blockage of vital energy called "anxiety." An even better term would be "anguish" or "intimidation," to distinguish from states of anxiety with organic causes, such as respiratory trouble.[27] These forces begin by blocking only the active expression of the affects, but continue by removing them from the sphere of consciousness, so that the individual or group ceases to be clearly aware of their existence. Finally even the nascent impulse of hatred, envy, or revenge can no longer cross the threshold of consciousness.[28] At the same time, the mass of previously repressed emotions attracts and assimilates the new affect, so that each earlier repression facilitates and accelerates the continuation of the process.

We must distinguish between several components of repression. First of all, there is the repression of the original object of an emotion. I hate a certain person or want to take vengeance on him, and I am fully conscious of my reasons—of the act by which he harmed me, of the moral or physical trait which makes him distasteful to me. If I overcome my impulse by active moral energy, it does not disappear from consciousness, only its *expression* is checked by a clear moral judgment. But if, on the contrary, the impulse is "repressed," it becomes more and more detached from any particular reason and at length even from any particular individual. First it may come to bear on any of my enemy's qualities, activities, or judgments and on any person, relation, object, or situation which is connected with him in any way at all. The impulse "radiates" in all directions. At last it may detach itself even from the man who has injured or oppressed me. Then it turns into a negative attitude toward certain apparent traits and qualities, no matter where or in whom they are found. Here lies the origin of the well-known modern phenomenon of class hatred. Any appearance, gesture, dress, or way of speaking which is symptomatic of a "class" suffices to stir up revenge and hatred, or in other cases fear, anxiety and respect.[29] When the repression is complete, the result is general negativism—a sudden, violent, seemingly unsystematic and unfounded rejection of things, situations, or natural objects whose loose connection with the original cause of the hatred can only be discovered by a complicated analysis. A doctor told me about a man whom hatred has rendered incapable of reading books. Cases like this are confined to the domain of pathology. But in the stage I described, the repressed affect suddenly bursts across the threshold of consciousness whenever the repressive forces happen to relax their vigilance. It frequently finds release in unexpected inner paroxysms of invective without any specific object, and this in the midst of apparent peace of mind, during work or conversation. How often does *ressentiment* betray itself through a smile, a seemingly meaningless gesture, or a passing remark, in the midst of expressions of friendship and sympathy! When a malicious act or remark, apparently unfounded, is suddenly inserted into amicable or even loving behavior which can have lasted for months, we distinctly feel that a deeper layer of life breaks through the friendly surface. Paul suddenly recommends Christ's precept to offer the other cheek by citing Solomon's metaphor (wonderful in itself) that "coals of fire" are thus heaped on the enemy's head. Jesus' original love and humility is here made to serve a hatred which cannot content itself with revenge and seeks it satisfaction in the deeper injury of making the enemy blush with shame.[30]

But repression does not only stretch, change, and shift the original object, it also affects the *emotion itself*. Since the affect cannot outwardly express itself, it becomes active within. Detached from their original objects, the affects melt together into a venomous mass which begins to flow whenever consciousness becomes momentarily relaxed. Since all outward expression is blocked, the inner visceral sensations which accompany every affect come to prevail. All these sensations are unpleasant or even painful, so that the result is a decrease in physical well-being. The man in question no longer feels at ease in his body, it is as though he moves away from it and views it as an unpleasant object. This experience has frequently been the source of dualistic metaphysical systems—for example, in the case of the Neoplatonists and in that of Descartes. It would be wrong to follow a well-known theory which believes that the affects are entirely composed of such visceral sensations.[31] But they do make up a substantial component of hatred, wrath, envy, revenge, etc. Yet they determine neither the particular intentionality or quality of an impulse nor the moment of its greatest intensity, but only its passive and static aspect, which varies for the different affects. In wrath it is greater than in the more "spiritual" emotions of hatred or envy. But when the visceral sensations are greatly stressed and intensified, their influence on the vital and communal instincts very often makes the affective impulses change their direction. The latter now turn against their own bearer. The result is "self-hatred," "self-torment," and "revenge against oneself." Nietzsche wanted to explain "bad conscience" itself in this way: the "warrior" is blocked in the expression of his impulses—for example, when a small warlike nation suddenly feels included in a large and peaceful civilization—and now attacks himself. This explanation is certainly unjustified. It only accounts for a pathological form of pseudo-remorse, a false interpretation of self-directed revenge as "remorse"—a delusion which presupposes true "remorse" and a genuine "bad conscience." [32] Yet the state of affairs described by Nietzsche does exist. The example is Blaise Pascal, a man filled with *ressentiment* as few others, who succeeded with rare art in hiding the fact and in interpreting it in Christian terms: "Le moi est haïssable." Guyau tells us that a savage who cannot commit vendetta "consumes" himself, weakens, and finally dies.[33]

Thus far about *ressentiment* itself. Now let us see what it can contribute to our understanding of certain individual and historical *moral judgments* and of entire moral systems. It goes without saying that genuine moral value judgments are never based on *ressentiment*. This criticism only applies to false judgments founded on *value delusions* and the corresponding ways of living and acting. Nietzsche is wrong in thinking that genuine morality springs from *ressentiment*. It rests on an eternal *hierarchy of values,* and its rules of preference are *fully as objective and clearly "evident"* as mathematical truths. There does exist an *ordre du coeur* and a *logique du coeur* (in Pascal's words) which the moral genius gradually uncovers in history, and it is eternal—only its apprehension and acquisition is "historical." [34] *Ressentiment* helps to subvert this eternal order in man's consciousness, to falsify its recognition, and to deflect its actualization. This should be kept in mind in the following discussion.

Basically Nietzsche says the same when he speaks of a "falsification of the value tablets" by *ressentiment*. On the other hand again, he is a sceptic and relativist in ethics. Yet "false" tablets presuppose others that are "true," or else there would be nothing but a "struggle of value systems" none of which would be "true" or "false."

Ressentiment can account for important developments in the history of moral judgments as well as for small everyday events. However, we must introduce an additional psychological law. We have a tendency to overcome any strong tension between desire and impotence by depreciating or denying the positive value of the desired object. At times, indeed, we go so far as to extol another object which is somehow opposed to the first. It is the old story of the fox and the sour grapes. When we have tried in vain to gain a person's love and respect, we are likely to discover in him ever new negative qualities. When we cannot obtain a thing, we comfort ourselves with the reassuring thought that it is not worth nearly as much as we believed. Initially there is only the verbalized assertion that something—a commodity, a man, or a situation—does not have the value which seemed to make us desire it. The man whose friendship we sought is not really "honest" or "brave" or "intelligent"; the grapes are not really savory, indeed they may be "sour." This is not yet a falsification of values, only a new opinion about the true qualities of the desired object. The *values* as such—intelligence, courage, honesty, the sweetness of the grapes— are acknowledged as before. The fox does not say that sweetness is bad, but that the grapes are sour. At first, such statements are only supposed to deceive the "spectators" whose mockery we fear. It is only later that their contents modify our own judgment. Yet there is a deeper motive even in the simplest cases. The negativistic statement relieves the tension between desire and impotence and reduces our depression. Our desire now seems *unmotivated,* it weakens and the tension decreases. Thus our vital energy and feeling of power rises by several degrees, though on an illusory basis. There is a tendency to modify not only our public statements, but also our own judgment. Who can fail to detect this tendency when he is told that this "inexpensive" ring or meal is much "better" than the expensive one, or to feel that it underlies the praise of "contentment," "simplicity," and "economy" in the moral sphere of the petty bourgeoisie? In this context, let us point to such sayings as "a young whore, an old saint" or "making a virtue out of necessity," and to the different evaluation of debts by merchants or nobles.

This law of the release of tension through illusory valuation gains new significance, full of infinite consequences, for the *ressentiment* attitude. To its very core, the mind of *ressentiment* man is filled with envy, the impulse to detract, malice, and secret vindictiveness. These affects have become fixed attitudes, detached from all determinate objects. Independently of his will, the man's attention will be instinctively drawn by all events which can set these affects in motion. The *ressentiment* attitude even plays a role in the formation of perceptions, expectations, and memories. It automatically selects those aspects of experience which can justify the factual application of this pattern of feeling. Therefore such phenomena as joy, splendor, power, happiness, fortune, and strength magically attract the man of *ressentiment*. He cannot pass by, he has to look at them, whether he "wants" to or not. But at the same time he wants to avert his eyes, for he is tormented by the craving to possess them and knows that his desire is vain. The first result of this inner process is a characteristic *falsification* of the *worldview*. Regardless of what he observes, his world has a peculiar structure of emotional stress. The more the impulse to turn away from those positive values prevails, the more he turns without transition to their negative opposites, on which he concentrates increasingly. He has an urge to scold, to depreciate, to belittle whatever he can. Thus he involuntarily "slanders" life and the world in order to justify his inner pattern of value experience.

But this instinctive falsification of the worldview is only of limited effectiveness. Again and again the *ressentiment* man encounters happiness, power, beauty, wit, goodness, and other phenomena of positive life. They exist and impose themselves, however much he may shake his fist against them and try to explain them away. He cannot escape the tormenting conflict between desire and impotence. Averting his eyes is sometimes impossible and in the long run ineffective. When such a quality irresistibly forces itself upon his attention, the very sight suffices to produce an impulse of hatred against its bearer, who has never harmed or insulted him. Dwarfs and cripples, who already feel humiliated by the outward appearance of the others, often show this peculiar hatred—this hyena-like and ever-ready ferocity. Precisely because this kind of hostility is not caused by the "enemy's" actions and behavior, it is deeper and more irreconcilable than any other. It is not directed against transitory attributes, but against the other person's very essence and being. Goethe has this type of "enemy" in mind when he writes: "Why complain about enemies?—Could those become your friends—To whom your very existence—Is an eternal silent reproach?" (*West-Eastern Divan*). The very existence of this "being," his mere appearance, becomes a silent, unadmitted "reproach." Other disputes can be settled, but not this! Goethe knew, for his rich and great existence was the ideal target of *ressentiment*. His very appearance was bound to make the poison flow.[35]

But even this apparently unfounded hatred is not yet the most characteristic achievement of *ressentiment*. Even here, it is still directed against particular persons or (as in class hatred) particular groups. Its effect is much more profound when it goes beyond such determinate hostilities—when it does not lead to a falsification of the worldview, but perverts the *sense of values* itself. What Nietzsche calls "falsification of the tablets of value" is built on this foundation. In this new phase, the man of *ressentiment* no longer turns away from the positive values, nor does he wish to destroy the men and things endowed with them. Now the values themselves are inverted: those values which are positive to any normal feeling become negative. The man of *ressentiment* cannot justify or even understand his own existence and sense of life in terms of positive values such as power, health, beauty, freedom, and independence. Weakness, fear, anxiety, and a slavish disposition prevent him from obtaining them. Therefore he comes to feel that "all this is vain anyway" and that salvation lies in the opposite phenomena: poverty, suffering, illness, and death. This "sublime revenge" of *ressentiment* (in Nietzsche's words) has indeed played a creative role in the history of value systems. It is "sublime," for the impulses of revenge against those who are strong, healthy, rich, or handsome now disappear entirely. *Ressentiment* has brought deliverance from the inner torment of these affects. Once the sense of values has shifted and the new judgments have spread, such people cease to be enviable, hateful, and worthy of revenge. They are unfortunate and to be pitied, for they are beset with "evils." Their sight now awakens feelings of gentleness, pity, and commiseration. When the reversal of values comes to dominate accepted morality and is invested with the power of the ruling ethos, it is transmitted by tradition, suggestion, and education to those who are endowed with the seemingly devaluated qualities. They are struck with a "bad conscience" and secretly condemn themselves. The "slaves," as Nietzsche says, infect the "masters." *Ressentiment* man, on the other hand, now feels "good," "pure," and "human"—at least in the conscious layers of his mind. He is delivered from hatred, from the tormenting desire of an impossible revenge, though deep down his poisoned sense of life and the true values may still shine through the illusory ones. There is no more calumny, no more defamation of particular persons or things. The systematic perversion and reinterpretation of the values *themselves* is much more effective than the "slandering" of persons or the falsification of the worldview could ever be.

What is called "falsification of the value tablets," "reinterpretation," or "transvaluation" should not be mistaken for conscious lying.

Indeed, it goes beyond the sphere of judging. It is not that the positive value is felt as such and that it is merely declared to be "bad." Beyond all conscious lying and falsifying, there is a deeper "organic mendacity." Here the falsification is not formed in consciousness, but at the same stage of the mental process as the impressions and value feelings themselves: *on the road* of experience into consciousness. There is "organic mendacity" whenever a man's mind admits only those impressions which serve his "interest" or his instinctive attitude. Already in the process of mental reproduction and recollection, the contents of his experience are modified in this direction. He who is "mendacious" has no need to lie! In his case, the automatic process of forming recollections, impressions, and feelings is involuntarily slanted, so that conscious falsification becomes unnecessary. Indeed the most honest and upright convictions may prevail in the periphery of consciousness. The apprehension of values follows this pattern, to the point of their complete reversal. The *value judgment* is based on this original "falsification." It is itself entirely "true," "genuine," and "honest," for the value it affirms is really felt to be positive.[36]

Notes

1. [Here is a list of Scheler's terms for the various emotions of this kind, with the English translations which have been used and consistently maintained: *Rache* (revenge), *Hass* (hatred), *Bosheit* (malice), *Neid* (envy), *Scheelsucht* (impulse to detract), *Hämischkeit* (spite), *Groll* (rancor), *Zorn* (wrath), *Rachsucht* (vindictiveness, vengefulness). The term *Schadenfreude* (= joy at another's misfortune) has been left in German.—Trans.]

2. Steinmetz, in his interesting studies on the genealogy of revenge, assumes that "directed revenge" is preceded by "nondirected revenge." He argues that in the most primitive stages of civilization even animals (such as the nearest horse), trees, or inanimate objects are destroyed when an injury has been experienced. Steinmetz misinterprets the essential nature of revenge, which is always *directed,* in contrast with nonactive affects such as wrath, anger, rage, etc. There are outbursts of rage even on a civilized level, for example, when someone whose anger has been aroused "cuts everything to pieces." These have nothing to do with revenge. Even if the examples given by Steinmetz should be cases of revenge, there are still several possibilities. The object destroyed may stand in a real or supposed property relation to the object of revenge or may be connected with it in a symbolic function which can be momentary and need not be permanent ("let this object stand for that person now"). Not only the destruction of books or the piercing of photographs, but also the crumbling of a piece of paper or a handkerchief may fall under this heading. Or revenge can be "without an object" in the sense that it may

be directed against no *particular* object, but may comprise the whole region where the injury has been inflicted—a district, a city, or even the whole world in its "otherness." Such a case occurred only recently in the mass murders committed by the teacher Wagner. [Cf. Robert Gaupp's monograph *Zur Psychologie des Massenmordes: Hauptlehrer Wagner von Degerloch* (Berlin, 1914), to which the author's remark refers.—M.S.] But revenge is "directed" even here. It has been wrongly assumed that vendetta is a secondary transference of the object of revenge to the offender's tribe or family members, caused by the awareness that the offender would suffer in sympathy with his stricken companion. But the true basis of vendetta is the view that the tribe or family is the real *perpetrator* and that the individual member is only its organ. It is as if I punish the man who cut off my hand by chopping off his foot.—It seems, moreover, that revenge is in the last analysis not limited to injury or the diminution of one's value inflicted by another individual. It may also be caused by our own depreciation of ourselves or of others with whom we sympathize. This is the case when we say: "I could hit myself, I could tear my hair," etc. These phenomena have nothing to do with the act of repentance or the desire for atonement and expiation, which are spiritual acts rather than vital impulses and are exclusively connected with the realm of moral values. Cf. S. R. Steinmetz, *Ethnologische Studien zur ersten Entwicklung der Strafe* (Leyden, 1894). Cf. also my essay on "Reue und Wiedergeburt" in *Vom Ewigen im Menschen*. [In the second edition of the essays and treatises *Vom Umsturz der Werte* (1919)—in this footnote as well as in some others—the work *Vom Ewigen im Menschen* is announced for as early as 1918. In fact it did not appear until 1921.—M.S.]

3. M. Guyau cites such examples in his book *Esquisse d'une morale sans obligation ni sanction* (1885).

4. The enormous explosion of *ressentiment* in the French Revolution against the nobility and everything connected with its way of living, and indeed the very emergence of this *ressentiment,* would have been entirely inconceivable if (according to Werner Sombart's calculation in *Luxus und Kapitalismus* (Munich 1912), pp. 10–24) more than 80% of the nobility itself had not been intermingled with bourgeois elements, who acquired names and titles by buying aristocratic estates. Besides, the nobility was racially weakened by money marriages. The *ressentiment* of the insurgents was sharpened by the new feeling that they were *equal* to the ruling class.

[There exists a mimeographed translation of Sombart's *Luxury and Capitalism* (New York, 1938), carried out under the auspices of the Works Progress Administration and the Department of Social Science of Columbia University, under the supervision of W. R. Dittmar.—Trans.]

5. Our present-day semi-parliamentarianism in the German Empire is conducive to the inner health of the people, since it serves as a discharge mechanism for accumulated *ressentiment*. But to the degree that the parliament is eliminated from active government, or at any rate from the function of selecting those men of the nation who have the strongest will and the most acute

political intelligence, it attracts only a certain section of the men of *ressentiment:* those who accept that their votes of nonconfidence strengthen the position of the ministers rather than weaken it.

[Of course Scheler is referring to the German Empire prior to the First World War.—Trans.]

6. In the experience of envy, the mere fact that the other person possesses the coveted good is therefore felt to be a "deprivation." This is because our original mental attitude is characterized by an illusory *appropriation* of the good. The other person's suddenly discovered ownership of the good appears as a "deprivation," as a "force" which takes it away from us.

7. [This quotation is from *Maxims and Reflections,* "From the Elective Affinities." 45.—M.S.]

8. Thus pride is always based on a *lack* of this natural self-confidence.

9. [On *arriviste* and *ressentiment,* cf. Max Scheler, *Der Formalismus in der Ethik und die materiale Wertethik.* Cf. index of the 4th ed., 1954.—M.S.] [In English, *Formalism in Ethics and Non-formal Ethics of Values,* trans. Manfred S. Frings and Roger L. Funk (Evanston, Ill.: Northwestern University Press, 1973.—Ed.]

10. [On this and what follows, cf. the essay "Der Bourgeois" in *Vom Umsturz der Werte.*—M.S.]

11. Cf. Leopold von Ranke, *Über die Epochen der neueren Geschichte* (Munich, 1921), 1st lecture.

12. Cf. what follows.

13. Cf. *Formalismus,* part II. [On feeling, preferring, and loving as cognitive acts, and on the relation between value consciousness and acts of aspiration, cf. *Formalismus,* section I3 and section V2.—M.S.] Cf. also my article "Ethik" in *Jahrbücher der Philosophie,* II. Jahrgang (Berlin, 1914), ed. Max Frischeisen-Köhler.

14. In an interesting study on "Christus und das Ressentiment" (supplement to Hambg, Korresp. of 28 Sept. 1913) A. Gustav Hübener, continuing the above, points out that in the view of the Christian Church even the devil has a glimmer of direct knowledge of the good. John Milton makes Satan acknowledge his principle as follows:

> "Farewell remorse: all good to me is lost;
> Evil be thou my good."

But still, heaven shines into his soul, so that he must cast furtive glances at it and stir up the infernal fire in his heart:

> "... the more I see
> Pleasures about me, so much more I feel
> Torment within me, as from the hateful siege
> Of contraries; all good to me becomes
> Bane, and in Heaven much worse would be my state."

15. Cf. my analysis of English "cant" in my book *Der Genius des Krieges und der deutsche Krieg* (Appendix, 3rd ed., 1917).

16. [Cf. the essay "Zum Sinn der Frauenbewegung" in *Vom Umsturz der Werte.*—M.S.]

17. Cf. the views of the great eighteenth-century writers and philosophers on this matter, collected by Havelock Ellis in his book *The Evolution of Modesty* (Philadelphia, 1910). They all reduce modesty to "upbringing" and mistake it for "propriety." [Cf. the author's study on "Scham und Schamgefühl," published posthumously by the German editor in *Schriften aus dem Nachlass,* vol. I, *Zur Ethik und Erkenntnislehre.*—M.S.]

18. The well-known inquiry of the "Verein für Sozialpolitik" shows how soon the qualified industrial worker is nowadays pushed down into the ranks of unqualified workers. [The title of the inquiry mentioned by the author is "Untersuchungen über Auslese und Anpassung (Berufswahl und Berufsschicksal) der Arbeiter in den verschiedenen Zweigen der Grossindustrie" (Leipzig, 1911/12).—M.S.]

19. Cf. *Luxus und Kapitalismus* (Berlin, 1912), p. 115.

20. Cf. Wilhelm Hasbach, *Die moderne Demokratie* (Jena, 1912).

21. All assertions in the book by Innocence III, *De contemptu mundi sive de miseria humanae conditionis,* are dictated by extreme priestly *ressentiment.*

22. Cf. *Genealogy of Morals,* part I, section 15.

23. Cf. the characterization of Tertullian by Johann Adam Möhler, *Patrologie* (Regensburg, 1840). "He was bitter and gloomy by nature, and even the mild light of the Gospel could not brighten his gloom" (p. 703). Tertullian's conversion to Montanism (about 203 A.D.), after which he knew no limits in ridiculing and deriding the principles and customs of the Church, is merely a renewal of the act of apostasy, which had become the very structure of his vital reactions.

24. Already Sigwart (*Logik II*) rightly points out that Darwin's theory as well uses the basic Hegelian idea of the "creative importance of negation." According to Darwin, all evolution is essentially determined by the elimination of the useless within purely contingent variations of the species. Thus the impression of positive development and creativity which is conveyed by the sight of organized species is a mere epiphenomenon, behind which there is nothing but negation and elimination.

25. [In the first version of the present study (1912), before its extension, this passage followed.—M.S.]

26. No other literature is as full of *ressentiment* as the young Russian literature. The books of Dostoyevsky, Gogol, and Tolstoy teem with *ressentiment*-laden heroes. This is a result of the long autocratic oppression of the people, with no parliament or freedom of press through which the affects caused by authority could find release.

27. We must exclude the type of anxiety which is genetically a fear that has lost its object. As all fear, it once had a definite object which has merely ceased to be clearly conscious. We must further except that type of anxiety which is primarily a mode of a person's vital feeling (*Lebensgefühl*) itself and which conversely *makes* him fear ever new objects, far beyond the danger they

might hold. The former kind of anxiety can be easily removed, the latter almost never. The general pressure of anxiety which weighs on individuals and whole groups varies greatly in degree. It is highly important for the total behavior of the subjects concerned.

[The German terms used by Scheler are: *Furcht* (fear), *Angst* (anxiety), *Verängstigtheit* (anguish), *Eingeschüchterheit* (intimidation).—Trans.]

28. Cf. the author's essay "Die Idole der Selbsterkenntnis" in *Vom Umsturz der Werte.*

29. Cf. the case of the captain of Köpenick. If one paid even slight attention, he certainly did not look like an officer. But the mere vague appearance of the "uniform," which he did not even wear according to regulars, was enough to make the mayor and the others obey all his orders.

30. We do not wish to decide here to what degree Paul, in his quotation, may be thinking of the salvation of him who blushes, who is awakened to new love by his shame and remorse.

31. Cf. William James, *Psychology* (New York, 1891).

32. Cf. the author's essay "Die Idole der Selbsterkenntnis" in *Vom Umsturz der Werte* and his treatise "Reue und Wiedergeburt" in *Vom Ewigen in Menschen.*

33. J.-M. Guyau, *Esquisse d'une morale sans obligation ni sanction.*

34. Cf. the author's book in *Formalismus,* where he attempts to prove this affirmation. [On "ordre du coeur," "moral genius," and "historical apprehension of values," cf. *Formalismus,* section V6; furthermore, the essay "Ordo Amoris," written about 1916, published posthumously in the previously mentioned *Nachlassband* (1933).—M.S.]

35. Antonio's behavior toward Tasso (in Goethe's *Torquato Tasso*) is strongly colored by *ressentiment.* This is certainly a reflection of this Goethean experience of life.

36. [In the first version of the present study (1912), there follows an account of a pathological case.—M.S.]

II

KNOWLEDGE AND SOCIAL LIFE

7

Love and Knowledge

"One knows nothing save what one loves, and the deeper and more complete that knowledge, the stronger and livelier must be one's love—indeed passion," wrote Goethe in his youth. He repeated this thought in countless variations all his life. Next to this judgment we may place the view of Leonardo da Vinci, that "every great love is the daughter of a great knowledge." The German poet (also the philosopher Giordano Bruno) agreed with the genius of the Renaissance in bringing *love* and *knowledge* together into the most profound and intimate connection, although for Goethe the movement of *love* grounds the act of knowledge, whereas for Leonardo the movement of *knowledge* grounds the act of love. However, both contradict the common, and as far as I can see, specifically modern bourgeois judgment, prevalent since the Enlightenment, that "love makes one blind," that all true knowledge of the world can rest only on *holding back* the emotions and simultaneously ignoring differences in value of the objects known. Framed as a conflict between amateur and expert, the opposition of these types is threaded through modern history. Even so, against this judgment that prevailed after the Enlightenment, no less than Blaise Pascal, in his "Conversation on the Passions of Love," dared to assert the clear, incredibly resonant proposition, "Love and reason are one and the same." Pascal's deeper meaning was that love first *discloses* objects, which appear to the senses and which reason later judges. Even Spinoza, who fought against all "anthropomorphic" worldviews, who wanted to conceive the passions as "lines, planes, and circles," spoke in his teaching of an intellectual love of God, an "amor Dei intellectualis." Spinoza considered the highest level of knowledge, where knowledge is most comprehensive and adequate to being, as the plane where "God comprehends and enjoys Himself," thus where knowledge is inseparably blended with loving attention to the object.

This essay was originally published as "Liebe und Erkenntnis," in *Gesammelte Werke*, vol. 6, *Schriften zur Soziologie und Weltanschauungslehre*, pp. 77–98. I have translated it with the assistance of Peter Haley.

If one ignores the finer nuances, the solution to the question of the relation of love to knowledge is revealed in certain world-historical *types* whose characterization I will be content to hint at here rather than portray in great historical detail.

Despite deep oppositions between the Indian and Greek mentalities, one can speak in a nongenetic and world-historic sense of an *Indian-Greek* type of solution to our question, a solution that is theoretical as well as factual. For the Indians as well as the Greeks, value was viewed ontologically, as a function of *being*. However, noetically—as a strict mental correlate—love is a dependent function of *knowledge*. In the Indian case, the object that has raised itself beyond the ground of being is of the highest value. But in the Greek case, the object that has achieved the highest degree of being, Plato's ὄντος ὄν, is of the highest value.[1] It is precisely because value is a function of being in both cases, but in such basically different ways, that the objective unity of their teachings can be seen.

The direction of the *Indian* mentality sets so much dependence on the ontological side that the positive and most central value adheres to *not-being*. This means that the way to salvation consists in emptying the reality coefficient of the world of its "whatness," its contents. In the Indian experience it is this "reality coefficient" that must be exorcised, for we drown in the depth and breadth of the contents of the world the more passionately bound to these contents we are by our desires. The world is "real" or "unreal" for us only as acting beings, driven by desires, not as pure knowing spirits or intellects. It is real to the degree it is desired, but at the same time poor to the degree it is real. Only when the world stands before us as not real, not desired, is it rich and its amplitude fully revealed.

By analogy, "knowledge" in the Indian view is gained, first of all, by increasingly overcoming the positive and negative reality accents of the world. As these accents are correlated with desires, their overcoming is set into motion by taking an ascetic path in which the appetites are rendered progressively arbitrary and their fading and eventual loss occurs automatically and naturally. In this way, desires that envelop and obscure the pure subjects of knowledge disappear and with them the associated reality accents. In the *Mahabharata* it is written that the spirit of reality continually captivates desires and deeds anew. "One must consider the paths taken before a man reaches self-containment and wisdom. His actions advance him from an involvement in bare nature to a true self. Only those blinded by the earth place the ground of their actions solely in themselves; the wayward are not constrained by modesty."[2]

The content of "love" in the Indian sense is located in the transition that occurs within the "actual," however, in the movement that is begun when desires are opposed and objects of knowledge are chosen. The more desires are opposed, the *fuller* knowledge *becomes.* Viewed from the side of action, love is merely the experience of transition from not-knowing to knowing. The love emotion is not independent; it is not an original, positive act of spirit that affects the mind, but merely the experience of the growth of knowledge itself. If we wish to understand Indian writings on love we must see the essential connection between ontic (existential) processes of the actualization of the world, brought about by the steady flow of desires out of the center of the ego, and intellectual processes in men. This is a presupposition to everything said of love in Indian writings. Above all, we must understand that love appears as a *consequence,* not as the origin, of knowledge. Whatever religious or ethical value may attach to love is solely a fruit of this knowledge. In no way does love here play a role similar to the Christian love of God and neighbor. For the Christian, love is given a place equal in primacy to, even greater than, knowledge. The Indian axiom stands in sharpest opposition to this. Augustine, the greatest Christian thinker, expressly made love the *original* power of movement of the divine as well as of the human spirit. In obvious opposition to Aristotle's doctrine of nous, Augustine said that love "makes holy *more* than reason."

The Indian idea of love is, therefore, as purely intellectual as the ideas of the *Greeks.* For Plato too eros is a transition from a lesser to a greater knowledge, a tendency of objects of sense, still belonging to the "material" domain, to win participation in the "idea," the essential. Eros is the drive and longing of not-being for being, of the bad for the good.

The most basic elements of love and knowledge for both Indian and Greek, consequently, may be expressed as follows. For the Christian, the process of *salvation* is begun by an earlier act of love and grace of a superhuman power. This is a transcendent act of *redemption* whose *consequence* is communication of *knowledge,* the revelation necessary for salvation. But for Indian and Greek, salvation is only *self*-salvation of the individual through knowledge. In Indian thought there is no savior who bears the attributes of God, only a *teacher of wisdom* whose teachings point the way to "holiness." This consequence follows necessarily whenever love is thought of as a dependent function of knowledge. Compared to such self-found knowledge, however, for the Christian each communication of knowledge necessary for salvation is based on love of the communicator for the communicant.

Moreover, the idea that one may arrive at complete knowledge through pure contemplation is in striking contrast to the Christian conception of the infinite worth and true substantiality of each individual soul. The contemplative *act*, for Indian and Greek, is bound up completely and solely with the *individual* and is the way to the end. But the end—"there" for the Greek (ὄντος ὄν, completed being), "here" for the Indian (not-being)—may coincide with the *extinction* of individuality, its disappearance in the sphere of the supraindividual being. According to Möhler's profound and little-understood essay "On the Unity of the Church," in original Christianity adherence to a religious conviction in the united community of love of the *whole* church was a criterion of *truth* of the doctrine corresponding to this conviction. The "heretic" must be wrong, no matter what the evidence for his view. He must be wrong, that is, because the essential Christian connection between love and knowledge binds any true knowledge to being proved in the community of love of the church. There is nothing of this in the Indian view: love is a consequence, not a condition, of the healing found only in knowledge.

The particular ethical character of the Indian idea of love is fixed with the above axiom. According to the pregnant, ever-repeated expression in the preaching of Buddha, love is the "redemption of the heart." [3] This means that love is positively valued for salvation, but not as something added to some other positive value, whether to God, to neighbor, or to beauty and life in nature. Love is a way "away from oneself," therefore a *denial* of being and reality. This is accomplished by a successive transcendence of one's individuality conditioned by one's desiring body. The contemplation of the self and things outside the self is thus an *ontic* process, an actualization of self and other from which, however, one gains increasing distance. Access to this "way away from oneself" can be had through neighboring human beings and also through nature. Love of nature, especially plants and animals, like love of neighbor, is included in the offering of love. Always, however, the cause of this act of love is merely the experience of "otherness," of a "*not*-I" as such, not because of any positive value this other being may have but only because it is not-I. Part of the Indian axiom, according to which the object's worth increases the farther it is removed from the sphere of being, becomes effective in shaping the basic character of the Indian *movement* of love. This movement is entirely altruistic, going beyond its object; the object is a terminus a quo, a point of departure, which serves as an *inducement* for the "redemption of the heart." The fulfillment of love in the object, love as a terminus ad quem, an arrival, is a matter of complete indifference. The only role that such accidental inducements are allowed to play is to lead to a radical change of life, as in the meetings with the sick and the beggars that prompted the young Buddha to repent and change.

To this structure of the Indian experience of the world a third strand is connected that is maintained constantly throughout the development of Indian religious speculation. Love, as merely dependent on knowledge, on the unveiling of the actual, is not an experience that a real *individual person* has as something that begins or ends. Love is, on the contrary, the emotional insight into the *nothingness* of individual-personal existence *in general*.[4] For the Indian, the basis of individuation is not an autonomous, spiritual principle of the person as it is for the Christian. Individuation is only a matter of love and desire within whose plurality the *one* and *identical* subject of knowledge in man is peculiarly imprisoned. In love one is not supposed to grasp the meaning and worth of a being other than and separate from oneself and overcome the separation in a deep affirmation of the other's existence and worth. Rather, one is supposed to feel the other's existence and worth as *transcended,* simultaneously with one's own, as both disappear together by drowning in the fullness of "nothingness." To this corresponds (existentially) fully reached knowledge, the final transcendence of individuality, which must leave behind the love that was merely the growth of knowledge. Compared to this last great holy act and true "death" the bodily death of the individual is only a false appearance of death; this is actually only a wandering of the individual into the house of a new body, therefore only the beginning of a new "life" in which love and knowledge must constantly be overcome. Buddha is the great teacher of salvation who announced the possibility of a true, final "death"—not through individual eternity, which was increasingly feared by the Indian world, but by individual extinction through entrance into Nirvana.[5]

In sharp contrast to the Indian-Buddhist type of relationship between love and knowledge, being and value, the *Greek* type *positively elevates being,* indeed, looks upon the completion of being as the greatest value. This affirmation of being, rooted specifically in Greek sources, remains the a priori of *all* European religion and speculation. The richer and higher the being of the object of knowledge, the more absolute and pure the knowledge. Absolute knowledge, therefore, is knowledge of ὄντος ὄν. The positive worth of existing things is merely a function of how much *fullness of being* they contain, whereas the negative values of "evil," "the bad," "the hateful," and so on—in the most extreme contrast to Buddhism—are traced to their relative *lack* of being. Analogous to this, subjective love is also primarily a turning

toward positive value, toward a form of being that has a certain fullness. Love is a taking possession of being in knowledge, and therefore
is not salvation from being as is the case in India. Love and hate have
been understood, ever since the doctrines of Empedocles, as objective
cosmic agents, the two forces behind the four elements of the world.
Love is a principle of *procreation* that brings forth newer and richer
forms of being. As Plato says in his *Symposium,* love is "generation in
beauty," a concept that can span animal procreation as well as the
intellectual conceptions of the philosopher and the works of the artist,
the statesman, and the general, all in a huge, finely graded ladder of
ways and goals of creating. There is an *unbroken continuity* in the
conception of love as a positive drive and agent of creation that runs
from the oldest Aphrodite and Eros cults to the intellectual articula-
tions in Plato and Aristotle. Corresponding to the ontic (existential)
levels of creating are levels in the intellect, of love for the lowest toward ever-higher figures and forms of the world until, finally, love for
the highest plane, that of "ideas." And from among ideas there is the
idea of ideas, the good, which makes possible even the ὄντος ὄν: beginning with the beautiful horse, through beautiful bodies of youths,
up to the pure idea of beauty itself.

But from another no less essential direction, the Greek notion can
be seen to have a deep *commonality* with the Indian. First, love is
understood intellectually, as dependent on the progress of knowledge.
Love is a bridge, or better, a movement from poorer to richer knowledge. Love is an ontic agent, the drive of μὴ ὄν, the least, to win participation in ὄντος ὄν, the most. In a striking figure that blends erotic and
spiritual elements in friendship, Socrates taught that the inner reform
of the individual, not merely rearrangement of externals, is brought
about by the question and answer of dialogue. Eros acts as the muse
of philosophical investigation, as a kind of spiritual midwife by means
of which the souls of the young will be lured forth and *self-knowledge*
gained. Plato's view that Eros is closely bound to dialogue is of this
origin. That love, for Plato, is entirely reduced to knowledge, indeed
means only the striving of incomplete knowledge for the complete, is
shown in his stipulation that neither the ignorant nor the fully knowing (i.e., the gods) can *love,* but only philosophers, lovers of knowledge.

Love, Eros, is the son of riches and poverty, knowledge and igno-
rance. For this reason, divinity for the Greeks is only the object of love,
but not in itself loving, as it is for Christians. Wherever this double
stipulation concerning love occurs in history, that love in its dynamics
comes after rather than before knowledge, and is merely a teleological

means to the end, there one always finds the heathen image of divinity as something dumb, looking only upon itself and incapable of loving back in return. That the divinity is solely the object of supplications of its creatures, not a subject of an "intimate conversation of the soul with God," as Saint Gregory of Nyssa defined Christian prayer, was also Spinoza's view, which took up again the Greek principle. No one, he said, can demand that God reciprocate one's own "amor Dei intellectualis" fom His side with love. In reacting to this thought, Goethe made his Philine respond, "If I love you, what does this have to do with you!"

The Platonic conception of love as the striving of not-being for being contains the kernel of this entire theory. Factually, however, love and hate, as well as the taking of an interest, do not belong to the sphere of the striving and willing of our intellect, although, of course, all kinds of striving, longing, desiring, willing, and drives may be found there. All "striving" consumes itself in the satisfaction of desire. At the same time, striving aims toward realizing another, actual new thing that is opposed to itself. Love, on the contrary, rests entirely in the being of its object and wants the object to be nothing other than what it *is*. Love grows as it presses more deeply into its object. When understood as "striving" for knowledge, however, love must *disappear* with complete knowledge. Love can thus not be one with the divinity, which, as the complete being, lacks nothing but is precisely what it "wants" and "should be." Celsius, in his critique of Christianity from a Neoplatonic standpoint, tried to prove in a rigorously logical fashion that the Christian idea of a "loving God" was nonsensical. It is perhaps more to be marveled that the Platonic conception of love as "striving" entered Scholastic philosophy against the innermost intentions of Christianity, and that the Platonic proposition, "Everything is good inasmuch as it is," formed a part of Thomistic doctrine.[6]

In the ontic stipulation of eros as a power, however, in which Plato may have seemed to approach the idea of a world-creating love, "creation" also became completely modified. What Plato called "creating" is actually a mere *image* of a "creation for us," the sphere of "representation" (*doxa*). For knowledge in the strong sense, *epistemae*, apparent creation is *not* creation, not production, but only *re*production of form. Only the eternal striving of "always becoming" matter to gain participation in the *permanence of "form" and "idea"* appears to us, both ontically and subjectively, as the process of creation. For Plato, *natural* love as a cosmic agent is merely the drive of the animal's life principle to *maintain species form* by creating new individuals. But this is not the *completion* of some kind of species form. In the lust of an animal Plato saw the longing for an earthly immorality of form, the Platonic form. All maintenance of form in becoming matter, even in dead nature, is the victory of eros, which thirsts after permanence. "Creation," thus, actually conceals preservation. This restless over-emphasizing of the static over the dynamic in Plato, of plastic spatial form over temporal creative powers, turns into the highest kind of *intellectual love*. The "fame" of philosophers, artists, and statesmen in classical understanding is not "honor" or "respect" of contemporaries, but a secret, inward being of the creative person that is transferred to his work as an objective "image" of worth and thereafter radiates as genius in the work itself. This "image" is also a kind of earthly immortality. Not merely the art of the individual, but what may be seen as creation of self in the work—these are self-maintaining when viewed in the hindsight of lasting generations. But finally, the highest goal to which all intellectual capabilities and also love in its purest form can lead is to "glimpse the ideas" of the philosophers, a goal that is at the farthest remove from creating. This is a participation in being. For Plato, love in the inner workshop of the intellect merely exercises just this function of survival or maintenance. What love accomplishes in the continuation and creation of species of plant and animal, it also accomplishes in the individual soul by memory and the reproduction of images. Plato had already asserted in the *Symposium* that there is an essential identity between memory and heredity.[7] Whatever appears in our present consciousness consists of earlier experiences that, driven by eros, have succeeded in gaining survival and permanence. These experiences appear again because of their reproduction in memory. This is nothing other than how plants and animals maintain their species, through procreation and inheritance.

The idea of the "creative power" of love disappears even more when we add to it the doctrine of recollection. Just as Plato lacked the "idea of spontaneous, creative consciousness and intellect" (as Windelband observes), so he also lacked the idea of creative love. This is shown clearly by his quite romanticized doctrine of the longing of the soul to see again the incorporeal world of pure ideas. For the soul thus satisfies itself in the *remembrance* of something once seen in a "heavenly place" in which all "knowledge" seemed to appear.

In his teaching on love and knowledge, Plato anticipated the great historical movement of "romantic love." In this anticlassical type, love is not primarily a spiritual possession but a *longing* for something distant or past; this love seems to grow proportionately as its object recedes and to diminish as its object draws near. Plato obviously looked to India for his famous mystical rendering of the *love of husband and wife* as a striving toward one another of both parts of an originally undifferentiated human being.[8] A special form of the deep metaphysical error of Indian thought occurs in Plato also, namely, that love is no more than an intuitive knowledge of the unity of being, a penetration of the appearance of disparateness, individuality, plurality, a movement toward each other of parts that were originally "one and whole." *All pantheism, from Spinoza to Hegel and Schopenhauer, has accepted this essentially false proposition.* It is easy to see how, according to this scheme (which has remained the scheme of every false mysticism up to the present day), love is reduced to egoism. For what else is love here except a kind of egoism of the whole, which only assumes the appearance of "love" with the appearance of an individual whose independence from the larger whole is merely that of being a part? What else is this except "égoïsme à deux"? The love of an individual who merely appears must itself be merely an appearance, a seeming love. Even the description of sexual love between husband and wife in Plato's myth contains a romantic character. The differences between the sexes are not the root of a special kind of love whose consequence, sexual choice for *breeding,* could work to transform and raise the species.[9] For Plato, love is rather a tendency to a mere "return" to the *one* sexually not yet differentiated human being whose parts now search for each other. Love serves only to *preserve,* not to raise or create, the species. Plato's doctrine stands far above all modern naturalistic endeavors to connect the appearance of love with the ongoing differentiation of the sexes, to view love in all its forms as mere development of the sexual drive.[10] Indeed, the very opposite is true for Plato: the division between the sexes and their working together in procreation is only one of the techniques of nature through which the cosmic power, which is dependent on this division, acts to create life. But the romantic and mystical tones of this "longing" for former states—of undifferentiated androgyny, of restoration of the whole—convey the idea of sexual love. This love is conceived *retro*spectively, not prospectively.

One cannot say that the greatest experience of European humanity, the appearance of Christ, has embodied the relationship between *knowledge* and *love* in an ideal type as strict as the Indian and Greek. Nevertheless, it is precisely the *structure of experience* of the world, of one's neighbor, and of divinity, which the Christian conception has most changed. Yet just on this point, on this unique revolution of the human spirit, the Christian idea has, for unfathomable reasons, failed to be *intellectually* and *philosophically* expressed. This is only part of a much more universal fact. Christianity has never, or only in weak ways, come to a philosophical picture of the world and of life, a pic-

ture that sprang *originally* and *spontaneously* out of *Christian experience*. There never was and is not now a "Christian philosophy," unless
one understands by this an essentially Greek philosophy with Christian ornamentation. But there is a system of thought that, springing
from the *root* and *essence* of Christian experience, observes and discovers the world. The reason for this is a double one: Christians of the
first century were by neither background, profession, nor predilection
disposed to a philosophical posture toward existence. But as the
growth of the heathen church and struggle with Gnostic and other
sects demanded the intellectual creation of a fixed doctrine, the new
experience of God and world had to make itself comfortable within
the sturdy structure of Greek philosophy—without, however, bringing
forth its own new building. Once Christian dogma was articulated in
Greek concepts, further efforts were made to interpret dogma philosophically and theologically and to align this interpretation with
knowledge of the world to form a unified worldview. The simultaneous attraction between dogma and Greek philosophy then remained
fixed for a long time. Because of this fact, spontaneous *philosophical*
expression of the Christian experience was inhibited to the greatest
degree. Nevertheless, the continuity of the Christian experience remained deep and alive within the church. Indeed, it is a nonsensical
idea that this continuity was torn for centuries until Luther. Only in
Augustine and his school do we find concerted efforts to turn the content of the Christian experience into philosophical concepts. And even
the success of these efforts was inhibited by Augustine's great dependency on Neoplatonism and his authoritarian will for unity of the
church, which overcame his speculative will.

That in the Christian experience there occurred a *radical reversal* of
position of love and knowledge, value and being, I have tried to show
elsewhere.[11] I have called this a reversal of the *movement of love,*
which *invalidates* the Greek axiom that love goes from lower to higher
things, from not-being to being, from the bad to the good, from man
to God who does not Himself love.

In the Christian experience, love descended from the higher to the
lower, from God to man, from the holy to the sinner who is taken up
into the *essence* of the "higher," therefore also the "highest," which is
God. Just in this reversal in direction of love lies a *new way of founding* love and knowledge, value and being.

This new way expresses itself religiously, first, in that religious
knowledge is no longer a spontaneous act of the individual but is
transferred to the initial movement of *God Himself,* to the redeeming
will of God and His self-revelation in Christ. The process of the indi-

vidual's becoming holy through works takes place between a beginning, in which being comprehended by the grace of God precedes all the individual's activity, and an ending, in which a grace "makes holy." All human freedom and service lie only *between* these two points. The beginning as well as the end of all religious knowledge and healing processes lie, therefore, in God. The Indian-Greek notion of self-salvation through knowledge is replaced by the idea of *becoming* redeemed through divine love. There is no communication of a new knowledge or wisdom of God through Christ (as happened through Buddha, or the great "teachers," or Plato, or as when God spoke and gave laws through Moses and His prophets). Nor is there a communication whose *content* is merely the existence of a loving and merciful God. Rather, all new knowledge of God is conveyed by the act of love in His self-appearance in Christ.[12] Christ is only derivatively a "successor" of his teacher or lawgiver precursors; He is a teacher and lawgiver only as a consequence of His value as a divine savior, as the personal, incarnated figure of God and His loving will. Beyond this personal figure, according to the early, genuinely Christian notion, there is no "idea," no "law," no "real value," no "reason" by which He could be measured or with which He would somehow have to agree in order to be recognizable as "holy." Christ does not "have" the truth. He "*is*" the truth in its full concreteness. His actions, expressions, speeches count as true, holy, and good because it is He, Christ, from whom they come. Just for this reason, belief in the content of His message and in Him as "savior" and "holy one" are rooted in a preceding *counter-love* to His love, which is directed to each person. It is in the process of this love that an image grows in the mind's eye of His divine existence, which is the object of faith. Not "everyone" saw Him when He spoke to Magdalena after rising: Magdalena's love saw Him first. Some, however, didn't see Him because "God had closed their eyes." Only the eyes of the loving were opened—to the degree that they loved Him. Just as it is the *person* of Christ—not some kind of "idea"—which is the first religious object of love, so the point of departure of the love emotion is an ontically real person: the person of God. The form of existence of the person is not dissolved in the stream of love—as with the Indians and the Greeks. Here there is no penetration by so-called metaphysical nothingness of the person in the emotion of love. The more purely the person in the man raises himself in the love of God from dependence on nature and society, from the confusion of sensual, drive-ridden consciousness, the more he secures himself, makes himself "holy." The person gains himself when he loses himself in God.

To this quite new principle of Christian consciousness corresponds the fact that love of neighbor is made equivalent with true love of God. All deeper, knowledgeable penetration of divine things is founded, *simultaneously and equally*, by love of God and humanity. It is obvious that wherever love belongs to the essence of God, and the religious process of salvation has its point of departure from divine love rather than spontaneous human activity, love "toward" God must always include at the same time *love of humanity, even love of all creatures with God*—an *amare mundum in Deo*. Augustine's formula for the inseparable unity of this act is "Amore Dei et invicem in Deo." A love of God such as the Greek, which leads one completely away from community, that does not bring one into increasingly deeper and more comprehensive communal relations with one's brethren, can logically end only on a mountain on which the lonely anchorite puts himself outside of all human contact. The Greek-Indian principle, that knowledge founds love, has this isolating, lonely-making power from the beginning. Wherever, as in the Eastern church, this Greek-Gnostic element gained supremacy over the new Christian life structure, anchoritism has grown of inner necessity and freed monks, as in present-day Russian Orthodoxy, from service to society.[13]

An intense love of God that does not issue in the same degree of love of neighbor would simply be, according to Christian consciousness, not love of God but love of an idol. In the Christian view God is lovingly related to those who love and to His creatures by His very essence. For this reason, in the testing of every assertion concerning divine things in the religious community of love, the church can and must have as its criterion of truth its uniting, nondivisive power. To found knowledge of the truth on love leads to the notion that heretics must be wrong, not for the content of their teachings, but simply because they are heretics. A heretic is someone who has come to a conviction not by means of love of neighbor in the saving community of the *church,* which would condition the rightness of the heretic's religious knowledge and belief, but in some lonely way. According to my experience, it is exactly this idea that is most difficult for our modern consciousness to understand. One is not used to seeing the priorities of knowledge of the church, as church over the individual, contained in kernel in the basic founding of *love* and knowledge. This thesis later became formulated in many ways, for example, in the proposition that the decisions of the ecumenical councils are to be held as stemming from "the Holy Ghost," or again in the basic assertion that one must first listen to the church in all religious matters. The practical expression of this thesis occurs also in the Christian willingness to sacrifice the intellect in cases of opposition to the authority of the church. All these dogmas are only the consequence of this momentous proposition for the sense and construction of religious social structure.

Despite the fact that the proposition of the priority of love over knowledge belongs to the essence of Christian consciousness and is at the bottom of the church and all Christian ethics (in which always, in contrast to the Greek ethic, an act of love is valued more than an act of pure knowledge, virtue more than "dianoetic"), it must be considered all the more marvelous that attempts to test this proposition, philosophically or psychologically, have been infrequent. With the exception of the mystical literature and specifically the Augustinian tradition in which the proposition is generally held, the so-called Christian philosophy has actually approached more nearly the *Greek* type. The inner *disharmony* between Christian religious consciousness and the worldly wisdom attached to it springs from this. In deep images of pious belief, for example, the seraphim, glowing with love, are portrayed as standing *over* the knowing cherubim in the hierarchical ordering of angels at the foot of God; and Mary, who is at the peak of all the angels, is entirely love. Nevertheless, the Greek stipulations are maintained by *Thomas Aquinas:* that love for an object presupposes knowledge of that object, that value is only a function of degree of perfection of being, and that love is not an elemental act of mind but only a special activity of the willing and *striving* capacities of the soul. Aquinas, accordingly, recognized only *two* basic powers of the soul, the appetitive and the intellective. Each, in his view, was split into a higher and lower activity. The appetitive was divided into the passive reaction to sensuality, concupiscence, and the active reaction to sensuality, irascibility; the intellective into the sensible capacity for knowing, perception, and that which corresponds to the "species intelligibiles" in things, reason. Each activity of the striving capacity must precede an activity of reason. By the presence of "species sensibilis" in perception and the stirring of the will in an act of intentional knowledge, the conceptual essence of a thing is grasped. According to this view, love, hate—the whole universe of emotions—present themselves merely as modifications of the striving capacity of the soul.

It is obvious that in this intellectualistic, psychological system love takes a subordinate place. This reflects back upon the *theology* of the system, however, principally upon the doctrines of the *creation of the world* and the relation of *salvation* and *revelation* through God. In the original Christian sense, "God" created the world out of "love." The creative power of love, which is nothing like the tendency toward survival or reproduction in Plato's view of creation, cannot be brought out more sharply than through the doctrine that God's creative act of will is founded in a previous act of love. The natural drive of all creatures toward their creator is, therefore, only an answering reaction to the creative love from which it proceeds. However, this doctrine must disappear in a system in which the human as well as the divine are completely broken up into intellect and power of will (sociologically represented in priesthood and worldly power). For Aquinas, God created the world for His own glorification. This goal now shines over His first servers, the priests. They are no longer the humble servers of the Christian community, the successors of Christ, but now appear quite like romantic-antique rulers on the great stage of the world as popes, the bishopry, and so on, in whom the life of the church culminates. The Christian followers (in the sense of *imitatio Christi*) become "successors of Christ" who derive their right from mere legal tradition, as princes derive their "office" and "dignity." On the other central point, the *revelation* of God in Christ is no longer a *consequence* of a divine act of *redemption;* rather, redemption through Christ is the most central content of a now completely intellectually understood revelation. Formulated in dogma, this revelation is to be believed, together with the other new central content, in total. Love of God and neighbor was supposed to make the original Christians, as children of God, superior to all "law" and "duty," able to achieve everything commanded by law without obedience to commands. But quite analogously, love of God and neighbor is now degraded to a mere partial content of the law prescribed by the divine will. Jesus appears as a new, second Moses who has comprehended the Ten Commandments in a single commandment: in "the law of love," "the command to love." [14] The inner contradiction of this concept is overlooked. [15] With this restoration of the Greek idea of the relation between knowledge and love, the primacy of love and will is indirectly articulated, and the self-sufficient Aristotelian God of *knowledge* is placed over the Christian God of *redemption.* Thus are teaching and regimental priests also placed over *homo religiosus,* the powerful over the good, law over the love and humility that are superior to law.

Even the Thomistic-Franciscan opposition between intellectualism and voluntarism, in which it was argued whether God commands what is good because it is good in itself or whether something is good because He has commanded it, completely misses the true Christian experience of God and the world. At first this was only a struggle between regimental and teaching functions and powers within the church. But later this became, for example, with William of Occam, a struggle between worldly powers and religious-churchly powers in general. The Franciscans' peculiar renewal of the *basic* Christian *experience* did not succeed, therefore, in effecting a corresponding conceptual-philosophical understanding.

If we ignore the mystical literature, which lacked a specific philosophical sense, we find serious beginnings in conceptual understanding of the basic Christian experience of the relation of love to knowledge as well as to extrareligious problems solely in *Augustine* and the Augustinian tradition through Malebranche and Pascal. It is incorrect to attribute to Augustine a doctrine of the "primacy of the will" and to make him, in this respect, a precursor of Scotus. What is called primacy of will in Augustine is actually primacy of *love*. The act of love takes primacy not only over knowledge, but also over willing and striving. Love is simultaneously the primacy of taking an interest, as a lower stirring of "love," and the primacy of an act over other acts, such as perceiving, representing, remembering, and thinking—all of which mediate images and meaning contents ("ideas"). No doctrines could be further removed from Augustine than those of Scotus and Descartes. They held that the ideas of good and bad owe their sense and meaning to the commands of a divine *will*, that the essences and ideas of things do not precede but follow the existence of things, and that ideas are only human products, creations to which nothing at all in the sphere of objects may correspond (the nominalism of William of Occam). These doctrines are derived from the necessary predicate of the primacy of the will. (It was from the propositions of the later Scotists, whose ideas entered modern philosophy, that conceptual expression was first given to the modern *bourgeois spirit of limitless work*. This spirit, of course, stood in opposition to a contemplative-intellectual priestly class.) Augustine's "volo ergo sum" should not mislead us by the choice of an unfortunate expression, *volo*. Love, the taking of an interest, is for him the most basic tendency of the human spirit. Indeed, in the final analysis love, for Augustine, is directed not toward happiness as a feeling but toward *the "holy."* In his view, representations and concepts stand only as stationary points compared to *love's* progressive movement, which penetrates, like the flames of a fire, ever deeper into God and the world. All actual "striving" and "willing" are viewed by him as only internal or external organs of expression, instruments for the completion of love.

Thus, for Augustine willing and representing follow love *equally* as a *third* original *source* of unity for all consciousness. But this happens because love *first* moves knowledge, and then, *mediated* by knowledge, love is enabled to move striving and willing. The relationship between knowing and willing is therefore exactly the same as in Thomas Aquinas. Both are in the most extreme opposition to all Scotist doctrines of the "primacy of will over the understanding."

Corresponding to this, love makes up the kernel, the essence, of *divinity*. Love, for Augustine, *precedes* and determines even the "ideas" (which have a Platonic sense in his doctrine) that he sees as "the thoughts of God" and that he understands to be, simultaneously, exemplars for the creating will. Creation "out of love," "according to ideas," becomes the idea of creation in his theology. For the *first* time the idea of the pure, creating nature of love is announced without a romantic-Platonic reduction of the new in creation to mere return to something that already exists, to mere maintenance of form. But secondarily, love of God shows itself in the divine act of *redemption* in Christ whose *consequence* is solely the self-revelation of God in Christ. Finally, love of God is revealed in the free, groundless forgiveness of some, while others, who remain corrupted by the word of the law and by commission of sins and original sin, are damned to eternal punishment. Augustine's doctrine of the election of grace is only one of the consequences of his giving primacy to love over all justice meted out rationally. This consequence necessarily resulted from the biblical presuppositions of a fall into sin, of original sin, and the proposition that according to the law we have all been made guilty of eternal death.

More important than the theological consequences of Augustine's proposition of the primacy of love over spirit, however, were his attempts to build from this proposition a wholly new *psychology* and *epistemology*. These attempts were, of course, few and never much elaborated. But it is of the greatest importance that they are there, as they still represent the first and only attempt to procure a new psychological and metaphysical insight from the *Christian structure of experience*.

Augustine anticipated in an extraordinary way the deepest insights of contemporary psychology. He maintained that all intellectual acts, images, and meaning contents, the simplest sense perception to the most complicated imaginative thought, are rooted in several things. Intellectual acts have their origin not only in the existence of external objects, the sensations that come from objects, the reproduction stimulus in memory, but above and beyond these, in the act of taking an interest. The attention derived from taking an interest is essentially and necessarily linked to the acts of *love* and hate. For Augustine, love and hate are not simply added to the content of a sensation or perception already given in consciousness, a given that owes everything simply to intellectual activity. Rather, taking an interest "in something" and "love for something" are the *most primary* acts that *found* all others acts, in which our mind grasps a "possible" object. Interest in and love or hate for objects are simultaneously the basis for judgments, perceptions, representations, memories, and intentionalities that are directed toward those same objects. Three things must be distinguished here: (1) Without a willful and instinctual "interest" in something, there can be no "sensation" and "representation" of this something. Even the choice of that which comes to us out of the objective, perceivable sphere of objects, as in memory of the thing that we think about, is directed by our interest, and this interest by love or hate toward these objects. (2) Our representations and perceptions follow the direction of our interest and our love and our hate. (3) Finally, an increase of intuition or meaning in which an object stands before our consciousness depends upon an increase of our interest in the object, at bottom our love (or hate) for it. If it meant this exclusively, our interest and love would be factors that deform and make our worldview one-sided and ourselves more or less "blind." The statement expressly should hold for the simplest sense perception, even sensation— that is, the original source from which our consciousness of the world is nourished. But quite apart from this, much more is being said, namely, that the content, structure, and connection of the elements of our worldview are determined already in the process of *becoming* every *possible* worldview by the forming and directing acts of taking an interest and love. All deepening and widening of our worldview is connected to a *preceding* deepening and widening of our spheres of interest and love.

This doctrine could be interpreted as characterizing the subjective, limited way in which we humans succeed in knowing the world. In this case, Augustine's teaching would be essentially not much more than Plato's characterization of eros as leader and as method. There is psychological and epistemological meaning in Augustine's doctrine, but no apparent *metaphysical-ontical* (existential) meaning of any kind.

Yet Augustine gave his epistemological ideas this last-mentioned meaning by entwining them, barely visibly but infinitely deeply, with his other doctrines of creation and revelation. The appearance of an image or meaning in the intellectual act, even in the simplest perception, is for him not merely an activity of the knowing *subject* that penetrates the completed object. Rather, an image is simultaneously an answering reaction of the *object itself*, a "giving of itself" or a "*self-revealing*" of the object. An image is a consequence of a "question" asked with "love" that the world answers and in so doing reveals itself. In this revelation the world *comes to its full existence and value*. Thus, for Augustine, the coming into being of the "natural" knowledge of the world, viewed solely according to its objective condition, yields a "revelatory character" that bypasses the concept of "*natural revelation*." Natural revelation is in the last analysis a revelation of God according to His essence as determined by eternal love. Augustine's system of ideas on love and knowledge is thus concluded with remarkable consistency: all subjective understanding and choice of the contents of the world are founded by the directions of interest and love; all known things first come to their full value in self-revelation.

Augustine also speaks in mysterious ways, for example, of the tendency of plants, when looked at by humans, to be "redeemed" in this viewing from their particular existence of being closed into themselves. It is as though what happens to plants through knowledge derived from love is a kind of analogue to the redemption that leads people back to God through Christ. To this corresponds the distinction that later thinkers dependent on Augustine, such as Malebranche and the Port-Royal logicians, made between interest and attention, the "natural prayer of the soul" versus prayer to God. The word *prayer* here was not meant merely in the sense of a subjective, human cognitive activity, but includes the experience of the answer, of a "self-giving, self-revealing" of the object that is viewed with love and interest. In analogy to Saint Gregory of Nyssa's old definition of religious prayer, as an "intimate conversation of the soul with God," Pascal in his *Pensées* and "Conversation on the Passions of Love" validated and further extended Augustine's chain of thought.

With the increasing deemphasis of Augustine's ideas in the Middle Ages, the attempt to build a new understanding of the relation between love and knowledge out of the basic Christian experience broke entirely apart. Only in the Renaissance was a new *type* of understanding developed—in Bruno's doctrine of heroic love of the world and in similar ideas of Telesio, Campanella, and Vives, and finally, of course, in Spinoza's "amor Dei intellectualis." Bruno moved within the boundaries of the worldview that Dilthey characterized as "dynamic pantheism." However, not with Bruno but in the traces of insight of Augustinism is a purely factual investigation of the great question—whose answer I have endeavored to give in another place—and a certain harmony suggested.[16]

Notes

1. For further amplification see my study *The Nature of Sympathy,* esp. pt. 1, ch. 4, sec. 5, "The sense of unity with the cosmos in some representative temperaments of the past."

2. Cf. W. v. Humboldt, "On the Name of the Bhagavad-Gita in the Well-known Episode of the *Mahabharata,*" talks delivered at the Berlin Academy of Science, 30 June 1825 and 15 June 1826.

3. Cf. R. Pischels's translation of the pertinent materials in his booklet *The Life and Teachings of the Buddha,* Vallabh, Vidyanager, 1904.

4. This point is relevant to the detailed discussion in the metaphysical chapter of my book *The Nature of Sympathy.*

5. Cf. Pischel, *Life and Teachings of the Buddha.*

6. Put differently, and more broadly along the lines of Augustine (whose indications are followed), is the idea in the question of Nicolaus Cusanus (see his *De visione Dei aut de icone,* sec. 4), and Vincenz von Aggsbach and the anonymous tractate, "De intelligentiis," ed. Cl. Baumker. After them, love in man went before knowledge of God.

7. This was first taken up again by E. Hering. Cf. his *On Memory as a Generic Function of Organic Material,* Vienna, 1870.

8. The prominence of the androgynous ideal in German romanticism is strongly rooted in Plato's thought.

9. Cf. my discussion of metaphysical conceptions of sexual love in *The Nature of Sympathy,* pt. A, VII.

10. The nonsense of these naturalistic theories is fully shown in my book *The Nature of Sympathy,* pt. B, V and VI.

11. See my work *Ressentiment,* chs. 2 and 3.

12. In his rich and deeply meaningful polemic, Saint Bernard of Clairvaux continually reproved Abelard for making the words and death of Christ merely a manifestation of God's love instead of seeing in them, in the first place, an outpouring of Christ's love and redemption. Cf. A. Neander, *Der hl. Bernhard und sein Zeitalter,* 3rd ed., Gotha: 1865, pp. 200f.

13. Cf. my essay "Über ostliches und westliches Christentum," 6:99–114.

14. Cf. A. von Harnack's book on Marcion, 1921, in which these deep, early errors are seen through.

15. Cf. the discussion in my book, *Formalism in Ethics and Non-formal Ethics of Values,* ch. 4, pt. 2b, of the absurdity of the idea of an "obligatory belief" or an "obligatory love," which is no sooner commanded than done.

16. Cf. my essay "The Nature of Philosophy," in *On the Eternal in Man.*

8

Problems of a Sociology of Knowledge

The Essence and Concept of a Sociology of Culture

The following pages pursue a limited goal. They are an attempt to denote the *unity* of a sociology of knowledge as part of the sociology of culture, above all to develop systematically the problems of such a science. They do not pretend to solve any of these problems conclusively but only to discuss in detail the directions in which their solutions appear to lie for the author. They attempt to achieve some systematic unity in the disordered mass of problems, some of which have already received scientific formulation, while others have been conceived only vaguely or are barely suspected. These are problems posed by the fundamental fact of the *social nature* of all knowledge—its preservation, transmission, methodical expansion, and progress. The relationship of the sociology of knowledge to the theory of the origin and validity of knowledge (epistemology and logic), to genetic and psychological studies of the evolution of knowledge from brutes to humans, child to adult, primitive to civilized people, stage to stage within mature cultures (developmental psychology), to the positive history of various kinds of knowledge, the metaphysics of knowledge, other areas in the sociology of culture—religion, art, law, etc.—and to the sociology of real factors, i.e., blood (kin), power, and economic groups, and their changing organization—all this must necessarily be touched upon.

In establishing the overall concept of "sociology" *two criteria* will

This essay was originally published as "Probleme einer Soziologie des Wissens" in *Die Wissenformen und die Gesellschaft* (Forms of knowledge and society) (Leipzig: Neue Geist Verlag, 1926), and reprinted in vol. 8 of *Gesammelte Werke,* ed. Maria Scheler (Bern: Francke Verlag, 1960). The first published English translation of the essay was by Ernst Ranly in *Philosophy Today* 12 (1968), 42–70. A slightly modified translation by Manfred S. Frings was published in *Problems of a Sociology of Knowledge,* ed. Kenneth W. Stikkers (London: Routledge & Kegan Paul, 1980), pp. 33–63. Professor Donald Levine kindly supplied me with an unpublished translation of the essay by Kurt H. Wolff, n.d. The present translation is my own, although I have benefited by consulting all of the earlier translations. Frings's distinction between "mind" and "spirit" has largely been retained, and I have adopted some of Wolff's subheadings.

serve us. First, this science does not deal with individual facts and occurrences in history, but with rules, average and logical-ideal types, and, where possible, *laws*. Second, sociology analyzes the whole gamut, subjective and objective, of the chief human contents of life. Sociology does this descriptively as well as causally according to the *factual* determination of these contents only, not the "normative" or ideal projections of what the contents of life should be. These contents are investigated in the temporally successive or simultaneous forms of association that exist among people in experiencing, willing, acting, and understanding, in action and reaction, as well as in a real and causal way that does not necessarily involve the consciousness-of-something by the person involved.[1]

The principal divisions of sociology, which we introduce here without further analysis, can be arranged according to the following considerations: (1) Investigation of *essential* considerations in contrast to that of *contingent* facts, that is, a pure a priori sociology[2] in contrast to an empirical inductive sociology. (2) Investigation of simultaneous and successive relationships of people and groups, that is, sociological *statics* and *dynamics* (Comte). Sociological dynamics differs from all philosophies of history by excluding from consideration goals, values, and norms viewed as objective; this is a strictly causal and (artificially) value-free position. Of course, this does not exclude taking into account values, ideals, and the like as psychological and historical causal factors. (3) Investigation of the chiefly spiritually and intellectually conditioned activity of humans directed toward "ideal" goals, and investigation of activity resulting chiefly from drives of procreation, nourishment, and power which at the same time are directed toward the factual alteration of such realities.

Ideal and Real

This "chief" intention—for every human act is at once ideational and determined by drives—more precisely, the intention ultimately directed toward the ideal or the real goal is such that we have to distinguish between a *sociology of culture* and a *sociology of real facts*. Certainly the experimental physicists, painters, or musicians also change reality when they perform an experiment, paint, play music, or compose. They do this, however, only to reach an ideal goal—to acquire knowledge of nature or to obtain for themselves and others an aesthetically worthy meaning to be understood and appreciated. But surely, on the other hand, the business administrator as well as the simple unskilled industrial worker, man in general as a producing and consuming being, any worker whose goal is to change realities (e.g. the practical technician as distinct from the scholar and technologist), the prominent statesman as well as the voter in an election, still deal with a great many preparatory cognitive activities directed toward the ideal realm. They do so only for the sake of a real objective, however, to affect a change in reality. On one hand, the activity terminates in the ideal realm, on the other, in the real world. I reject as fatuous forms of spiritualism all theories that try to delimit the foundation of economics without going back to the hunger drive, of the state and kindred structures without reference to the drive for power, of marriage without reference to the sex drive. It is absurd to maintain that economics has nothing to do with the drive for nutrition and the feeding of humans because there are publishing houses and art shops, because one can buy and sell books and buttercups, and because even animals have a drive for nutrition and nourish themselves *without* economics. It is equally inane to maintain that economics is, thus, intellectually and rationally conditioned and achieved in exactly the same sense as art, philosophy, science, etc. This is simply not so! Without the hunger drive and the objective goal this serves biologically, namely nourishment, there would be no economics—and no publishing houses or art shops either. Without the drive for power there would be no state, no political culture, no law laid down by the state, no matter what affairs the state may deal with. The only thing correct about the above thesis is that without the mind and its normative regulation there would be no economics, no state, etc. Therefore, a spiritual-intellectual theory of humanity is a necessary presupposition for the sociology of culture, and an instinct-drive theory of humanity is a necessary presupposition for the sociology of real facts.[3]

The division of sociology into the sociology of culture and the sociology of real facts, the sociologies of the *super*structure and *sub*structure of human life, sets up two extreme poles between which there are a great many intermediate transitions. Technology, for example, depends for its growth on economic and political-juridical as well as on scientific factors; a purposive utilitarian kind of art, in contrast to a "pure" art, is conditioned by the values and ideals of those in power, say a religious ruling class. The main task of sociology is to characterize *typologically* and determine by specific rules a sociological event with reference to these two poles, to establish what in this event is conditioned by the autonomous self-development of *spirit,* such as the logical-rational development of law or the immanent logic of religious history, and what is conditioned by the relevant sociologically *real* factors, which have their own causality. Without the distinction between the sociology of culture and the sociology of real factors this task cannot be accomplished.

This division is not only "methodologically" but also ontologically grounded. Given sociology's ultimate aim, however, this is only a provisional division. The proper task of sociology is to examine the kinds and orderly sequence of reciprocal effects of ideal *and* real factors, the spiritual and drive factors—for social life is always conditioned by nature—which determine the contents of human life. Indeed, in my view the highest goal of all nondescriptive and nonclassificatory sociology, that is, of all *causal* sociology, is in attaining knowledge of a first *law of sequential order*. I do not mean this in the same sense as Comte's ideal of a law of mere temporal succession—which was absurd since history only passes once. I mean a law *governing the achievements of ideal and real factors in determining* all life contents belonging to human groups. These factors are sociologically conditioned through kinds of human relationships. This sociology treats not *only* the phase rules of temporal development of economic, political, and reproductive relationships of different groups and cultures, to name the most important kinds of real factors, or of the temporal development of the ideal factors of religion, metaphysics, science, art, and law. Important as this descriptive task may be as a preliminary undertaking, this sociology would also treat something altogether different, namely, *the law of order governing the realization of ideal and real factors*. Out of this realization there ensues, at each point of time within the historical-temporal passage of human life processes, the undivided totality of the life of the group. This is not a law of completed, temporally successive events, but a law of the *possible* dynamic development of any completed event in temporal order.

The Law of Realization of Ideal and Real Factors

I have sought such a law for years and believe I have found it in principle, but cannot give its full demonstration here.[4] However, it has a number of characteristics that can be accurately described.

1. First, this law defines the principal kind of interdependence in which ideal and real factors affect the potential movement of social-historical being in preserving itself and changing. My thesis is as follows:

Mind, in the subjective, objective, individual, and collective senses, determines only the particular *quality* of a certain *cultural* content that may come to exist. Mind as such has *no original* trace of "power" or "efficacy" to bring this content into existence. Mind may be called an "ascertaining factor" but not an "accomplishing factor" of possible cultural developments. The *negative,* or selective, factors of what is *possible* through understandable motivation are always the *real, drive-conditioned factors of life.* These are in each case the unique combination of political powers, economic production, and qualitative and quantitative conditions of populations as well as geographical and geopolitical factors. The "purer" the factors of mind, the less they affect society and history.[5] This is the great common element of truth in all skeptical, pessimistic, and naturalistic conceptions of history, whether economic, racial, power-political, or geographic-political. Only to the extent that "ideas" of any kind, whether religious or scientific, are united with interests, drives, and collective drives or "tendencies," as we call the latter, do they indirectly acquire the power of being realized. The *positive,* realizing factor of a purely cultural content is always the free act and free will of a few persons, primarily those who are leaders, models, and pioneers. By virtue of the well-known law of psychic contagion, of deliberate and fortuitous imitation (copying), these few are followed by a "large number," a majority. It is in this way that culture "spreads."[6]

Quite different is the relationship of existing ideal and real factors and their subjective correlates in humans (spiritual-intellectual and drive structures) in the determination of emerging real factors, such as a new international allocation of political power, economic relations of production, racial miscegenation and tension. The extent of the objective, possible development of such real factors is not determined by ideal factors at all but only by the particular makeup of real factors previously given. In such cases, which are precisely the inverse of the preceding ones, everything we call "mind" has only a negative "guiding," that is, a restraining or nonrestraining, causal role. In principle, this merely negative role of mind in the fulfillment of real possibilities does not determine their qualities in the slightest. The human mind and will of the individual and collective can do but one thing: retrain or release that which operates according to a strictly independent, real causality, is insensible to meanings, but presses to come into existence. If mind seeks to transform real factors in a way outside the scope of the causal relationships peculiar to them, it bites on granite and its "utopia" crumbles to nothing. A planned economy, a "constitution for world politics," a planned, legal eugenics, and racial selection are utopias of this kind.

On the other hand, it is always pointless to try to derive the positive meaning and value content of an existing religion, art, philosophy, science, or juridical system solely from real conditions of life such as kinship, economy, power politics, or geopolitics. The role of existing combination of real factors may be "explained" by considering that which did *not,* but *could* have, come into existence given the scope of the autonomous law of meaning intrinsic to the qualitative determination[7] of religion, law, and mind. Raphael needed a brush—his ideas and artistic visions did not create the brush; he needed politically and socially powerful patrons to employ him to exalt *their* ideals, otherwise he could not act out his own genius. Luther needed the interest of dukes, cities, territorial lords leaning toward particularism, and the rising bourgeoisie; without these nothing would have come of the dissemination of the doctrine of *spiritus sanctus internus* (internal spiritual sanctity) and *sola fides* (solitary faith), which Luther derived from his reading of the Bible.

Just as we reject all naturalistic sociological interpretations of the development of the meaning content of culture, so too we must reject on the basis of a pure sociology of culture any theory (reminiscent, for example, of Hegel) that holds that the course of cultural history is a *purely* spiritual process determined by its own logic. Without the negatively selecting forces of *real* conditions and without the *free* voluntary causality of "leading" persons—though, of course, this freedom refers only to the "if" or "if not" of the action, never to the "what" of logical meaning—absolutely nothing is affected by merely spiritual determining factors, even on the basis of the purest intellectual culture. And nothing at all is affected in the realities with which the sociology of real facts deals. These realities follow a strictly necessary course with respect to existence, quality, value, so-called progress or regress. This course is "blind" to the meanings and values held by the human mind, for it is a course of fate.[8] Only one sovereign changeless privilege remains to us: with our mind we are able to "reckon"—not calculate—the future, to formulate a hypothetical and probable expectation. And through our will we are able to restrain temporality, ward off something coming into existence, or accelerate or slow down something in its temporal succession (not, however, in the *order* of time, which is predetermined and unchangeable) much as a catalyst does for a process of chemical synthesis.

In the spiritual-cultural sphere there is, therefore, potential "freedom" and autonomy of the quality, meaning, and value of an event, yet in practical expression these can always be suspended through the causality of the "substructure" proper to it: "*liberté* modifiable" (or "suspendable") one might call it. Conversely, in the field of real factors there is only a "*fatalité* modifiable," which Comte aptly and correctly discussed. In the former case, the real circumstances have a suspending effect on that which is being realized from among the spiritual-intellectual potentialities. In the latter case, mind has a suspending effect, in the sense of temporal displacement, upon that which corresponds to the fate of historical tendencies.

2. A second characteristic of the law of causal factors is that it includes and joins in a unified way *three* dynamic and static modes and relations:

a. The relations of the ideal factors with one another—the static, the dynamic, and those such that in actual situations the static modes present themselves as the result, the relative momentary representation, of the dynamic ones, that is, as the stratification of older and newer power effects. Every concrete culture is in this sense stratified.

b. The relations of the individual kinds of real factors to one another—again from the three viewpoints above.

c. The relations of the three chief groups of *real* factors to the various kinds of *ideal* factors—within the scope, of course, of the universal laws of ideal and real factors already defined and described.

In each time and place that we find human society we confront some kind of "objective mind,"[9] a meaning incorporated in some material or reproducible psychophysical activity such as tools, works of art, language, writing, institutions, morals, customs, rites, ceremonies. Corresponding exactly to this subjectivity we encounter a changing structure of the "mind" of the group possessing a more or less binding significance and power for the individual, or at least experienced by the individual as "obliging." Is there an order in which these objective meaning contents of culture and the meaningful structures of acts are constituted, in which they "maintain," alter, mutually establish themselves according to laws? What is the relationship among myth and religion, metaphysics, science, saga, legend, and history; among religion, mysticism, and art; among art, philosophy, and science; between philosophy and science; between the realm of current values and the theoretically "assumed" existence and quality of the world?

The simultaneous relationships of meaning, and the relationships of motivations between these objective structures of meaning, are extremely numerous, and each requires extensive special study. One might think that although all these should somehow be "mutually" dependent and reciprocally motivating, there is no *lawful order* of foundation among them. But I am of the opposite opinion without being in the position to prove this in detail.

Laws of Culture

There are *essential,* not merely contingent, existential dependencies among the ideal factors in their being and becoming—difficult as it may be to discover them. There are such dependencies, for example, between religion, metaphysics, and positive science, philosophy and positive science, technology and positive science, religion and art, etc. These correspond exactly to the order of the genesis and structure of the acts inherent in the human mind. There are, for example, comprehension and preference of values on one side versus willing and doing on the other; perception or representation of objects versus drive impulses in a determined direction as a condition for such perception; practical impulses of movement and will versus goal-free impulses of expression, thinking, and speaking. All these build upon each other not "first this way, then that," but according to strict laws of their nature.[10] All empirical, factual dependencies of objective cultural contents are anchored ultimately in a *universal, basic theory of human mind.* Whoever speaks of random "reciprocal effects" is in error.

In this universal formal framework of the laws of spiritual acts in general, there are changing, incipient, and transient special structures and functional organizations of group minds or cultures. To discover these is the first goal of anyone setting out to acquire a descriptive knowledge of the culture of any particular historical group studied from all sides and according to all kinds of values and goods. Apart from these universal, basic laws of mind—which are not laws of "one" real mind, group, or individual being—mind exists beforehand only in the concrete multiplicity of endlessly many groups and cultures. To speak of some kind of *factual* "unity of human nature" as a presupposition of history and sociology is useless and even harmful. A *common* norm of structure and style permeates only the living cultural elements of *one* group—its religion, art, science, and law. To work out these norms for each group in the chief phases of its development is one of the highest goals that the discipline of the history of mind can set for itself.[11] We reject, therefore, the notion that there is a certain fixed "inborn" functional apparatus of reason present in all humans from the beginning—the idol of the Enlightenment as well as of Kant. I reject this as a premise of sociology and also reject the theory of the monophyletic origin of humans usually associated with it. Spiritual unity and blood kinship of all races may be the end of all history—and

all history is in fact also the history of the leveling of blood—but it is
certainly not a point of departure for historical events and a presupposition for sociology.[12] Rather, the pluralism of groups and cultural
forms is the premise from which all sociology has to start.

We can still "understand" in principle, though not concretely, the
occurrence of spiritual structures assumed to be relatively "original."
We can generally understand how spiritual structures of this kind, carried forward by tradition, can and must arise from an amorphous
mind through gradual "functionalization"[13] of the genuine grasp of
ideas and their association with contingent things. This "functionalization" is first performed by pioneers and subsequently carried on by
the masses along with and after the pioneers, but not "imitated" from
without as are bodily movements and deeds. To that extent, the spiritual and rational apparatus of each great cultural unit and period, notwithstanding the multiplicity and diversity of such, can be partially
true and ontically—that is, existentially—valid, though they need not
be so. For they all arise from the reach of the one ontically ordered
realm of ideas and values through which this "contingent" real world
passes. Thus, we escape a philosophical relativism, to which, for example, Spengler fell victim, despite our assuming a multiplicity of rational organizations. But we do not escape this kind of relativism by
denying or restricting, as is presently done by cheap extremist philosophers of value, the clearly recognizable fact of relativism even with
respect to rational organizations. This denial would simply mean falling into an equally cheap "Europeanism" or similar viewpoint, which
occurs when treating only one culture as the "model" supposedly valid
for all people and all history. We do not escape relativism either, as
Troeltsch strangely enough wishes to do,[14] by "affirming" our European model with a mere "postulate," a *sic volo, sic jubeo* (so I wish it
to be, so I rule it to be), in spite of our knowledge of its relativity. On
the contrary, we avoid relativism, as Einstein's theory does on its own
basis, by lifting up the *absolute realm of ideas and values* corresponding to the essential idea of humanity far above *factual* historical value
systems. We do this, for example, by viewing all orders of goods, ends,
and norms of human society in ethics, religion, law, and art, as simply
relative and conditioned by a historical and sociological standpoint,
preserving nothing but the *idea* of the eternal objective Logos. To penetrate the boundless mystery of that Logos in terms of a basic history
of mind is not the prerogative of one nation, of one cultural unit, or
even of all past ages of culture. Access to the basic history of mind can
be had only by all of these together, including those of the future, in

the solidarity of spatial and temporal cooperation among the irre-
placeably unique subjects of culture.

In particular concrete cases we can no more explain the presumably
"original" spiritual structures of groups than we can explain from the
psychic functions of humans' animal ancestors "mind" as such, when
considered as a basic premise of human history or of humans themselves (of the "idea" of humanity).[15] At best we can only show how
one structure developed from another in terms of their inherent laws
of sense and understandability, for example, in the sequence of Western styles of art or forms of religion.

In sharp contrast to this development of spiritual structures according to laws governing transition from one level of development to another stands the phenomenon of the *accumulation of works,* which
corresponds only to one spiritual structure and one cultural unit limited in time and place. Although I assume an authentic genesis of all
subjectively functional a priori structures of the human spirit—not
their constancy, as Kant does—I must reject all theories that see in the
history of humanity *only* an accumulation of achievements and works.
I hold that the history of humanity is also a development of spiritual
faculties which is first of all a development of humans' a priori subjective apparatus of thinking and evaluation. Since I unconditionally reject all culturally significant inheritance of so-called received psychic
attributes (along with Weismann, the recent scientific theory of heredity, and now also Bumke),[16] it is my view that the psychophysical human organism has not changed essentially in history, unless by the already assumed influence of culture itself. I reject, therefore, the theory
manifest in the whole of Spencer's sociology, that spiritual structures
could be acquired by the so-called species and then handed down
through heredity to the individual. However, Weismann's conclusion,
that the whole history of culture is only accumulation, I find equally
invalid. Weismann assumed, as did Spencer, that we not only share the
vital-psychic element with the higher primates, with which I agree, but
also that "spirit" and "reason" in humans is solely conditioned by
humans' psychophysical system, which I deny.[17] I maintain, rather,
that for sociology, psychology, biology, and history, human mind is
simply an assumption to be accepted, and that mind poses a problem
at most of a metaphysical and religious order, not of the order of positive empirical science.

If this is the case, then mind itself, including its powers—and all
that is not just the sum of the achievements of mind at a certain stage
of its development because of changing conditions of blood relations

and milieu—really and truly unfolds itself. This development can signify progress and growth of mind as well as its regression and decline, but in each case change in mind's constitution. The following types of change come under consideration in this respect: in the form of thinking and attitude, as in the transition from "mentalité primitive," recently described by Lévy-Bruhl, to the civilized phase of human thought that follows the principles of contradiction and identity; in laws of *value* preference, that is, not merely different preferences within the *same* law of value preference; in the feeling for styles and artistic sentiment (which since Riegl are assumed in the history of art); from the early Western organismic worldview, which extended into the thirteenth century to the mechanical worldview; from a grouping of men predominantly in clans without state authority to the age of "political society" and the state, or from a group form that is predominantly a "life community" to one predominantly "societal," or from a mainly magical form of technology to a mainly positive one. These changes are of an entirely different scope from, for example, those of "practical morality" adapting a form of ethos to changing historical circumstances,[18] such as the adaptation of the Christian ethos to the economic and social conditions of late antiquity, the Middle Ages, and modern times. For the sociology of the dynamics of knowledge nothing is more important than this difference: whether the forms of thinking about, evaluating, and viewing the world underlie a particular change, or whether only their application to the quantitatively and inductively expanded materials of experience are subject to change. A precise criteriology of this difference remains to be developed.

Process and Order of Intellectual Development

A universal phenomenon of all spiritual-intellectual development is a process already clearly seen by Spencer, namely, the *differentiation and integration of the spheres of culture* and the spiritual acts and value experiences that underlie them. This is reflected most strikingly in the gradual separation of leader and pioneer groups from the intellectual professions, for example, the magician, physician, priest, technician, philosopher (sage), researcher, scholar, etc.

In applying this principle of differentiation and integration, however, it is of first importance that these levels of differentiation be set in correct order. It is especially because the levels are falsely assigned that gross errors occur. For example, one must recognize that religious, metaphysical, and positive knowledge, or, as we can also say, knowledge of salvation or redemption, knowledge of culture, and knowledge for control of nature, differentiated themselves from their common origin in mythical thinking and began largely distinct lines of development. Comte already took myth for religion, for instance, and did not see that in the modern West religion by no means yields to metaphysics in importance but is only *differentiated* from it more clearly than in the Middle Ages, and that positive science and metaphysics are also more sharply distinguished from each other by the fact that the sciences now appear as an endless process, whereas metaphysics appears as a personally bound and closed "*system.*" Comte's confusion on the phenomenon of differentiation led him to the basically false theory of the so-called law of the three stages, which stipulates that metaphysical essence thinking "developed" out of religion, and science, in turn, out of metaphysics. Or, out of magical techniques over the powers of nature the positive technique of control differentiated itself from the expressive technique of *religious cults* and the ritual technique of representing sacred events. Comte took for a temporal stage of development what in fact was only a process of differentiation of the mind. If this distinction is acknowledged, serious mistakes are avoided. Similarly, art and crafts (tool techniques) doubtless have a common point of departure in structures that express activities of the psyche and at the same time are carried out in such a way as to serve some continued useful end.[19] But if one so misconstrues the situation as to derive art from work and technique (as, for example, G. Semper has done in his work on the development of style, and more recently C. Bucher in *Arbeit und Rhythmus*), or thinks that work and technology are derived from art, as the romanticists did and now quite rashly Leo Frobenius also does, then serious errors are the result. Similar distortions are found in theories such as that of Albert Langes, according to which metaphysics is "poetry in concepts," or in the theory of Wilhelm Ostwald, who holds that art is "the foreshadowing form of science," or in the "gnostic" error that religion is essentially a degraded popular metaphysics in "pictures" for the masses (Spinoza, Hegel, E. von Hartmann, Schopenhauer, etc.), or in the converse error of both Bonald and Maistre that metaphysics is only a subsequently rationalized folk religion that goes back to revelation through persons or to an original revelation, or in the theory that metaphysics is an illegitimately rationalized prophecy of a religious or poetical kind, which is subsequently compressed into a system (the "prophetic philosophy" of Max Weber and Karl Jaspers). In the general theories that without further ado look upon one or two of the above-mentioned three kinds of knowledge as "dying out" on the basis of quite particular levels of development within a narrowly confined culture such as that of late western Europe—as Dilthey did also but only with respect to "metaphysical" knowledge[20]—there are serious errors of the same kind. They arise from faulty assessment of the processes of differentiation and integration, especially of the degree of originality of particular patterns of mind, and from the fact that certain secondary meshing and mingling phenomena belonging to the highest cultural forms are taken for logical ideal types.

Thus, for example, mysticism—a general and strictly definable category of spiritual behavior, namely, an ecstatic and immediate knowledge of identification in intuition and feeling—can be found in a particular religion and its dogma (Indian, Christian, Sufic, Jewish, Taoist) as well as in philosophical metaphysics (e.g., in Plotinus, Spinoza, Schopenhauer, Schelling, Bergson); it can be found in a spiritualistic as well as in a naturalistic worldview (e.g., in the intellectually cool mysticism of Plotinus and in the Dionysian mysticism of entrancement); in a predominantly theoretical disposition (as contemplative mysticism) as well as in a practical one (practical ascetic mysticism and the belief that union results from acts of will of a certain superior kind, as in Thomas à Kempis). In all cases, mysticism "itself" remains an independent category of kinds of knowledge or of participation in a presupposed absolute Something or Value, which never proceeds from its own source of knowledge—a participation that is always, genetically, an entirely uncreative, secondary and belated phenomenon—a going back! When this is not seen a common mistake of ecclesiastical writers is the result, making orthodox Christian mysticism *the* mysticism and ignoring its entirely supraconfessional and even suprareligious nature. Others make mysticism a separate source of "religious" knowledge,[21] or a source of "metaphysical knowledge," as in the "intuitionism" of Schopenhauer or Bergson. The mixed forms of mysticism always presuppose the existence of the pure type.

Social Organization of Intellectual Activity

Closely allied to that part of the sociology of culture sketched above is another one that treats the more or less organized *social forms of spiritual-intellectual cooperation*. In each age the three basic types of knowledge first appear in social forms geared essentially to their highest intended ends. The types are necessarily distinct according to the quality of their accepted object. This is true for all basic kinds of specifically spiritual, cultural activity. For the chiefly religious forms of *knowledge of salvation* there correspond congregations, churches, sects, loosely organized "floating" mystical groupings, or directions of thought united only theologically. There are, on the other hand, "schools of *wisdom*" and *educational* communities, in the ancient sense, which bind the teachings, research, and life practice of their members into a union that spans life communities and often even nations, and which together recognize a system of ideas and values that pertain to the whole world. Finally, there are *instructional and research organizations of the positive sciences,* based on division of their proper objects and separation of work, more or less connected with technological and industrial organizations or with certain professional organizations such as those of lawyers, physicians, and officials— "scientific bodies" we may in general call them. The arts develop their "master schools" similarly. Each form develops dogmas, principles, and theories in formulas that rise above natural language to the level of "cultivated language," or are expressed in "artificial" systems of signs according to conventions of measurement and axioms that they recognize in common.

These organizations of knowledge are, of course, to be distinguished from forms of instruction and "schools" in which children of various age groups first acquire the average knowledge of the culture prevailing in the life community about them—in their family, clan, state, nation, or cultural units. In such schools the average and socially necessary level of knowledge is *merely transmitted* from generation to generation according to caste, estate, and class. In relation to teaching or educational organizations, the groups named above represent a superstructure from which newly acquired knowledge very slowly filters down to the teaching staffs in the "schoolhouses" of communities, cities, states, churches, etc.

Knowledge, Interests, Prejudice, and Ideology

The above-mentioned forms of knowledge are to be distinguished from the phenomena in which collective *interests* are mixed with (alleged) knowledge. This mixture occurs when people have in common their membership in a certain rank, profession, class, or party. I choose to characterize these phenomena under the inclusive title of "prejudice." The peculiarity of this *pseudo*knowledge is that those who share it remain unaware both of the collective root of interests behind this "knowledge" and of the circumstances that only they as a group, and only by virtue of belonging to one of these groups, have this knowledge in common. If after becoming automatic and unconscious these systems of "prejudice" try to justify themselves in conscious deliberation behind the aegis of religious, metaphysical, or scientific thinking, or by drawing on dogmas, principles, and theories originating in the higher organizations of knowledge, then we have those new mixed forms called "ideologies," of which the prime example in our modern history is Marxism as a kind of "ideology of the oppressed." To subject the origin of *all* knowledge to the laws of the rise of ideologies is a specific thesis of the economic interpretation of history. "Public opinion" serves here as a screen through which prejudices and ideologies are filtered;[22] it is the tendency to judge shared by the "educated" of a group.[23]

The Social Organization of Knowledge

The sociology of culture must distinguish the forms of spiritual-intellectual cooperation according to an *ideal typology* and also the *order of phases* within the process of these forms and within each single cultural whole. Phase orders must also be distinguished in the shifting power relations of such organizational forms of knowledge with one another; for example, of the church to philosophy, of both of these to science, etc. One must always consider the relation of the content of knowledge, such as the content of faith, whether dogmatically defined or not, to organizational forms. Some examples: the content of the Jewish religion of Yahweh necessitates its being a nonmissionary religion of a chosen people and that this one "people" be its carrier; the content of polytheistic and henotheistic forms of religion exclude universality even as a *claim;* the content of Plato's theory of ideas required to a great extent the form and organization of the Platonic academy; the content of Protestant faith is the primary determinant of Protestant churches and sects, which can exist *only* in this and in no other social form.[24] The object and method of positive science necessarily require the *international* form of cooperative exchange and organization, whereas the content and task of metaphysics demand a *cosmopolitan* form of cooperation of individually different, unique and irreplaceable minds of peoples or their representatives.

However, universal differences in possible organizational forms of knowledge are connected with the essential types of human groups. The primary types of groups range from nomadic *hordes, stable life community* (in the sense of Tönnies), and *society,* to the *personalistic system of solidarity* among independent individuals responsible to themselves and to one another.[25] As will be pointed out, these differences are always simultaneously accompanied by differences in forms of thinking and viewing. For example, the type of thinking in a predominantly stable life community must necessarily have the following characteristics: (1) It will be a preserve of traditional knowledge and truth that will not pertain to research and discovery. The vital logic and "form of thought" of this type will be an *ars demonstrandi,* an art of showing, not an *ars inveniende et construendi,* an art of discovery and invention. (2) Its method of thought will be predominantly onto-logical and dogmatic, not epistemological and critical. (3) Its "form of thought" will be conceptually realistic—not nominalistic as in a *society.* However, *words* will no longer be understood as *properties* and *powers* of things as was the case with the men of primitive tribes where, according to Lévy-Bruhl's exact wording, all acquisition of knowledge rested upon a "dialogue" of men with spirits and demons who express and divulge themselves in the phenomena of nature. (4) Its system of categories will be principally organological, that is, ori-ented to the organism and then generalized to everything else. The world will be a kind of "living being" for it, not a mechanism as is the case for a *society.*

Despite the quite different paths that can be taken by the concrete history and structure of a spiritual culture, certain phases of a formal kind are sociologically prescribed, from whose realm even that which is genuinely "historical," that is, individual and nonrepeating, cannot escape. Thus the historical facticity of the medieval university (of Paris, Prague, Heidelberg, etc.) and its dramatic transformation into the modern university of the absolutist state—first in the Reformation and humanism, then in the Age of Absolutism, finally through the era of liberalism following the French Revolution—is certainly something that can be described only *historically* as it developed within the vari-ous emerging nations. Yet the fact that the medieval university in its course structures and plan, which clearly reflect the dominating rela-tions among theology, philosophy, and science in medieval society and establishment, was not essentially a research institute where a living language was spoken but an institute with a "learned" tradition to be handed on in a dead language—this is not a historical but a *sociologi-cal* fact. We can, therefore, study this university in certain phases of Arabic, Jewish, and Chinese cultural history, such as the educational traditions of old China since the fall of the dynasty. So too, the dura-tion of the so-called dispute about universals in medieval philosophy[26] is a fact to be known only *historically.* That conceptual realism itself prevailed as a living mode of thought—not as a logical "theory"—in the Middle Ages, however, while in the modern age the mode of thought is nominalistic, is again a *sociological* fact. That the *organol-ogical* categorical structure of the medieval worldview reveals the dominance of Platonism and Aristotelianism, and that *mechanical-*

technical thought took over with Gilbert, Galileo, Ubaldi, Leonardo, Descartes, Hobbes, Huygens, Dalton, Kepler, and Newton are historical facts. However, the kind of thinking that subordinated all reality, the inanimate world *and* the spiritual one, to forms of thought and being primarily seen in the *living organism* ("form" and "matter"), and then subordinated this latter kind to one that sees in the "motion of inanimate masses" and its laws forms to which, as soon as they are functionalized, even the living, social, economic, spiritual, and political worlds are, or at least "should" be, successively subordinated— these are not historical facts but sociological ones. They are inseparable from the replacement of the hand tool by the machine, the incipient transformation of community into society, production for the free market (merchandise economy), the disappearance of the vitalistic principle of solidarity in favor of an exclusively individual responsibility, and the rise of the *principle of competition* in the ethos and desires of Western society.

An idea totally alien to Aristotle and the Middle Ages was that in an essentially unending process of methodical "research," detached from specific persons and particular technical tasks, knowledge of nature would be accumulated and stocked to be used at will. That this "positive" science should be ever more *cut off* from theology and philosophy, both of which at the beginning of the modern age appeared as personally bound, closed systems, was not possible without a simultaneous collapse of the medieval economy of demand and the rise of the new spirit of gain (limited chiefly by mutual competition) in business. These were supported, moreover, by the new covetousness of the absolutist mercantile states, which, in sharp contrast to the "Christian West" under pope and emperor, formed the "European concert" held together by the principle of "balance of power."

Dynamics of Culture and Knowledge

A further task of general cultural sociology is the problem of determining to which essential forms of change—i.e., of flowering, maturing, and decaying—the cultural domains, or certain components of them, such as styles and techniques in art, are subject. The forms of change in kinds of knowledge are only a special case of this larger, more comprehensive question concerning the sociological dynamics of culture.

It seems to me that this area breaks down into several large complexes of questions.

First, is spiritual culture at all subject to the basic mortality of the mainly biological collectives and units of descent that bore and produced it? Or with what (nonmeasurable) degree of durability does one area of spiritual culture relate to another, i.e., religion as compared to philosophy and philosophy as compared to science, etc.? Let us call this problem the extent of a "culture's capacity for surviving" the groups that produced it. In what areas is culture merely a onetime, unrepeatable, vital, psychic expression (Spengler calls it "physiognomy," mistakenly applying this form of change to all culture) of the collective psyche of the people that bear it, so that culture necessarily disappears with collective biological existence, for example, with the hereditary races, peoples, and clans and their sociological real factors and conditional states?

Second, in what areas of values and things does there predominate that special kind of "growth" of culture that—based on an entirely spiritual-intellectual transference from people to people in time (tradition and acceptance)—both preserves the culture already acquired and surmounts and surpasses it in a new and living synthesis? I refer here to the process of sublation (*Aufheben*), in the double sense of Hegel, so that (a) no living meaning of a culture of a past period will thereby lose its value, and (b) not the validity and sense of a culture, but its origin will remain attached, in an irreplaceable and nonsubstitutive manner, to certain individual subjects of culture over time. In this dynamic form it is not only possible but also desirable to speak of a suprabiological cooperation of cultural contents independent of racial, political, and economic existence of peoples. One should, for example, speak of the "spirit" of ancient culture, or the "spirit" of Confucian ethics or Buddhist art in the growth of "world" and universal culture—a cooperation that rests on the fact that an individual cultural subject (an age or cultural unit) is so composed that only one particular subject is affected through it. It is easy to see that in the sphere of "knowledge" this form of dynamics can apply only to a certain type. This type is, first, independent of inductive experience and is thus knowledge of essences; second, has been functionalized in categorical structures; and third, is "accessible" only to one certain phase and one definite concrete subject within the universal development of history.

I call the dynamics of this type "cultural growth through the interweaving and acceptance of available spiritual structures into a new structure." I avoid the Hegelian expression, "dialectical growth," used by E. Troeltsch, K. Mannheim, and others—although I grant that Hegel saw this form of growth, even though the application of this category in his philosophy of history was totally inadequate due to the narrowness, which reached the point of extreme naïveté, of his European horizon. The fact that Hegel perceived this form is shown by his theory of a development of the categories—in contrast both to Kant's theory of a static organization of reason and to the theory of a mere progress in reason's *application* to quantitatively expanding materials of experience. Hegel's theory also explains that only the transtemporal (though continuously disclosed in historical time) context of *all* historical cultures makes up the total meaning of world history, not some temporal, distant goal of a so-called end condition of continuous "progress," as in the positive systems of Comte and Spencer. The deep truth expressed by Leopold von Ranke, that every phase of culture is "immediately near God," that every age and people has "its own self" against whose ideal nature it is to be measured, and that there is no "mediation of epochs through succeeding epochs," is an element, though only a partial element, of this idea of "growth." Let it be added that too little attention has yet been given to the possible monopoly and privilege, so to speak, of early, "youthful," as compared to the more mature, periods of particular cultures on certain achievements, productions, and irreplaceable kinds of knowledge, for example, knowledge of salvation and knowledge of form.[27]

Only the third form of dynamics is the one I term *cumulative progress* or retrogression in temporal succession or "international cooperation" if it is of simultaneous character. Religion, art, and philosophy in their supratechnical core mainly belong to the second form. However, the *exact sciences* insofar as they are based on numbers and measures, medicine based on the progress of medical science and technique (such as surgery) in contrast to the "physician's art," the positive techniques of controlling nature, and the techniques of social organization (in contrast to forms of political art) belong to the third. They are the chief substrates of possible cumulative progress. The difference between the dynamics of the third and second forms is evident. The third form pertains only to goods that build upon one another cumulatively without requiring a change in mode of thought, ethos, or spiritual structure, so that each generation stands upon the results of the past. Moreover, in the cumulation of value goods that can be handed down and accepted continuously from age to age and people to people, the acquisition or enhancement of the members of any one culture can in principle be replaced and substituted for another once the "methods" have been found. This discovery, however, can only be the product of the structure of an individual historical culture, such as the unique structure of the late Western cultural situation, with our positive science and technology. This dynamic form moves ever onward, continuing across any possible fall of nations, if I may say so, and, of course, right athwart of the *expressive features of national psyches*. It strides without friction, so to speak, across the kinetic phases and syntheses of the culture of the second form. The form of time in which this "cosmos of civilization" (as Alfred Weber called it) advances is sequential, as it is in the case of cultural growth. Although the "progress" of cumulative culture appears equivalent to temporal sequence, however, it is in fact bound exclusively to humankind's fortuitous experiences and to the magnitude of the achievement at hand—not to a positive individual "calling" or to a cultural determination of the concrete subjects. For this reason, and no other, in sharp contrast to the second dynamic form, a devaluation of the older state necessarily accompanies the "progress" of its successor. There is, thus, nothing here like a transtemporal interconnective sense to culture contents, and no "cosmopolitan" cooperation in ever-new cultural syntheses. There is but a single, steady, potentially unlimited progress toward a final goal.

This goal is characterized by (a) a vision of control of the world whose elements are selected according to the value of and will for domination of nature (living, social, inanimate) on the part of a vital, cultural subject. All laws of the space-time coincidences of phenomena are epitomized in this vision. Therefore, the goal is independent of both psycho-vital nature and the individuality of the personal bearer of the culture, but allows nature to be controlled to desired ends; (b) the aggregation of the necessary apparatus for this control (technology). This third dynamic form surpasses the others in unity, continuity, predictability of stages, generality, universal validity, increase of positive (progressive as opposed to retrogressive) values, character, certainty, linearity, and unlimitedness. Yet the content and evaluation assigned to this progressive form are, in turn, totally conditioned by the content of metaphysical knowledge.

Intellectual and Real History

The problems so far touched on concern only conditions of regular growth that prevail among the products of mind. But the most profound and fruitful questions for the sociology of culture lie within a different problem area marked out by the question, In what lawful order do the real institutions, corresponding objectively to the drive structures of the leading elite, affect the production, preservation, advancement, or obstruction of that *ideal meaning world* that, at every point of time in the real history of events and situations, hovers *above* this history of realities and also in front of the possible history of the future as a project, an expectation, faith, or program? We obtain a possible answer to this question only through reflecting on human history, not at all through cognition of nature or so-called natural history. We, in human history, can not only conjecture about and interpolate becoming from fixed processes; we can also follow the development of what has become by reliving the interests, efforts, programs, plans, projects, and unsuccessful "experiments" from which this or that historical reality has sprung. This possibility is always borne as a small fraction of the desires, ideas, projects, and plans that precede given realities, and has a basically different makeup from any group or individual who played, willed, knew, or expected a historical role. We are in a position to know clearly the immense quantitative and qualitative difference between the history that is possible and becoming at each point of time and *the actual* history, event, work, condition that has already occurred. We know this difference because of the twofold source of our knowledge—the reliving of plans, projects, and ideas on one hand, *and* all that which becomes known as actually having happened.

The ever-present difference between what is happening and what has happened points to the place where the real factors in the history of mind and its ideal works take effect, at times blocking the realization, or disrupting the "continuity of meaning," or promoting and "extending" what was logically expected. The basic error of all naturalistic explanations of history is that they ascribe to real factors, which they set up as decisive—whether of race, geopolitics, or economic production—the role of *solely* determining this ideal world of meaning as we find it comprised in and understood by our minds. Their error is to assume they can "explain" this ideal world from the world of *real* history. The contrary error of all ideological, spiritual, and personalistic interpretations of history is no less grave, for they suppose one can understand the history of real data, institutions, and conditions of the masses directly or by a roundabout, rectilinear extension of the history of mind.

It is my view, however, that in the course of real history the human spirit and will are capable only of directing and guiding[28] a fixed phase order of events and situations that have their own laws. Indeed, mind cannot do one bit more! For these laws operate automatically, independent of human "will," and are blind to mind and value. Where ideas are not objectified institutions, forces, interests, passions, and drives, they are utterly meaningless in real history whatever their spiritual value may be. There is no such thing as the "cunning of the idea" (Hegel) enabling an idea to steal upon interests and affections from behind, as it were, and capture and control them. Conditions and events are indifferent to such "cunning." What Hegel called the "cunning of the idea" is only a transfer of the liberal and static system of harmony of the eighteenth century to the dynamism of the sequence of historical periods. The course of real history is completely *indifferent* to the logical requirements of spiritual production! But neither does the course of real history solely determine the meaning and value of spiritual culture.[29] The course of real history releases, restricts, or limits only the mode and the effect of spiritual powers. That which can be and is effected is always incomparably too complex and rich to correspond to a sole determination by real factors. This implies the history of real conditions and events can explain only the difference between potential and actual achievements in the history of mind. The "fatalité modifiable" of the history of real factors, therefore, does not at all determine the positive *meaning content* of works of mind, though it does hinder, release, delay, or hasten the development of these works and the realization of their meaning content. To use an image, real history opens and closes the sluices of the spiritual stream.[30]

Nevertheless, it must be recognized that in spite of this sovereign indifference of the real history of institutions, conditions, and events to spiritual history and the demands of *its* inherent logic of meaning, the prevailing constellation of economy, political power, and the qualitative and quantitative character and racial admixture of the populace do, beyond doubt, show certain similarities of overall style to contemporaneous spiritual culture—even though the masses (the "large number") and the elite leadership (the "small number") seldom make a good match. This similarity of style between spiritual and real factors does not exist because one of these shaped the other to its image, as is assumed by both the ideological-personalistic and the naturalistic-collectivistic theories of history. These "agreements" arise, rather, from the fact that the higher spiritual structures of an epoch and group, which direct and guide the history of real factors, also produce works in the history of mind; they are *one and the same* structures for both.

I mention in passing that the extent of "directing" and "guiding" influences on the sequence of the real history of a relatively closed, coherent cultural process is not always the same. In the course of the three principal phases of a culture—its youth, fruition, and decline— the extent of directing and guiding decreases markedly. As they decrease, the collectivistic moment of fatality, and with it humanity's sense of determinism, increases, and the real process of history becomes less amenable to direction and guidance. The final phase of such a process is the massing of life, a mass society. Moreover, in this final phase the spiritual and ideal cultural content, and the personal groups who represent and carry these, detach themselves to an ever greater degree from the "service" of directing and guiding real history, and they exist and live for their own sake. What had once been a causal factor, or cofactor, in real history (even if only in the service of direction and guidance) becomes increasingly an end and value in itself. "L'art pour l'art," "La science pour la science," etc., are the slogans of such late periods. The individualist, living completely for himself and his own occupation, for example, in "dandyism," is one of its outstanding phenomena.

Still, for cultural sociology the central question is this, Is there in human history one *constant or lawfully changing order* of real factors, the openers and shutters of the sluices we believe are basic to the history of mind, applicable to the order of phases of cultural units? I raise this question because the long years of controversy among the three chief trends in historical and sociological thought, which can be described as *racial nativism, politicism,* and *economicism*—an opposition that primarily concerns the sociology of real facts—must also find expression in the history and *sociology of spiritual culture.* Gumplowicz, Gobineau, the Rankeans and neo-Rankeans, and the economicism of Karl Marx represent one-sided lines of thought in this respect. All three fall into the error of "naturalism" when they replace the opening and closing of the sluices with a single determination of spiritual cultural contents. We have already rejected this kind of "naturalism." But the opposition between them remains if we introduce our rule of universal dependency and ask, Which of the real factors in their particular forms are *primary, secondary,* or *tertiary* in closing and opening the "sluices" for the realization of spiritual potentialities?

In answer I can only introduce here a number of theses whose complete grounding will be given elsewhere.[31]

A mostly tacit, unconscious assumption in the controversy among the sociological tendencies described above, it seems to me, is that the independent variable among the three factors, blood, political power, and economics, remains constant throughout history or, as the purely empiricist opportunists of methods assume, there is no firm order of history-forming forces at all—things are just one way and then another.

The earliest crack in this false assumption was made by the ethnologists. They discovered ever more clearly a large variety of *pre*state, *pre*political societies, namely, an immense era in which *family and blood ties* predominated. The ethnologists thus broke through the ancient as well as Christian prejudice, unfortunately still very widespread among historians and philosophers, that the "state" is an essential condition of human nature. *Social life in general* is undoubtedly such an essential condition, as is the formal law of a "great number" of followers and a "small number" of leaders, which pertains even to animal groups. The more we penetrate into the past or even early stages of cultural peoples—not only the half and fully primitive races—the more our investigations terminate in the major ties of kinship and clan. The fact is that everywhere in the beginning of the "state" there were centuries of conflict in which the youthful followers of the first enduring warlord class opposed the order of clans and their many forms of organization, i.e., law, sites of worship, morals, customs, ceremonies, rites, worldviews, and mentalities. This opposition left the prepolitical world of humankind, which in each aspect rested upon the *primacy* and order of blood relations, age, and *their* socializing and history-forming powers, in a shambles. This fact is to be looked upon today as one of the most certain results of the investigation of primitive races.[32]

The second crack in this common prejudice comes from a completely different source, late Western history. To my knowledge, it was Werner Sombart's special service to historical sociology to have first pointed out in his disputes with Karl Marx, to whose views he was close in his youth, that the *pre*capitalist world of Europe was definitely not determined by the primacy of economic factors, but by *another* law of history-generating processes that existed between state and business, polity and economy, the power structure and the wealth of groups, processes that were different from the way the capitalist world has realized itself ever more forcefully since its beginning. He saw that the economic basis of history (in Marx's sense) does not apply even remotely to the *whole* history of the West, or to all humankind for that matter, or even to the time of that mystical "leap into freedom" of the socialistic society of the future that will eliminate all class struggle. Once freed from the "naturalistic" character that makes it a total economic "materialism" according to which economic conditions alone explain the content of spiritual nature, however, economism is approximately valid *only for a narrowly limited epoch of late Western history.* After I had contributed some detail to this insight,[33] Sombart developed it extensively, especially in the second edition of his major work on modern capitalism and the chapter entitled "Power Rule and Ruling Power."

From these insights, it follows, I think, that there is no *constant* independent variable in history among the three chief groups of real factors: blood, power, and economics. There are, however, laws ordering the respective primacies in their repressing or releasing effects on the history of mind, i.e., there is a *different* law of order for particular *phases* in the history of culture. Because of this, the opportunism popular among historians of the empirical and methodological schools is just as untenable as the false assumption, mentioned above, common to the three lines of thought, namely, that one factor is primary.

Laws of the Three Historical Phases of the
Primacy of the Real Factors

In years of work on the problems of sociological dynamics, primarily in real history rather than its effect on the history of mind—which alone is under discussion here—I have sought to strengthen the base of these ideas in a number of directions. In particular, I have sought to ground them in a theory of the *developmental order of human drives*.[34] The result of these efforts is the law of sequence of which I have spoken. Its content is this:

During any coherent cultural process relatively bounded in time and place, *three* large phases are to be distinguished. It is presumed here without argument that nowhere is there *in fact* any such coherent process in one and the same biologically unified people. But the attempt will be made, by the abstract methods of distinguishing and comparing as well as by thought experiments, to discriminate the independent, endogenous developmental causes from the more or less "catastrophic" exogenous ones such as wars, migrations, natural calamities, etc. In this conceptual format the following are the phases for the course of events conditioned only by endogenous causes:

1. A phase in which *blood relationships* of each and every kind and the corresponding institutions regulating them (rights of fathers and mothers, forms of marriage, exogamy and endogamy, clan groups, integration and segregation of races, together with the "limits" set for them by law or custom) form the independent variable of events and determine at least primarily the form of groupings, i.e., the scope of that which can happen through other real causes, such as political or economic ones.

2. A phase in which this effective primacy—understanding this word in the same limited sense as constraint of scope—passes over to the political power factors, primarily to the workings of the state.

3. A phase in which economics holds effective primacy and in which "economic factors" are the first to determine the conditions for real events, "opening and closing the sluices" for the history of mind.

In this theory the old dispute among various conceptions and explanations of history becomes historically relativized. Moreover, the theory is also coordinated with all other phase orders, the chiefly personally conditioned courses of history and the chiefly collectively conditioned (such as tribe, life community, society, union of personal solidarity between irreplaceable individuals in a "collective person") and with the internal principles that permit these groups to construct an image of the world when they are in one or another phase. As to the first phase, it appears a rule can now be established with considerable universality, namely, all high cultures in their development represent a nonadditive cultural mixture of both mainly indigenous matriarchal animistic cultures as well as patriarchal cultures of active personalities, entailing and fostering distant trade. Further, those among them that have the richest and most varied historical life also have the greatest racial stratification. These two characteristics provide the strongest motive force for the birth of all high culture with its separations of caste, rank, class, and division of labor.[35] Only in these mixtures and stratifications are the dynamic oppositions and tensions that discharge themselves in the birth of high cultures engendered. Family tensions, racial strife, and the unceasing adjustments of these through the intervention of political "state power," which rises considerably precisely because of the increasing leveling of such conflicts, are the most important factors in the genesis of high cultures. The prime causes of the distinction of caste, rank, and class are by no means found in the differentiation of economic ownership classes, as the Marxists and also C. Bucher, among others, assert. In this economistic view a law pertaining to the third phase has been transferred onto the first. Nor are these several kinds of differentiation based on a distinction of professions that become hereditary, as G. Schmoller was inclined to suppose.[36] These differentiations can be found in the stratification of races on the basis of their inborn dynamic powers, and above all, of their urge for domination or submission. To have seen all this clearly, it seems to me, is the outstanding contribution of Gumplowicz to the sociology of real facts. Wherever views on religious and metaphysical fate are different in the higher and lower classes, or men and women have different views on mortality, immortality, or life after death,[37] or where the distribution of religious and metaphysical knowledge is ordered according to caste (for example, the "holy books" are withheld from the Sudras in India), there also is a cultural effect of the facts of the sociology of race.

Religious-metaphysical democracy has throughout history been the highest presupposition of every other kind of democracy and its progress, political as well as social and economic. However, it has always been political authority with blood ties (usually in the form of monarchy) which, with the help of relatively "lower" strata, has leveled differences of blood, race, and clan and prepared for that metaphysical-democratic view—a way of thinking that became the chief presupposition and starting point for the entire development of the West, as far as we can survey it, in contrast to Asia. Apart from Russia, whose whole history is characterized by changes of alien rulers (Tartars, Swedes, Poles, Germans, Jews) who lorded it over her submission-happy racial conglomeration, the Western history of social orders and classes, from the very beginning, has been determined chiefly by *political* causes. The primary law governing the formation of social strata is more veiled than exhibited by this feature of Western history alone. Only in the transition from late antiquity to the historical phase of the "German and Romance" peoples (Ranke) does the primacy of blood factors appear again, but along with so many other inner "reasons for the decline" of late ancient civilization that here also this primacy can be questioned, as Max Weber did in his agrarian history of Rome.

The political principle of power, which secondarily leads to the formation of classes, remains the springboard and germ of all class divisions, and, at the same time, is the regulator for the extent of all potential economic formations until the end of the absolutistic and mercantilistic era. Moreover, up to that point capitalism was primarily the instrument of politically derived powers not based on economics at all, however much simultaneous economic development may have come to their aid. Only in the age of high capitalism (the age of coal) does an era gradually dawn that can be described in a historically relative way as chiefly economic, whose special laws of motion Marx not only exaggerated naturalistically into historical materialism but also erroneously for *all* of history. Only in this way could he make "all" previous history the outcome of economically based class conflict.[38]

Our law of the three phases of primary causality governing the real factors should not be taken as applying to three phases of a single coherent universal history. This law is valid, with the above restriction, for a purely interior coherent process of history that never occurs empirically. It is, moreover, valid only in a relative sense for the smaller, not the larger, group units that are already meshed in a jointly destined historical process. Examples will clarify this. In the formation of the great "national" political units, political power invariably preceded economic unification. Liberalism and free trade *follow* state capitalism in the absolute and mercantile era. Even the German Customs Union is entirely of political origin and a political instrument.[39] Once the economic unity of business and trade has been prepared in this way for the unit "nation," then within this unit—and only within it and not yet in the relation of European nations with each other—the *primacy of economics* gradually comes to the fore in all intranational relations. In spite of this, however, political power maintains its primacy within the larger unity of "Europe," notwithstanding an incipient so-called world economy, which is in fact only an interweaving of national economies. The changing economic motives of European alliance politics before the world war, especially the battles over markets outside Europe for the rapidly expanding population and industry of European society, should not cause us to overlook the fact that the highest positions of power as well as the goals of politics—quite distinct from the above motives—were not of economic origin at all but first of all a residue from the age of European power politics. Schumpeter's profound discussion of this question in his *Imperialism/Social Classes* explains this in detail.[40] The economic expansionism and imperialism of the greater European powers could never have led to the world war had not *political* and military power complexes existed whose reality, nature, and outlook originated in the precapitalist era of power politics in Europe, reaching back even to the feudal period. The rescue of economics that Schumpeter undertakes after his excellent refutation of the popular Marxist thesis that "world capitalism" was the main cause of the world war,[41] when he remarks that the present political superstructure of the economic conditions of production would correspond to a much *older economic* phase than that of the present, is quite artificial. A strange bargain! If economic conditions of production in the course of the entire period since the beginnings of capitalist economy—the "dynamic" economy in Schumpeter's view—did not have within them the power to transform the political and juridical superstructures, then is not the whole economic thesis false?

The Theory of Drives and Aging

I have tried within the framework of this essay, in what is more an intimation than a detailed treatment, not only to verify inductively, in this restricted sense, the above "law of the order of causal factors" in the three phases of history, but also to make it understandable *deductively* according to a *"theory of the origin of human drives"* as well as from the laws of psycho-vital aging according to which certain basic human drives became dominant over others in the most important stages of aging. I have made this theory fundamental to the sociology of real facts in the same sense that the theory of mind is fundamental to cultural sociology. I understand here under basic drives those drive systems from which all special drives proceed, partly through the process of psycho-vital differentiation, partly through association of drive impulses with spiritual interaction. The *sexual and reproductive* drives, serving primarily the species; the drive for power, serving both the individual and groups; and the nutritive drive, directed toward the preservation of the individual—all are objectified only in institutions based on tangible, real sociological factors. At the same time, these drives appear in various ways as repressed or released in the form of legal stipulations. The drives can be transformed, to be sure, in the dynamic relationship of their dominance or subordination to one another. This transformation will perhaps make it clear, in the not too distant future, that the phase law governing the ordering and reordering of real historical causal factors is a simple *law of aging* of the peoples who carry and underlie all cultures. This would be the law of a process largely irrelevant to the ideal cultural sphere—a sphere that initially embraces all real factors and institutions alike and is in principle "immortal"—but touches this sphere only secondarily.[42]

We have to reject completely all those theories that merely revive the theses of the utopian, rational socialism of the eighteenth century in the pseudoform of historical evolutionism. These utopian theories assume the possibility that at any future point the relationship between ideal and real factors can in principle be reversed, namely, that human spirit and ideal factors can govern real factors according to plan. I have countered this utopia by establishing a twofold relation of ideal and real factors, namely, as the restraint or release of spiritual potencies by real factors and as the "direction and guidance" of real history through the spiritual, personal causality of the elite. The dream of Fichte, Hegel (the "Age of Reason"), and, following them, Marx— in whose theories the "leap into freedom" is deferred to the future (in this he is a complete disciple of Hegel and his prejudice of the "*self-power* of the idea," derived from antiquity)—will remain for all time a mere dream. It is well to note that only against the assumption of a positive "rule of reason" over real history—rather than the mere direction and guidance by reason of a process that is itself fated—could there occur the accusing caricature of human history found in Marxism, or the patently "Messianic" theory of the historical "call" of the proletariat to put an end to all class conflicts, and thus the doctrine of the ending of the economically determined world of historical ideal structures. Our view is exactly opposite to that of Karl Marx, namely, *there is no constant effective primacy among real factors; among them there is only ordered variability.* There is, however, a *basic relationship of ideal to real factors in general* (as described above), which does not deviate but is strictly constant throughout the history of humankind.[43]

Ideal Factors Affected by the Phases of the Real Factors

The manner in which the three real factors, operating in the different orders within their phases, work upon the realm of ideal factors, which take their course according to their own special laws, indicates to us an undoubted "developmental progress"—though only in the restricted sense that the *discharge of spiritual-intellectual potencies* in the three phases of blood, politics, and economics becomes richer and more diverse. This progress, however, refers only to the quantity of intellectual potentialities released, aside from any questions of valuation, and can in no way be measured by such value contrasts as "true and false," "good and evil," "beautiful and ugly," etc. The realization of the spiritual potencies of the group is partly hindered, partly released by the institutional conditions of all three kinds of real factors. But this restraint and release are not of one and the same extent and power in the three phases of the different kinds of causal primacy. The restraint and selection of spiritual-intellectual potencies in periods and groups characterized principally by economics is the *least,* but the release of the potencies is the *greatest.* The more the first selection of spiritual-intellectual potentialities is made by conditions of production, property, and the organization of labor, that is, by economic conditions, the more abundant will be their realization. But in the case where ties of blood, clans, or age groups directly or indirectly decide the discharge of spiritual potencies, the degree of restraint is *greatest* and the possibility of their release is smallest. *Power* politics occupies a middle position. In its very highest stages of life, therefore, where the amount of work and the accumulation of possessions become more important in determining the possible discharge of spiritual potencies, spiritual culture need not have the greatest positive "value," but it is nevertheless always the richest, most differentiated, colorful, and stratified. Furthermore, the energy, generally so meagerly imparted to the human mind, directed to the course of real conditions fated in their order, direction, and guidance, is at its maximum here. Romantic sentiment and thought, which Karl Marx took over far more than he knew—especially in the form of the bitter criticism of romanticism against finance and "liberalism"—plays in vain on the sentimental theme of "soul" against "spirit," "life and blood" against "money and spirit" (O. Spengler), and futilely tries to sever the unbreakable connections between economics and the maximum freedom and release of the mind. For it is the tragic fact, definitely rooted in a metaphysical field, I think, that the "death and birth" of all development of *real* history and society is in principle different from the development of the fullness of the ideal realm of human culture.[44]

Notes

1. I therefore reject Max Weber's restriction of sociology to understandable subjective and objective "meaning content" (objective spirit). If anyone ever had a conviction about the divine, or the course of his people's history, or the structure of the stars of the heavens "because" he belonged to a privileged or an oppressed class, or was a Prussian officer, or a Chinese coolie, or his blood represented this or that racial mixture, neither this man nor any other need "know" or even surmise that this is the case. In the last analysis I agree with Karl Marx's statement that it is the being of man (though not merely his economic or "material" being, as Marx implies) toward which his whole possible "consciousness," "knowledge," and the limits of his understanding and experience are directed.

2. A major part of my pure sociology, the theory of the *essential forms* of grouping, is given in my *Formalismus in der Ethik und die materiale Wertethik* (1913–16), sec. 6, B4, ad 4 (5th ed., ed. Maria Scheler, vol. 2 of the *Gesammelte Werke*). [This has been translated into English as *Formalism in Ethics and Non-formal Ethics of Value*, pp. 519–42.—Ed.]

3. I shall develop both theories in my *Philosophical Anthropology*. A theory of the development and energetics of human drives as the foundation of the sociology of real facts was clearly seen recently by W. McDougall.

4. A much more thorough grounding of this law will come with the concluding volume of my series, *Schriften zur Soziologie und Weltanschauungslehre*. [The essays under this heading are published in vol. 6 of *Gesammelte Werke*. Scheler envisioned entitling his concluding volume *Probleme der Geschichtsphilosophie*, but it was never completed. Manuscripts for this as well as other writings on the philosophy of history will appear as vol. 13 of the *Gesammelte Werke*, ed. Manfred S. Frings.—Ed.]

5. *Lowering* of the value level of everything spiritual, such as a particular religion or a form of art, through its increased propagation and its growth among the masses is, thus, an inescapable law of the human realization of meaning and value.

6. The law of the few pioneers and the many imitators was first explained by G. Tarde in the book *Les Lois de l'imitation* (1895). This appeared in English as *The Laws of Imitation*, trans. Elsie Clews Parsons (New York, 1903).

7. I need hardly say that the logic of *meaning* has nothing to do with the contrasts "true/false," "good/evil," "beautiful/ugly," "sacred/profane," and similar oppositions of value.

8. I do not wish to discuss here the metaphysical "meaning" of this fate.

9. A notable categorization of kinds of "objective mind" has been given by Hans Freyer in *Zur Theorie des objectiven Geistes* (Leipzig, 1923).

10. Besides the key laws of the foundations of static acts, there are also developmental phase laws whose logical importance is scarcely recognized. These have nothing to do with the so-called phase rules of a majority of actual developmental series, nor with mere lines of direction or lines of *singular* factual development such as the development of *one* earthly humanity or *this* Prussian state (it being meaningless to speak of law in the latter case). A "direction" can be disclosed by a temporal phase comparison of a group (a major direction, a secondary one, a cul-de-sac, a tangent, etc.), but this is never a law. A developmental phase law is an *essential* law of transition from stage to stage such that the unique factual beginning and ending of development remain variable. This law controls all *possible* factual development.

11. That is, the history of the formation, growth, decline, and structural changes of mind *itself*, not of its accomplishments and works.

12. The theory rejected here is that of the unity of "rational human nature." This theory is assumed throughout by humanism, which is *only European*, as Troeltsch observes in his *Historismus* (*Der Historismus und seine Probleme*, vol. 1, *Das logische Probleme der Geschichtsphilosophie*, vol. 3 of *Gesammelte Schriften*, ed. Hans Baron, Tübingen, 1922). This theory was taken over from the church's teaching, eliminating only original sin and inherited guilt.

13. I have dealt with the "functionalizing" of the objective knowledge of essences at length in my "Problems of Religion," in *On the Eternal in Man*, pp. 105–356.

14. *Der Historismus und seine Überwindung* (Berlin, 1924); see also Ernst Troeltsch, *Christian Thought: Its History and Application*, ed. Baron F. von Hügel (New York, 1957), pp. 53–77.

15. I will supply strict proof of the above statements and justification for the term "idea of humanity," in contrast to the empirical concept "human-animal," in my *Philosophical Anthropology*.

16. O. Bumke, *Kultur und Entartung* (Berlin, 1922).

17. Here I must refer to the *Philosophical Anthropology*, which I have worked on for many years and will appear soon. References to this problem were already given in my study "Zur Idee des Menschen," in *Vom Umsturz der Werte*, vol. 3 of *Gesammelte Werke*. ["On the Idea of Man (1915)," trans. Clyde Nabe, *Journal of the British Society for Phenomenology* 9 (October 1978), 184–98.]

18. See my book, *Formalism in Ethics*, especially the chapter concerning relativity of values and valuation, pp. 275–95.

19. This holds generally for all primitive discoveries and tools, such as primitive ground-working instruments (shoe and plowshare) or ways of making fire (fire bore, etc.) All these are at once tools *and* cultic forms of expression of an inner experience. The idea of human generation and the concept of the earth as the fructifying mother are always the principal modes of these discoveries.

20. Wilhelm Dilthey, *Einleitung in die Geisteswissenschaften* (1883), in *Gesammelte Schriften,* vol. 1 (Leipzig, 1924); also, *Die geistige Welt,* I and II in *Gesammelte Schriften,* vol. 5, ed. George Misch. In his admirable introduction Misch observes that Dilthey departed more and more from the views of his early period, strongly influenced by positivism, that metaphysics was a poetry of concepts, pp. XXXVII, LXIff. However, even in "Das Wesen der Philosphie," in *Gesammelte Schriften,* vol. 5, we still read, "Hereafter metaphysics, as a universally valid science, is destroyed." [See the English translation of this book by Stephen A. Emery and William T. Emery, *The Essence of Philosophy* (Chapel Hill: University of North Carolina Press, 1954), p. 54.—Ed.]

21. For example, H. Scholz in his *Religionsphilosophie,* 2nd ed. (Berlin, 1923).

22. See the distinguished work by F. Tönnies, *Kritik der öffentlichen Meinung* (Berlin, 1922).

23. On the essence and source of national ideologies see my *Schriften zur Soziologie und Weltanschauungslehre,* in *Gesammelte Werke,* vol. 6, and also my study on "cant," "Zur Psychologie des englischen Ethos and des Cant," in *Politische-pädagogische Schriften,* in *Gesammelte Werke,* vol. 4, ed. Manfred S. Frings.

24. See Ernst Troeltsch, *The Social Teachings of the Christian Churches,* trans. Olive Wyon, 2 vols. (London, 1931).

25. I have presented a precise characterization of these essential forms of human groups in *Formalism in Ethics and Non-formal Ethics of Values,* sec. 6, B, ad 4. The divisions made there are expanded by Edith Stein in *Beiträge zur philosophischen Begründung der Psychologie und der Geisteswissenschaften* in *Jahrbuch für Philosophie und phänomenologische Forschung,* vol. 5, 1922 [; 2nd ed. (Tübingen, Niemeyer, 1970)]. Theodore Litt has a similar aim in his work *Individuum und Gemeinschaft* (Leipzig, 1924).

26. For the exact course of this dispute consult even today K. Prantl, *Geschichte der Logic im Abendlande,* 4 vols. (Leipzig, 1855–70).

27. See the chapter "Problems of Religion" in my book *On the Eternal in Man.* In a lopsided way, such monopolies and privileges of early periods are taken as metaphysical knowledge by Bachofen, whose method is criticized very learnedly by C. A. Bernoulli in his great work *J. J. Bachofen und das Natursymbol* (Basel, 1925). More radical than Bachofen is L. Klages in *Mensch und Erde* (Jena, 1920), *Von Wesen des Bewusstseins* (Munich, 1921), and *Von kosmologischen Eros* (Munich, 1922). In this theory, spawned by romanticism (Savigny), the whole history of human knowledge is a progressive "decadence"—a view as unbalanced as that of positivism, which makes history a steady progress.

28. "Direction" is the primary, "guidance" the secondary function of mind. Direction holds out a value idea, whereas guidance is the *repression or release of the instinctive impulses* whose assigned movements bring the idea to realization. Direction conditions the *kind* of control.

29. As assumed, for example, by the economic view of history.

30. I believe I can show—elsewhere—that on the basic relationship between the history of mind and the history of real factors in general such otherwise divergent scholars as Wilhelm Dilthey [see *Die Einbildungskraft des Dichters,* Leipzig: Fues's Verlag, 1987], Ernst Troeltsch (see introduction to *Social Teachings of the Christian Churches,* vol. 1), and Max Weber (see his volumes on the sociology of religion) are in essential agreement on the above.

31. This occurs in my *Philosophical Anthropology* along with the fourth volume of my series on sociology and the theory of weltanschauung (*Probleme der Geschichtsphilosophie*).

32. See W. Wundt, *Völkerpsychologie,* vol. 3, "Die politischen Gesellschaft" (Leipzig, 1917). The recent work of Fr. Oppenheimer, *System der Soziologie,* vol. 1 (Jena, 1922), is also relevant. More critical is A. Vierkandt in *Gesellschaftlehre* (Stuttgart, 1922), pp. 320ff. I do not accept the view of Vierkandt that the state could "also" have arisen purely by association—not only as a dominating organization.

33. See my treatise on capitalism (1914) in *Vom Umsturz der Werte,* where I first demonstrated the significance of the contrast between wealth born of power and political power born of wealth.

34. The theory of this order of development of drives is an important part of my forthcoming *Philosophical Anthropology.*

35. See Fritz Graebner, *Das Weltbild der Primitiven* (Munich, 1924). This book explains unusually clearly the contrast between patriarchal and matriarchal cultures, affecting the whole worldview, technology, and character of law. He also pursues brilliantly the idea that high cultures represent mixtures of the two and always have the tendency to equalize this inner contrast through political monarchy of a more or less despotic form.

36. Georg Schmoller, *Die soziale Frage,* vol. 1 (Munich, 1918).

37. See the examples cited by Graebner, *Das Weitbild der Primitiven,* pp. 48ff.

38. A good historical treatment of the rise of the theory of class conflict is given by Werner Sombart in his article "Die Idee des Klassenkampfes," *Weltwirtschaftliches Archiv* 21, no. 1 (1925), 22–36.

39. See Max Weber's economic sociology, [*Economy and Society: An Outline of Interpretive Sociology,* trans. Guenther Roth, Claus Wittich, et al., 2 vols. (New York, 1968)]. Weber points out the political nature of the Customs Union and its antagonisms to the economically determined tendencies of the industry of Rhenish Westphalia and Silesia, and East Prussian agriculture.

40. Joseph Schumpeter, [*Imperialism/Social Classes,* trans. Heinz Norden (New York, 1955)].

41. What is meant here are not the causes of the war in the historical sense of a single causality that includes the free-will acts of ruling persons, but only the sociological cause of the tensions underlying the war, therefore the causes of the potentiality of war. Between France, the leading player in the creation of the power coalition hostile to the Central Powers, and the Central Powers

themselves, there existed no outstanding economic tensions. (The question of "guilt," which concerns only the spiritual repression or nonrepression of given tensions, continues in any case; it is not at all touched by a sociological explanation of the possibility of war.) However, even if we assume that, with the eventual new structure of Europe, the economy and its interweaving of interests had won a victory over power politics and its spirit, there would still have continued between this new Europe, in which economy as a history-making factor had first achieved its complete victory over the power politics of the states, and the *non*-European world, even Russia, the essentially and primarily *power* political relationship of the past. In a third case, a possible confrontation with Japan by the nations of America and Australia, blocking the expansion of the productive Japanese people, the opposition of *race* and *blood,* and the cultural differences between the Whites and the Yellows founded therein, would overshadow all other conflicts of whatever kind, and a victory by Japan, as the *new* "pioneer" of Western civilization, would resurrect the *oldest* motive for the birth of political power structures and again raise racial conflict as the primary causal factor in history.

42. For demonstration I must refer to my *Philosophical Anthropology,* the sections on "Trieblehre" (theory of drives) and "Theorie des Altes and des Tod" (theory of aging and death). For the order of the origin of the basic drives, see Paul Schilder, [*Medical Psychology,* trans. David Rapaport (New York, 1953)].

43. I cannot show more precisely here that there is a connection between this point and metahistory, or the metaphysics of history.

44. We in no way need to be concerned with the spiritual culture of the coming distinctly and purely economic age. The industrial wealth of the segments controlling production and energy for the economy could extensively replace the present state and what the state has done for spiritual culture without subjecting that culture to the service of interests of political governing classes to the same degree as the state was accustomed to doing. This latter, I think, is already being achieved in North America, not only on the continent but also in what Americans are doing outside their country (China). This is an important model for European industry, which along these lines is hardly enlightened. In this sense the disadvantages of capitalism and industrialism were only temporary; they can be ameliorated by a sharply delineated economism.

9

Formal Problems of the Sociology of Knowledge

Several formal problems closely link the sociology of knowledge to epistemology and logic as well as to developmental psychology. They all rest on three possible basic relations of knowledge to society. First, the knowledge members of a group have of each other, and the possibility of their mutual "understanding," is not something added to the group, but coconstitutes human society. However, collections of mere objective data, for example, classification of races by traits such as color of skin or shape of skull, or statistical data such as the number of dead in Cologne in 1914, do not yield a *sociological* object. Second, there belongs to any group a knowledge, however vague, of its own existence as well as its commonly recognized values and aims (therefore, no class without class consciousness, etc.). All knowledge, especially common knowledge of "the same" objects, determines in some way the characteristics of the society. Third, all knowledge is, conversely, also ultimately determined by the society and its structure.[1]

Chief Principles of the Sociology of Knowledge

The significance of the chief principles of the sociology of knowledge are still too little appreciated. They are

1. The knowledge each person has of being a *member of society* in general is not empirical but a priori. The origin of this knowledge pre-

This essay appeared as "Probleme einer Soziologie des Wissens" in the anthology edited by Scheler, *Versuche zu einer Soziologie des Wissens* (Munich: Duncker & Humbolt, 1924). A revised version appeared as part of *Die Wissenformen and die Gesellschaft* and was reprinted in *Gesammelte Werke*, vol. 8. The first English translation was by Rainer Koehne, published in *The Sociology of Knowledge: A Reader*, ed. James E. Curtis and John W. Petras (New York: Praeger Publishers, 1972), pp. 170–86. Manfred S. Frings has also published an English translation in *Problems of a Sociology of Knowledge*, pp. 67–81. I have benefited by the two previous translations, but the present version is my own.

cedes the stages of the consciousness of oneself and one's value: no *I* without a *we*. Genetically, the *we* always has content before the *I*.[2]

2. The actual participation of a man in the experiences of his fellow men depends on the essential structure of the group. These can be grasped by ideal types. At one pole of participation is identification, found, for example, in primitive humans, the masses, hypnosis, certain pathological states, and the relation of mother to child.[3] At the other pole are inferences by analogy from bodily gestures to specific contents of experience. This kind of participation is characteristic of an individualistic society in which the "other" is understood as a stranger with whom a conscious *contract* is made. When a contract binds wills in law, the knowledge the parties have of each other is inferential.

Between these forms of participation there are several others I will merely enumerate. First is coexperience among human beings by contagion without recognition of such coexperience. Second are types of involuntary *imitation* of actions, at a later phase imitation of expressive movements, and yet later copying of purposes. This latter is called *tradition* when it occurs between different generations of a group. Tradition must be clearly distinguished from historical knowledge, however, for tradition is not knowledge of history but the possibility of history, the historicity of life. All these forms of transmission of experience are found in the higher animals. In sharp contrast to them is the immediate, subjective *understanding* of others' feelings and experiences according to laws of motivation and objective understanding of meanings. These meanings are either of material things (works of art, inscriptions, monuments, tools, etc.) or are associated with repeatable acts that mean or name something. An example of the latter is *language* as distinguished from expressions of inner states, however rich, specialized, or differentiated such expressions may be. In higher apes, twenty-two distinct sounds expressing affect were observed, but even if there were one thousand, this would not mean the presence of even a trace of a language or naming function. But representation, for example, self-representation in singing, dancing, or the representation of meaning in objective materials such as pictography and art, customs, mores, rites, cults, ceremonies, and descriptions of persons, are all understandable, objectified forms of conduct common to the group. The different types of understanding, as well as all types of sympathy as distinct from contagion, are proper only to human society—animals do not have them.

Thus far we have imperfect knowledge as to whether there are other forms of transmission than the ones mentioned, including the specifically social acts of mind that have meaning, such as teaching and learning, disclosing and concealing, commanding and obeying, making and receiving announcements, suffering and forgiving, and so on. Are there nonconscious forms of transmission accomplished by heredity? What seems certain is that there is no innate recognition of particular objects, only general or specific innate functions for acquiring knowledge of a certain kind. It also seems certain that inherited aptitudes and talents, both of individuals and hereditary races, are originally different for the acquisition of knowledge. The chief ground for qualitative differences among castes, estates, and occupations within nations lies in original differences of talent, not of class dispositions, demands of society, or any kind of milieu influences. According to scientific studies in heredity, talent and perhaps also psychic factors are accumulated hereditarily, although acquired functions are not.

The case is altogether different for *genius*.[4] A genius enters life like a meteor. He is strangely independent of the accumulations of talent whose inheritance seem to be governed by Mendel's laws. Genius is a quality separable from particular accomplishments in a way not true for talent. But it is by combining with specific talents (musical, technical) that genius takes a certain direction in which to act. Genius is everywhere marked by *love of a cause,* an ecstatic devotion to ideas and values—it is an excess of mind beyond the biologically important and beyond the originality of the work created according to no rules (Kant).

In whatever way the combinations among willing, loving, hating, etc., may occur genetically, they are the basis for two categories also essential for the sociology of knowledge, the *group soul* and the *group mind*. We do not hold these to be metaphysical entities that precede all human living and experiencing with one another. They are merely the subject of psychic and mental contents that always produce themselves anew in experiences with others.[5] These categories are not simply the sums of the knowledge of individuals "plus" a subsequent communication of that knowledge. Only for the individual's knowledge of himself and his nature does "collective knowing" represent a limit, the more so the more primitive and less developed the group. We call "group soul" only those psychic activities that are not spontaneous but acted out in forms of expression and other automatic and semiautomatic psychophysical activities. We call "group mind" the subject that constitutes itself with others through conscious, spontaneous acts intentionally related to objects. Thus, myths and fairy tales that are not individually formed, "natural" folk language, folk songs, folk religion, folkways, customs, costumes, are based on the group soul, whereas the state, the law, refined speech, philosophy, art, science, public opinion rest largely on group mind. The group soul "lives and grows" in everyone even when they are asleep; its effects may be called "organic" in the romantic sense. The group soul's origin is *impersonal* and anonymous. The group mind, in comparison, appears only in *personal representatives*. Its contents, values, aims, and direction are always determined by personal leaders and exemplars, at any rate by a "small number" (Wiese), an "elite" (Pareto) who beget its objects and goods in spontaneously performed acts. The objects and goods of the group soul would collapse if the acts that generate them were not *spontaneously performed*. Thus each cultural possession is a continuous regeneration, which at the same time is an original acquisition, a *creatio continua*. The group soul acts on the group from "below" to "above," as it were, the group mind from "above" to "below."

The sociology of knowledge must trace the laws and rhythms by which knowledge of those at the top of the society, the intellectual elites, filters downward and is distributed over time among various groups and strata. This discipline must, therefore, also understand how such knowledge is socially regulated, partially through the institutions that disseminate it, such as schools and the press, and partially through the social barriers that restrict it, such as secrets, indexes, censorship, and prohibitions that forbid particular castes,[6] estates, or classes to acquire certain kinds of knowledge. These are issues chiefly of the group mind.

3. A third principle of the sociology of knowledge, which is also a principle of epistemology, states that there is a *fixed law ordering* the origin of our knowledge of reality, that is, of what "achieves effects." This is the law of the order of fulfillment of the spheres of knowledge, which are constants of the human mind, and their correlated objects.[7]

Before stating this law, let us enumerate the spheres of being and objects that are not reducible to each other. They are (a) the absolute sphere of reality and value, the sphere of the sacred; (b) the sphere of a coworld, anteworld, and postworld, that is, the world of society and history, or the world of the "other"; (c) the sphere of the outer and inner worlds as well as the sphere of one's own lived body and environment; (d) the sphere of what is "alive"; and (e) the sphere of the corporeal but inanimate world that appears to be dead.

To this date, epistemology has never ceased attempting to reduce these spheres to each other, although their contents have changed continuously in history. We can only touch on these reductive efforts here. Some, for example, have attempted to assimilate the inner world to the outer, as in the work of Condillac, Mach, Avenarius, and the materialists. Others, such as Descartes, Berkeley, and Fichte, have taken the opposite tack. Some have attempted to reduce the Absolute to other spheres by establishing "causes" for the essence and existence of the divine. Some have endeavored to reduce the living, vital world to the pregivenness of the inanimate, dead world—as in the empathy theory of life espoused by Descartes and Theodor Lipps, among others. Some have tried to reduce the shared, mutual world to the pregivenness of one's inner world and an outer corporeal world—in theories of analogy to and empathy with another's consciousness. Some, such as Avenarius, have tried to reduce the distinction between subject and object to a pregivenness of "fellow men" into whom an environmental element, such as "this tree," is introjected, which is followed by the introjection of themselves by an observer. Some have tried to reduce one's own lived body to a merely associative relation between consciousness of one's ego and organic sensations, on one side, and the external perceptions of one's body, on the other. All such attempts are fallacious. These spheres are irreducible and are given equally genuinely in each human consciousness. Yet, it is demonstrable that there is an order to the givenness and pregivenness of these spheres that remains constant in human development. That is, one of these spheres, in any phase of development, is already filled while another is not. Also, the reality of the objects that furnish one of these spheres can be doubted or left undecided *if* the reality of objects in other spheres is certain.

If we leave aside the place of the Absolute in this order, the following basic proposition is valid for purposes of the sociology of knowledge: the *reality* and *general and particular contents* of the shared social world and the world of the historical past are given before all other spheres. "You-ness" (the "thou") is the most fundamental existential category of human thinking. That is why primitives apply this category to all phenomena of nature, for nature is to them a field of expression, a grammar of spirits and demons dwelling behind natural appearances. Let me add a few more relevant laws of pregivenness of the spheres. (1) The sphere of the outer world is always given before that of the inner. (2) The world perceived as animate, as alive, is given before the world perceived as inanimate, as dead. (3) The outer world of cosubjects, belonging to the shared, common world, is always given prior to what I, as an individual, have and know of the outer world. Also, the outer world of my coworld is given before the inner world of my coworld. (4) The inner world of the shared world, and its past and future as perspectives of expectations, is given before the sphere of my own self-observations. As Thomas Hobbes put it, all self-observation is behaving toward myself as if I were another; it is not a condition but an imitation and result of the observation of others. (5) As a field of expression, not as a corporeal object, my own and every other body is given before any distinction between body and psyche.

The assumption of the reality and specific form of society and history in which a person is located is, thus, *not* based on the assumption of the reality and specific form of the corporeal world or of the contents of inner self-perception, as many still hold. It is not by chance that many philosophers, such as Plato, Aristotle, Berkeley, Fichte, Leibniz, and Kant, among others, have denied the existence of a real, extended, inanimate world, but few have denied the existence of an animal or even a plant. Even the radically idealistic Berkeley had doubts whether his formula of *esse = percipi,* to be is to be perceived, could be applied to plants. Nowhere has there ever existed a solipsist! Apart from ample proofs of our law from genetic psychology, which cannot be discussed here, this shows clearly how much more deeply the conviction of the *reality of society* is rooted in us than the reality of all other objects of any other sphere of knowledge or being. We can doubt all other realities or leave them in abeyance, but not *this* reality.

What are the consequences of these laws for the sociology of knowledge? First, that all knowledge, all forms of thought, perception, and cognition are undoubtedly of sociological character. This proposition does not refer to the content of knowledge, and still less to its objective validity. It means that selection of the objects of knowledge is made according to the *ruling social-interest perspective.* The "forms" of the mental acts by which knowledge is acquired are always necessarily co-conditioned sociologically, that is, by the structure of the society.[8] Since explaining consists of reducing the relatively new to something better known, and since society is always "better known" than anything else, we may expect what a profusion of sociological studies has shown: the subjective forms of thought and perception, as well as classification of the world into categories—indeed classification of knowable things in general—are coconditions by the division and classification of the groups, for example, clans, that make up the society.[9]

In light of this, two things in particular now become fully understandable. One consists of the curious facts of the collective worldviews of primitive men discovered by Lévy-Bruhl, Graebner, and Thurnwald and also reported in many other ethnological studies. The other consists of the far-reaching structural analogies between knowledge of nature and knowledge of the psyche,[10] knowledge of metaphysics and religion, and knowledge of the structure and organization of society, particularly of the hierarchy of the parts of society during a political age. It is an especially inviting task for the sociology of knowledge to trace the structural parallels between views of the world, the psyche, and God and all developmental stages and kinds of social organization as these pertain to the basic forms of knowledge—religious, metaphysical, and scientific. A systematic investigation of these structural identities is still lacking.[11] Also lacking is an attempt to formulate some *simple* laws. All such attempts are ultimately justified by our formal principle of the laws of the givenness of the spheres. These laws fully explain the fact that in the development of knowledge a "biomorphic" worldview always genetically precedes any view that recognizes the distinctive character and laws of the inanimate and dead, or tries (as modern mechanistic biology does) to reduce the living to the dead. It is on the basis of these laws, furthermore, that the fallacy of the theory of projective empathy is revealed, which is as inapplicable to the sociology of primitive humans as it is to the psychology of children.[12]

The Major Types of Knowledge

The formal problems of the sociology of knowledge also require identifying the major types of knowledge and their social origin and forms of movement, all of which must be investigated sociologically.

Epistemologists consider knowledge of every kind to be based on a "natural worldview"—whether it is knowledge of salvation, education, history, science, religion, metaphysics, or values. They seem to mean by this a constant minimum set of factors informing the way the world is viewed at any time and place that human beings live. Epistemologists are inclined to take this "natural worldview" as their point of departure, and sometimes refer to it as a view "naturally grown," "practical," and the like. However, this concept is as deceptive as the famous notion of a "state of nature" found in the old ecclesiastical or antiecclesiastical doctrines of natural law. Ecclesiastical natural law likened "Paradise" to this conception, and the *status naturae* was made to be more or less similar to the sinful state, depending on the significance attributed to the "Fall." In a deliberate counter to the church, Hobbes equated the state of nature as the "bellum omnium contra omnes," the war of all against all. Rousseau equated this state as the idyll in which private property was absent. And the Marxists have equated this state with "the free and equal" men who "originally" lived together with common property and in promiscuity. But in fact, we know nothing of any "state of nature." The content of such a state is in each case a political foil and background for future interests each of these typical ideologies seeks to justify. Is the "natural world view" of the epistemologists any better? I do not think so.

Berkeley, for example, held that natural man is an idealist, in his sense, and said that "matter" was an invention of crotchety "scholars." Others conceive the natural worldview realistically and ascribe to it only one categorial structure—e.g., a plurality of dead things in space and time, uniformity of occurrences, reciprocity, etc. Kant, Avenarius, Bergson, and now N. Hartmann—all give entirely different versions of the "natural worldview." Unfortunately, each version is exactly constructed to serve as the point of departure for the preconceived theory of knowledge the philosophers intend to prove.

The traditional concept of a constant natural worldview must be totally rejected by the sociology of knowledge. In its place I introduce the concept of the *relatively* natural worldview, which may be defined as follows: The relatively natural worldview of a group consists of everything the group accepts as given *without question*. This means that every object and meaning in the structural forms of the given is accepted by the group, without special spontaneous acts, as something *that cannot and need not be justified*. Such objects and meanings can be entirely different for other groups and for the same groups during different developmental stages.[13] One of the most certain insights gained by the sociology of knowledge of so-called primitives, the biomorphic view of the child, and the entire West up to the beginning of the modern age, is this: *there is no one,* constant, natural view of the world held by all human beings. This insight is also supported by comparing the relatively natural worldviews of the largest cultures. To the contrary, the diverse worldviews extend into the various categorial structures of the given itself. For primitive people, demons and spirits are given in the act of perception just as "naturally" and unquestioningly as they are *not* given to us. One absolutely natural worldview is, thus, no more than a limit concept to assess developmental stages of the relatively natural worldviews.

The "absolutely constant" natural worldview is an idol of traditional epistemology that must be replaced by an attempt to discover *laws of transformation* among the structures of relatively natural worldviews.[14] Spengler was correct when he wrote, in the first volume of *Decline of the West,* the very words I wrote in 1914: "Kant's table of categories is just a table of the categories of the European mind."[15] A theory of such transformations can succeed only if the sociology of knowledge is closely allied with genetic psychology and adapts for its own purposes the parallel coordinations of developmental stages already discovered there. Indeed, such parallels exist between a great variety of different series.[16] Any of the organizations of psychic stages that have been discussed in what is already a large literature could be of great significance for the sociology of knowledge of the relatively natural views of the world and their transformations into each other. In many respects they already are significant, as shown by the studies of Edinger, McDougall, Thorndike, Köhler, Koffka, Bühler, Stern, Jaensch; the psychiatrists and neurologists Schilder, Birnbaum, Storch, and Freud; and the ethnologists and sociologists Preuss, Graebner, Lévy-Bruhl, Durkheim, Niceforo, etc. After all, the sociology of knowledge has for its subject not only the sociology of truth, but also the sociology of delusion, superstition, and socially conditioned errors and forms of deception.

Relatively natural worldviews are organic growths that advance over great reaches of time. They are untouched by preachments, but can probably be changed fundamentally only by racial, cultural, and linguistic mixing. They belong to the lowest centers of the automatically functioning group "soul," not at all to the group "mind."

Rooted in the great cultural promontories, so to speak, of relatively natural worldviews are the forms of knowledge of *relatively artificial* or *"educated" worldviews*. Ordered by degree of artificiality, from least to most, they are (1) *myth and legend,* as undifferentiated, predecessors of religious, metaphysical, natural, and historical knowledge; (2) everyday *natural language,* and the knowledge implicit in this (in contrast to learned, poetical, or technical language), as has been elucidated by Wilhelm von Humboldt's studies of inner forms of language and worldview,[17] and recently by Finck and Vossler; (3) *religious knowledge* in various amalgams from the devout, emotive, vaguely intuitive, to the fixed dogmas of a priestly church; (4) *mystical knowledge* and its forms; (5) *philosophic-metaphysical* knowledge; (6) the *positive knowledge* of mathematics, the natural sciences, and the cultural sciences; and (7) *technical* knowledge.

Historical shifts are slowest and most ponderous in relatively natural worldviews, but accelerate as knowledge becomes more artificial. The positive religions obviously move much more slowly than metaphysical systems that are distributed among various groups in all the world religions. Within a given culture there are a comparatively few main types of metaphysical system, and their recognition and validity endure over time much longer than the positive sciences whose results change hourly.

Each type of knowledge develops its own language and style of expression. Religion and metaphysics necessarily remain attached to natural folk languages to a greater degree than mathematics and the sciences, which develop purely artificial terminologies.[18] As every publisher knows, mathematics and the natural sciences are vastly more internationalized than the cultural sciences, which, aside from differences in their subjects, is due to the artificiality of their languages. Only mystical knowledge is, as it were, inherently antithetical to language and formalized expression. For this reason alone, mystical knowledge has a powerful individualizing and isolating tendency— but this is also combined with cosmopolitan tendencies. As we know, mystical knowledge is supposed to be "ineffable." This holds both for the "light" intellectual mysticism of ideas and the "dark" vitalistic mysticism of identification with the primeval ground of creative nature (*natura naturans*). These different mysticisms can be found in all societies; they probably originate in the tension and contrast between matriarchal and patriarchal cultures. The religious as well as metaphysical mystics, from Plotinus to Bergson, view language as inadequate to express what is experienced, thought, and envisioned in mystical *union* and *ecstasy*. Indeed, mystics are inclined to see in language an ineradicable *source of deception and error* for the "knowledge" they desire. All mystics believe what Schiller says: "When the soul speaks, it already speaks no more." Thus, the concept of *sanctum silentium*, silent sanctuary, is basic to each kind of mystical community, order, and sect the world over. This is explained by the sociology of knowledge, for the concept applies both to the "dark," orgiastic, vital mysticism that empties the mind as well as to the "light," intellectualized mysticism that empties sensations and drives. This concept is independent of the contents of the given religious or metaphysical system whose presence is necessary for mysticism to appear. Silence on the "mysteries" is not only a rule analogous to the keeping of professional or state secrets that is directed to outsiders: this rule is part of the method of finding mystical knowledge. Among Quakers, for example, the union of minds and wills is expected to occur through silent prayer until one member, seized by the "Holy Ghost himself," finds the word of the hour and expresses the true purpose of the community and of God.[19]

A basic problem in the sociology of knowledge is the *origin* of the more or less artificial types of knowledge. But only the origins of the principal types of artificial knowledge can be examined here.

In all these types, the striving for knowledge emerges from an innate drive that humans have in common with the higher vertebrates, especially the apes. The apes already exhibit a distinct curiosity when they investigate objects and occurrences that seem to be neither biologically useful or harmful to them individually or as a species. Anything strange, anything that disrupts the familiar pattern of expectations, triggers this impulse which is doubtless part of the power drives and also closely related to the drives to construct and play. From these affective impulses of stupor and curiosity some new emotional factors emerge. An impulse somewhat higher than curiosity is desire for knowledge. This may be directed not only at new things, but at things already known. Only from this impulse is there a transformation to the affects and drives associated with higher types of knowledge.

Of these higher types of knowledge, there is, first, the irresistible urge, primarily of the *group,* secondarily of the individual, to "rescue" and "safeguard" their existence, welfare, and fate by achieving a knowledge of an "overpowering and sacred" reality. This reality is valued as the highest good and ground of existence, and is the enduring affective root of all *search for religious knowledge.*

Second, there is the more intellectual feeling of *wonder* that serves as the foundation for a new type of knowledge. In its intention, this affect is profoundly different from all stupor affects such as fright, bewilderment, amazement, etc., and from all impulses for rescue, security, or salvation. Any object, even the most familiar, may evoke this wonder, but on condition it is understood as an *exemplification* of an ideal type or an *essence.* To see an object in this way is to grasp it not as related to its immediate or mediate surroundings in time and space, to what philosophers refer to as "secondary causes," but as something that poses the questions, why, how, for what, does something like this *exist at all,* and *not not exist?* Should these questions be directed to the essential structure and existence of the entirety of the world, pure "metaphysical" wonder will have been reached. Aristotle clearly recognized that wonder and the feelings accompanying it are the constant source of all searching for *metaphysical knowledge.* The essence of this attitude is such that any object cognized, placed "into an idea," is examined with no concern for its accidental, immediate characteristics and existence or for their causes. No question is asked as to why this object is here and not there, and why it is now and not then, that is, what its positional value in a spatiotemporal order may be—an order that primitive people, according to recent studies of Lévy-Bruhl, cannot yet discriminate clearly from material things.[20] Rather, seen as representing an ideal type of essence, the object is immediately and directly related to its *prima causa,* its first cause.[21]

The third emotion that excites desire for a new kind of knowledge is animated by a search for experiences that at first occur accidentally in *acting* and *working* in the world and only after this, secondarily, become something sought after. This is the emotion of *striving for power and domination* over nature and people—over social, psychic, and organic processes. This striving extends even to the attempt to guide and dominate supernatural, or what appear to be supernatural, powers and to "foresee" phenomena in order to control them.

The deeper source of the drive for power is in the purposeless impulses to construct, play, examine, and experiment. But although purposeless, these impulses are at the same time the source of the drives for all positive science and technique—drives whose emotional springs are closely related. Perfectly correlated with this intellectualized urge to control and dominate is the ability, doubtless already found in the highest vertebrates, to adapt to new, *atypical* situations through insight rather than instinctive action or trial-and-error behavior. Insight serves life-enhancing, biological behavior in such a way that *practical-technical intelligence* (which we cannot yet define well[22]) is the result. Crucial to practical intelligence is that our natural world of perception, which science has established is conditioned by our drives, can register constant and temporally regular processes of nature better than the irregular or unique ones. Thus, thresholds of noticeability, which are always directed by thresholds of excitation, invariably favor the constant and uniform, a unified pattern of meaning in space and time, for example, or things ordered symmetrically. Furthermore, E. Jaensch has suggested that the tendency to select the constant and regular is probably not transferred from perceptual to imaginative-representational images but originally inheres in both. Perception and imagination develop from fundamental forms of intuitional image, which, in adults, are far more common in perception than in excitation.[23] Thus, neither the rationalist and Kantian views of so-called pure reason nor the empiricists' view of sensual experience (which is actually formed according to and thus follows the selective tendency of attention) is the basis of the ultimate conviction of a spatiotemporal natural law that guides all positive research. The basis of this law is *entirely biological*. It is the *drive for power and control* which originally determines intellectual behavior toward the world in perception, imagination, and thought as well as practical behavior in acting upon the world and altering the environment. The unity of both theoretical and practical action in the world, and the common structural forms of each, are founded on this biological drive.

The need that arises to find "secondary" causes governed by laws is as distinct from the religious need for protection and salvation as it is from the metaphysical need to find in the representation of a thing, its "idea," the primary cause of the thing's existence. Indeed, the object of positive science is in sharpest contrast to that of metaphysics. Whereas the object of metaphysics is beheld in wonder—why death? why pain? why love? why man?—the object of natural science is viewed in terms of its positional value in space and time, as something to be foreseen and thus to be controlled. (*Voir pour prevoir, Wissen ist Macht*, knowledge is power, etc.) The question positive science asks is, Why is such and such a thing here and not there? This is also the basic question for every sort of technique. Technique strives to divide things, reassemble them into a more desired spatiotemporal pattern, and foresee the outcome of such interventions in the course of nature.

Comte's and Spencer's positivism—which is not a philosophy but an ideology of late western European industrialism—acknowledge only the third root of the human desire for knowledge, but without seeing its biological origins. This ideology was, therefore, destined to misapprehend the essence of religion and metaphysics and their history. Positivism has made what are in fact three constant, totally irreplaceable forms of knowledge into mere temporal stages of the development of knowledge. However, the emotions and cognitive methods of religion and metaphysics are the sole *monopolies of "Homo sapiens,"* whereas technique and positive science, notwithstanding their coconditioning by the mind, are merely gradual outgrowths of the faculty of practical-technical intelligence that animals already have. The later positivists were thus also compelled to deny the *essential psychic-mental differences between human and animal.*[24]

Only by understanding the three distinct sources of the three different types of knowledge can one also clearly grasp (1) the distinct ideal-typical leader qualities in these fields of knowledge (*homo religiosus,* sage, and scientist and technician), (2) the distinct sources and methods of their acquisition of knowledge (God contact of the charismatic leader, idea thinking, inductive and deductive inference), (3) the distinct forms of the development of the three types of knowledge, (4) the distinct social forms in which the acquisition and preservation of knowledge are embodied, (5) the different functions of such knowledge in human society, and (6) the different social origins of such knowledge—classes, vocations, estates.

Notes

1. The Age of Enlightenment one-sidedly saw only the conditioning of society by knowledge. It was an important realization of the nineteenth and twentieth centuries to see there was also a converse relation, that knowledge is conditioned by society.

2. The detailed epistemological reason for this proposition is found in my book *The Nature of Sympathy.*

3. See *The Nature of Sympathy* for a clarification of these issues.

4. See also *The Nature of Sympathy*, p. 122.

5. That cooperation is "productive," when correctly understood, is an important insight of Othmar Spann; cf. *System der Gesellschaftslehre*, Berlin, 1914.

6. A radical example is the withholding of the sacred writings of Hindu religion and metaphysics from the lowest caste, the Sundras. One might also think of the withholding of free reading of the Holy Scriptures by the medieval church from the laity, although this occurred only to a limited extent. This policy is similar to secret diplomacy.

7. I refer to the complete foundation of these laws of order contained in vol. 1 of my metaphysics, to be published soon. [See *Erkenntnislehre und Metaphysik*, ed. by Manfred S. Frings, vol. 2 of *Gesammelte Werke*.]

8. I say "coconditioned." To be rejected is sociologism, which is analogous to psychologism, for neither distinguishes forms of thinking and intuition from forms of being. Also, neither separates the successive, reflexive *cognition* of these forms from the forms themselves. Both reduce forms of being to forms of thinking and perception, as does Kant, but unlike Kant, sociologism reduces these objective forms to forms of work and "speech" in society. This theory of origins corresponds to a conventionalism in epistemology and logic first advocated by Hobbes ("Truth and falsehood are attributes of propositions, not things") and recently avowed by Poincaré. For sociologism, history and the entire scientific worldview is a "conventional fable." Bonald took a wrong turn in wanting to make social consensus the criterion of truth and placing all knowledge in the "tradition of language" while reducing language to primal revelation. His theory is merely an ecclesiastical-orthodox analogy to the positivist "sociologism" exemplified by Durkheim. Such false paths in sociology can be avoided if all functional forms of thought are reduced to *functionalized comprehension of essences* in the *things themselves*. In this way, the particular *selection* to which this functionalization is subject may be seen as the work of society and its *interest perspective* rather than a "pure" realm of essences. I have shown briefly that there *can* also be a "prelogical" level of society, as Lévy-Bruhl justifiably assumes. See my "Bemerkungen" on W. Jerusalem's paper in *Kölner Vierteljahrsschriften für Socialwissenschaft*, vol. 1, no. 3, 1921.

9. On such divisions based on patriarchal-totemistic culture, see Graebner, *Das Weltbild der Primitiven;* also Lévy-Bruhl, *Das Denken der Naturvölker*, Vienna, 1921, trans. Jerusalem.

10. See the conclusion of my essay "Die Idole der Selbsterkenntnis," in *Vom Umsturz der Werte* ["The Idols of Self Knowledge," in *Selected Philosophical Essays*, Evanston, Ill., Northwestern University Press, 1973, trans. David Lachterman, pp. 3–97.—Ed.] Thus the faculties of the psyche assumed by Plato correspond exactly—in accordance with his proposition that the state is a "great man"—to the natural estates he assumes are parts of the state.

11. In Germany, M. Weber, C. Schmitt in his distinguished book *Politische Theologie*, Munich, 1926, and O. Spengler in some of the penetrating insights

of his well-known work have also begun to develop these problems for the better-known areas of society. On the structural identities between political monarchies and monotheism, see Graebner, "Gottesglaube und Staatsgedanke," in *Das Weltbild der Primitiven*, pp. 109ff.

I have described such structural identities between Greek city particularism and Greek polytheism (and in Plato's pluralistic conception of "ideas"). I have also established an identity between the Stoic doctrine of the world as cosmopolis, a single, embracing community, and a large-scale empire in which increasing universalism and individualism are interdependent; between the conception of the world as a realm of levels of teleological forms and the feudal estate structure of society; between the images of world and psyche of Cartesianism and Malebranche and the absolute monarchy; between Calvinism, in which intermediary forces and secondary causes are eliminated, and a new, analogously founded sovereignty; between deism, in which God is conceived as an engineer and machinist, and free trade, political liberalism, associational psychology, and the static notion of "balance of power" in foreign policy; between the monadological system of Leibniz and the social individualism of the Enlightenment; between the conception of organic nature as "struggle for existence" (Marx, Malthus, Darwin) and the practical-ethical-utilitarian–class struggle attitude of the economic system of competition; between Kant's theory that the understanding must produce the order of nature and the moral world from a chaos of sensations and the development of the Prussian state (see my book *Die Ursachen des Deutschenhasses*, 1917, reprinted in vol. 4 of *Gesammelte Schriften*), and finally, between the religious thinking of Eastern orthodoxy and the sociological bases of czarism. Cf. also my discussion of structural likenesses between theism, materialism, and monism and certain constitutional forms of the state in *The Nature of Sympathy*. Cf. also Schmitt, *Politische Theologie*.

12. Cf. my *Nature of Sympathy*, p. 277ff.; also Graebner, *Das Weltbild der Primitiven*, p. 132: "In primitive thought attributes play a much larger role, substances a much smaller role, than with us, but the concepts of the animal and human organisms are more substance-like." Also see Lévy-Bruhl's *Denken der Naturvölker* and his new book, *La Mentalité primitive*, Paris, 1922 (*Primitive Mentality*, London, George Allen & Unwin, 1923, trans. Lilian A. Clare); see also Jerusalem's article in the volume I edited, *Versuche zu einer Soziologie des Wissens*, Munich, 1924. It would be a great mistake to think these analogies are mere primitive anthropomorphisms; they also occur in high cultures.

13. See my article "Weltanschauungssetzung," in *Schriften zur Soziologie und Weltanschauungslehre*.

14. The greatest categorial differences are most likely between matriarchal and patriarchal cultures. See Graebner, *Das Weltbild der Primitiven*.

15. See the chapter "Die geistige Einheit Europas" in *Der Genius des Krieges*, 1915.

16. I will only mention the most important ones here since I will deal in greater detail with such parallel coordinations in my *Philosophical Anthropol-*

ogy: (1) between developmental stages of a human's psychic functions up to the end of the second year, i.e., the actual "becoming human," and psychic functions and aptitudes of adult higher vertebrates (Edinger); (2) between the image of the human psyche altered by pathological symptoms and those animal psyches in which the said function is not yet developed (e.g., absence of frontal brain functions in apes); (3) between normal psychic behavior of primitive groups and pathological (or abnormal) psychic behavior of adults in higher levels of civilization (see Schilder, Storch, and others); (4) between the psychic life of primitives and human children (see W. Stern, E. Jaensch, Bühler, Koffka, Lévy-Bruhl); (5) between elimination of the higher psychic centers in the composition of the mass psyche in higher civilizations and the animal psyche, or animal societies (see Scheler, *Nature of Sympathy*); (6) between the moment-to-moment formation of the mass psyche within civilization and the more enduring direction of the psyche within primitive hordes (see Freud, *Group Psychology and the Analysis of the Ego,* New York, W. W. Norton & Co., 1959, trans. James Strachey); (7) between mass psyche and pathological or abnormal consciousness (hysteria, depersonalization, hypnosis; see Freud, *Group Psychology,* and Schilder, *Über das Wesen der Hypnose,* 1912); (8) between the behavior of masses and children; (9) between normal child behavior and pathological adult behavior; (10) between growth and decay of psychic functions in individual stages of life and the parallel stages of aging peoples and civilizations (see my article "Altern der Kulturen," in *Kölner Vierteljahrsschrift für Sozialwissenschaft*); (11) between the psychic life of children and women (the childlike "constitution" of the female organism), and also between the psychology of the sexes in matriarchal and patriarchal cultures; (12) between the mentality and degree of cultivation of the lower classes and the cultivation of elites that lived two, three, or more generations earlier ("stratification theory" of knowledge and class structure).

17. Cf. Graebner, *Das Weltbild der Primitiven,* ch. 4, "Weltanschauung und Sprachen."

18. Cf. Tönnies's profound attempt to write a history of philosophical terminology, *Philosophische Terminologie in psychologisch-soziologischer Ansicht,* 1906. This was originally published as "Philosophical Terminology" (Welby Prize Essay, 1898), *Mind* 8 (1899), 289–332, 467–91; 9 (1900), 46–61, trans. Mrs. Bosanquet.

19. The association of the "Word of the Holy Ghost" with the groups, techniques, and authorities in Christian religious communities, for example, papacy, church council, parish, and the "spiritus sanctus internus" of Luther, are perhaps their most important socioreligious feature.

20. Cf. *La Mentalité primitive,* p. 520, *Primitive Mentality,* p. 445; "In it space is felt rather than imagined; its directions are weighted with qualities, and each of its regions, as we have already seen (*vide supra,* ch. VII, pp. 208–215), participates in all that is usually found there."

21. On the lack of a sense for secondary causes among primitives, see Lévy-Bruhl, *La Mentalité primitive,* especially the conclusion.

22. On the issue of "insight" in animals, cf. Wolfgang Köhler, *Intelligenzprüfungen bei Menschenaffen,* 2nd edition, Berlin, 1921 (*The Mentality of Apes,* New York, Harcourt Brace, 1925, trans. Ella Winter); see also the partly critical discussions in K. Bühler, *Die geistige Entwickling des Kindes,* 3rd edition, Jena, 1923 (*The Mental Development of Children: A Summary of Modern Psychological Theory,* New York, Harcourt Brace, 1930, trans. Oscar Oeser); K. Koffka, *Die Grundlagen der psychischen Entwicklung,* Osterwieck am Harz, 1921 (*The Growth of the Mind: An Introduction to Child-Psychology,* New York, Harcourt Brace, 1924, trans. Robert Morris Ogden); O. Selz, *Über die Gesetze des geordneten Denkverlaufs* (Bonn, 1913–22); and G. Kafka, "Tierpsychologie," in *Handbuch der vergleichenden Psychologie,* Muen, 1922, vol. 1.

23. Cf. E. Jaensch, *Über den Aufbau der Wahrnehmungswelt,* Leipzig, 1924.

24. The essential distinction between human and animal should not be confused with empirical differences, that is, the anatomical, physiological, psychological species differences between primitive humans and apes. See my forthcoming *Philosophical Anthropology;* see also my essay "Zur Idee des Menschen," in *Vom Umsturz der Werte.*

III

VALUES AND SOCIAL LIFE

10

The Spheres of Values

In the *totality* of the realm of values there exists a singular order, an "*order of ranks*" that all values possess among themselves. It is because of this that a value is "*higher*" or "*lower*" than another one. This order lies in the *essence* of values themselves, as does the difference between "positive" and "negative" values. It does not belong simply to "values known" by us.[1]

The fact that one value is "higher" than another is apprehended in a special act of value cognition: the act of *preferring*. One must not assume that the height of a value is "*felt*" in the same manner as the value itself, and that the higher value is *subsequently* "preferred" or "placed after." Rather, the height of a value is "given," by virtue of its essence, only *in* the act of preferring. Whenever this is denied, one falsely equates this preferring with "*choosing*" in general, i.e., an act of conation. Without doubt, choosing must be grounded in the cognition of a higher value, for we choose that purpose among others which has its foundation in a higher value. But "preferring" occurs in the absence of all conation, choosing, and willing. For instance, we can say, "I prefer roses to carnations," *without* thinking of a choice. All "choosing" takes place between different deeds. By contrast, preferring also occurs with regard to any of the goods and values. This first kind of preferring (i.e., the preferring between different *goods*) may also be called *empirical* preferring.

On the other hand "preferring" is a priori if it occurs between different *values themselves*—independent of "goods." Such preferring always encompasses whole (and indefinitely wide) complexes of goods. He who "prefers" the noble to the agreeable will end up in an (inductive) experience of a *world of goods* very different from the one in which he who does not do so will find himself. The "height of a value" is "given" not "prior" to preferring, but *in* preferring. Hence, when-

Reprinted with permission from *Formalism in Ethics and Non-formal Ethics of Values*, trans. Manfred S. Frings and Roger L. Funk (Evanston, Ill.: Northwestern University Press, 1973), pp. 87–109. This was originally published in two parts as *Der Formalismus in der Ethik und die materiale Werthethik*, in *Jahrbuch für Philosophie und phänomenologische Forschung* (Halle: Niemeyer, 1913, 1916).

ever we choose an end founded in a lower value, there must exist a *deception of preferring*. But this is not the place to discuss the possibility of such a deception.

But one may not say that the "being-higher" of a value only "means" that it is the value "preferred." For if the height of a value is given "in" preferring, this height is nevertheless a relation in the *essence* of the values concerned. Therefore, the "*ordered ranks of values*" are themselves absolutely *invariable,* whereas the "rules of preferring" are, in principle, variable throughout history (a variation which is very different from the apprehension of new values.)

When an act of preferring takes place, it is not necessary that a multiplicity of values be given in feeling, nor is it necessary that such a multiplicity serve as a "foundation" for the act of preferring. . . .

Since all values stand essentially in an order of ranks—i.e., since all values are, in relation to each other, higher or lower—and since these relations are comprehensible only "in" preferring or rejecting them, the "feeling" of values has its foundation, by essential necessity, in "preferring" and "placing after." The feeling of values is by no means a "foundation" for the manner of preferring, as though preferring were "added" to the values comprehended in a primary intention of feeling as only a secondary act. Rather, all *widening* of the value range (e.g., of an individual) takes place only "in" preferring and placing after. Only those values which are originally "given" in these acts can *secondarily* be "felt." Hence, the *structure of preferring and placing after circumscribes* the value qualities that we feel.

Therefore, the order of the ranks of values can *never be deduced or derived.* Which value is "higher" can be comprehended only through the acts of preferring and placing after. There exists here an *intuitive "evidence of preference"* that cannot be replaced by logical deduction.

But we can and must ask whether or not there are a priori *essential interconnections* between the *higher* and *lower levels* of a value and its *other* essential properties.

We can find, in this respect, different characters of values—already to be found in everyday experiences—with which their "height" seems to grow. But these may be traced back to *one* factor.

It appears that values are "higher" the *more* they *endure* and the *less* they partake in "*extension*" and *divisibility.* They are higher the *less they are "founded"* through other values and the "*deeper*" the "*satisfaction*" connected with feeling them. Moreover, they are higher the *less* the feeling of them is *relative* to the *positing* of a specific bearer of "feeling" and "preferring."

1. Since time immemorial, the wisdom of life has been to prefer

enduring goods to transient and changing ones. But for philosophy this "wisdom of life" is only a "problem." For if it is a matter of "*goods*," and one understands "*endurance*" in terms of the objective time in which they exist, this proposition makes little sense. "Fire" or "water" or any mechanical accident, for example, can destroy a work of art of the highest value. As Pascal states, a drop of "hot water" can destroy the health and life of the healthiest being; a "brick" can extinguish the light of a genius! . . .

The aforementioned proposition takes on a very different meaning if it is the higher *values* (and not goods) that, in their relation to lower values, are given in "*enduring*" by a phenomenal necessity. "*Endurance*" is, of course, basically an *absolute* and *qualitative phenomenon of time*. It has nothing to do with an absence of "succession." Endurance is, *eo ipso*, a positive mode, i.e., a mode of contents filling time as well as succession.[2] Whatever we may call "enduring" in this sense of the term may be relative (with respect to something else); however, endurance itself is not relative but a phenomenon absolutely different from "succession" (or change). A value is *enduring* through its quality of having the phenomenon of being "able" to exist through time, no matter how long its thing-bearer may exist. "Endurance" already belongs to something of value, in the particular sense of "being of value." This is the case, for instance, when we execute the act of loving a person (on the basis of his personal value)! The *phenomenon of endurance* is implicit in both the *value* to which we are directed and the experienced value of the *act of love;* hence there is also an implicit "*unceasing endurance*" of these values and this act. An inner attitude which would correspond to expressions like "I love you *now*" or "for a certain time" therefore contradicts the essential interconnection concerned. But there *is* this essential interconnection, no matter how long *in practice* love toward a real person may last in a span of objective time. If, on the other hand, this factual quality of the love for a person is in practical experience *not* filled in terms of endurance, so that we "do not any longer love" at a certain time, we tend to say, "I was mistaken; I never loved this person; there were only common interests that I held to be love," or "I was deceived by this person (and his value)." For there belongs to the *essence* of a genuine act of love a *sub specie quadam aeterni*. This shows us, too, that the mere de facto endurance of a partnership does not at all prove that love is the bond on which it rests. For a partnership or a bond of interests and habits can last for any length of time—as long as, or longer than, a factual "love between persons." Nevertheless, it lies in the *essence* of a *bond of interests,* as opposed to love and *its* implicit values, i.e., in the essence of such an intention and its own implicit value—namely, the value of use-fulness—to be "*transient.*" Something sensibly agreeable or its respec-tive "good," which we enjoy, may last for any length of (objective) time. Likewise, the factual *feeling* of the agreeable. But it belongs to the *essence* of this value, as opposed to, say, the value of health, even more to the value of "cognition," to be given "as variable." This vari-ableness is implicit in any act of apprehending the value of agreeable-ness.

All this becomes clear in considering the qualitatively and basically different *acts* in which we feel values and the very *values* of these ex-periences.[3] Thus, it lies in the *essence* of "blissfulness" and its oppo-site, "despair," to *persist* and "endure" throughout the vicissitudes of "happiness" and "unhappiness," no matter how long they may last in *objective* time. Likewise, it lies in the essence of "happiness" and "un-happiness," to persist and endure throughout the vicissitudes of "joy" and "suffering,"[4] and in the essence of "joy" and "suffering," in turn, to persist and endure throughout the vicissitudes of (vital) "comfort" and "discomfort." And, again, it lies in the essence of "comfort" and "discomfort" to persist and endure throughout changes in sensible states of well-being and pain. In the very "quality" of these feeling experiences there also lies, by essential necessity, "*endurability.*" Whenever, to whomever, and however long they are factually given, they are given as "enduring" or as "varying." Without having to wait for any experience of factual endurance, we experience in them a cer-tain "endurability" and, with this, a certain measure of temporal "ex-tendedness" in our souls, as well as a personal "permeation" by them as belonging to their *essence.*

No doubt, therefore, this "criterion" of the height of a value is of significance. For the lowest values are at the same time essentially the "*most transient*" ones; the highest values, at the same time "*eternal*" ones. And this is quite independent of any empirical "habitability" of mere sensible feeling or similar factors which belong only to psycho-physical characteristics of special *bearers.*

But whether or not this "criterion" can also be considered an origi-nal criterion for the height of a value is another question.

2. There is also no question about the fact that values are "higher" *the less they are divisible,* that is, the *less* they must be *divided* in *par-ticipation by several.* The fact that the participation of several in "ma-terial" goods is possible only by dividing these goods (e.g., a piece of cloth, a loaf of bread) has this final *phenomenological* basis: the *values* of the *sensibly agreeable* are clearly *extensive in their essence,* and their felt experiences occur as localized and as extensive in the body.[5] For

example, the aggreeableness of sweet, etc., is spread over sugar, and the corresponding sensible feeling-state over the "tongue." From this simple phenomenological fact, based on the essence of this kind of value and this particular feeling-state that corresponds to it, it follows that *material "goods"* can only be distributed when they are *divided,* and that their value corresponds to their material extension—to the extent that they are still unformed, i.e., when they are "pure" material goods. Thus a piece of cloth is, more or less, double the *worth* of one-half of it. The height of the value conforms in this case to the extension of its bearer. In strict contrast to this there stands a "work of art," for example, which is "indivisible" and of which there is no "piece." It is therefore essentially impossible for one and the same value of the value series of the "sensibly agreeable" to be enjoyed by several beings *without* the division of its bearer and of the value itself. For this reason there are also, in the *essence* of this value modality, "conflicts of interest" relative to the striving for a realization of these values, and relative to their enjoyment—quite independent of the amount of goods (amount being important only for the socioeconomic value of material goods.) This, however, also implies that it belongs to the *essence* of these values to *divide,* not to unite, the individuals who feel them.[6]

The most extreme opposite of these values, the values of the "*holy,*" of "*cognition,*" and of the "*beautiful,*" etc., as well as their corresponding spiritual feeling-states, have a totally different character. There is no participation in extension and divisibility with these values; nor is there any need to divide their bearers if they are to be felt and experienced by any *number* of beings. A work of spiritual culture can be simultaneously apprehended by any number of beings and can be felt and enjoyed in its value. It lies in the essence of values of this kind to be *communicable without limit* and without any division and diminution (even though this proposition seemingly becomes relative by reason of the existence of their bearers and their materiality, by the limits of possible access to these bearers, e.g., in buying books, or the inaccessibility of material bearers of a work of art). Nothing *unites* beings more immediately and intimately, however, than the common worship and adoration of the "*holy,*" which by its nature excludes a "material" bearer, though not a symbolic one. This pertains, first, to the "absolute" and "infinitely holy," the infinitely holy person—the "*divine.*" This value, the "divine," is in principle "proper" to any being just because it is the *most indivisible* value. No matter how men have been *divided* by what came to be considered "holy" in history (e.g., wars of religion, denominational quarrels), it lies in the *essence* of the *intention toward the holy* to *unite and join together.* All possible divisions are based solely on *symbols and techniques,* not on the holy *itself.*

Although we are concerned here, as these examples show, with essential interconnections, the question remains whether the criteria of extension and divisibility reveal the basic nature of "higher" and "lower" values.

3. I maintain that a value *B* is the *"foundation"* of a value *A* if a certain value *A* can only be given on the condition of the givenness of a certain value *B,* and this by virtue of an essential lawful necessity. If this is so, the "founding" value, i.e., the value *B,* is in each case the *"higher"* value. Thus the value of what is *"useful"* is "founded" in the value of what is *"agreeable."* For the "useful" is the value of something that reveals itself as a "means" to something agreeable, not in terms of a conclusion, but in terms of immediate intuition. . . .

No matter how independent of *spiritual* values (e.g., values of cognition, beauty, etc.) the value series of the *noble* and *vulgar* may be, it remains "founded" in these values. Life *has* these values in fact only insofar as *life* itself (in all its forms) *is* a bearer of values that take on certain heights in an absolutely objective scale. But such an "order of value ranks" is comprehensible only through *spiritual* acts that are not vitally conditioned. For instance, it would be an "anthropomorphism" to consider man the most valuable living being if the value of this value cognition, with *all* its values (including the value of the cognition that "man is the most valuable living being"), were "relative to man." But this proposition is "true," independent of man, "for" man ("for" in the objective sense of the word). *Life simpliciter* has a value, apart from the differentiations among vital value qualities, only insofar as there are spiritual values and spiritual acts through which they are grasped. If values were "relative" to life alone, *life itself would have no value.* It would be a value-indifferent being.

However, *all* possible values are "founded" in the *value of an infinitely personified spirit* and its correlative *"world of values."* Acts which comprehend values comprehend absolutely objective values only if they are executed *"in"* this world of values, and values are absolute values only if they appear in this realm.

4. The *"depth of contentment,"* too, is a criterion of the heights of values. This depth accompanies the feeling of a value height. But the height does not *consist* in this depth. Yet it is an essential interconnection that a *"higher* value" yields a *"deeper* contentment."[7] "Contentment" here has nothing to do with *pleasure,* much as "pleasure" may result from it. "Contentment" is an *experience of fulfillment;* it sets in only if an intention toward a value is fulfilled through the appearance

of this value. There is no "contentment" *without* the *acceptance* of objective values. . . . But we must distinguish again between the "degree" of contentment and its "*depth*," which alone concerns us here. The contentment in feeling one value is deeper than the contentment in feeling another value if the former proves to be *independent* of the latter while the latter remains dependent on the former. For instance, it is a quite peculiar phenomenon that sensuous enjoyment or a harmlessly trivial delight (e.g., attending a party or going for a walk) will bring us full "contentment" *only* when we feel "content" in the more central sphere of our life, where everything is "serious." It is only against this background of a deeper contentment that a fully content laughter can resound about the most trivial joys. Conversely, if the more central sphere is not content, there arises a "discontentment" and a restless search for *pleasure values* that at once replace a full contentment in feeling the lower values concerned. One can draw a conclusion from this: the many forms of hedonism always reveal a token of "discontentment" with regard to higher values. There exists a reciprocal relation, then, between the degrees of *searching* for pleasure and the depth of contentment in a value of the value series in question.

Nevertheless, on whatever essential interconnections the above four criteria of value heights may rest, they do not give us the *ultimate* meaning of value heights. Is there another such . . . principle, then, one that can bring us nearer to the meaning of "being-higher," and from which the above criteria may be derived?

5. Whatever "objectivity" and "factual nature" are attributable to all "values," and however *independent* their interrelations may be of the reality and the real connections of goods in which they are real, there is yet another distinguishing element among values that has nothing to do with apriority or aposteriority: this is the *level* of the "*relativity* of values," or their *relationship* to "*absolute* values." [8]

The basic mutual interconnection between the act and its correlate implies that we must not presuppose any objective existence of values and their types (let alone of real goods that bear values of a certain kind) unless we can find types of acts and functions *belonging* to the experience of such types of values. For instance, for a non-sensible being there are no values of the agreeable. Indeed, such a being may know that "there are sensibly feeling beings," and that "they feel values of the agreeable"; and it may also know the *value* of this fact and its exemplifications. But the *value* of the *agreeable itself* does not exist for such an imaginary creature. We cannot assume that God, like men and animals, has a *lived experience* of all values of the agreeable. In this particular sense I maintain that the values of the agreeable and disagreeable are *"relative"* to a "sensibly feeling being," just as the values of "noble and vulgar" are relative to "living beings" in general. In strict contrast to this, however, I maintain that *absolute values* are those that exist in "pure" feeling (and preferring and loving), i.e., they exist in a type of feeling that is *independent* of the *nature* of sensibility and of life as such. This feeling possesses its own functional characteristics and laws. Among the values belonging to this feeling are *moral* values. In *pure* feeling we may be able to "understand" the feeling of sensible values (i.e., in a feeling manner) without performing sensible feeling-functions through which we (or others) enjoy the agreeable, but we cannot feel them in this manner. From this we infer that God can "understand" pain, for instance, but that he does so without feeling pain.

Such relativity of the being of *kinds* of values has, of course, *nothing* to do with another relativity: that of the *kinds of goods* that are the *bearers* of such values. For kinds of goods are, *in addition,* relative to the special factual psychophysical constitution of the real being that has such goods. The fact that the same object can be poisonous for one species and nutritious for another, for instance, or that something may be agreeable to the perverted drives of one living being and "disagreeable" or "harmful" to the normal drives of another being of the same species, determines only a relativity of values *in relation to* the *goods* in question. But this relativity in no way represents an ontic relativity of the values themselves. It is one of a "second order" only, which has nothing to do with the relativity of the above-mentioned "first order." One cannot reduce this relativity of *kinds* of values to that of goods (*in relation* to kinds of values). Both orders are essentially different. . . .

Taking the words *relative* and *absolute* in *this* sense, I assert it to be an essential interconnection that values given in immediate intuition *"as higher"* are values that are given as *nearer* to *absolute* values *in* feeling and preferring (and not by way of deliberation). Entirely outside the sphere of "judgment" or "deliberation" there is an *immediate* feeling of the "relativity" of a value. And for this feeling the variability of a relative value in comparison with the concomitant constancy of a less "relative" value (no matter if variability and constancy pertain to "endurance," "divisibility," "depth of contentment") is a *confirmation,* but not a *proof.* Thus the value of the cognition of a truth, or the value of the silent beauty of a work of art, has a *phenomenal detachment* from the concomitant feeling of our *life*—above all, from our sensible feeling-states. Such a value is also quite independent of an estimative deliberation about the permanence of such beauty or truth with regard to the "experiences of life," which tend more to detract us from true absolute values than to bring us nearer to them. In living an act of pure love toward a person, the *value* of this person is detached from all simultaneously felt value levels of our own personal world of values when we experience these as connected with our sense and feeling of life. Again, this value is also quite independent of any estimative deliberation about the permanence that an act of pure loving may have through happiness and sorrow, the inherent or accidental fate of life. *Implicit* in the very kind of the given value experience there is a *guarantee* (and not a "conclusion") that there is here an absolute value. This *evidence* of an absolute value stems neither from an estimative deliberation about the permanence it may have in practical life nor from the universality of a judgment which holds that "this value is absolute in *all* moments of our lives." Rather, it is the *felt absoluteness* of this value that makes us feel that a defection from it in favor of other values constitutes "*possible* guilt" as well as a "falling away" from the height of value experience which we had just reached. . . .

A Priori Relations of Rank among Value Modalities

The most important and most fundamental a priori relations obtain as an *order of ranks* among the systems of qualities of nonformal values which we call *value modalities*. They constitute the *nonformal* a priori proper in the intuition of values and the intuition of preferences. . . . The ultimate divisions of value qualities that are presupposed for these essential interconnections must be as independent of all factual goods and the special organizations of living beings that feel values as is the order of the ranks of the value modalities.

Rather than giving a full development and establishment of these systems of qualities and their implicit laws of preferring, the following presents an explanation through examples of the kinds of a priori orders of ranks among values.

1. The values ranging from *the agreeable to the disagreeable* represent a sharply delineated value modality. The function of *sensible feeling* (with its modes of enjoying and suffering) is correlative to this modality. The respective feeling-states, the so-called feelings of sensation, are pleasure and pain. As in all value modalities, there are values of things, . . . values of *feeling-functions*, and values of *feeling-states*.

This modality is "*relative*" to beings endowed with sensibility in general. But it is relative *neither* to a specific species, e.g., man, *nor* to specific things or events of the real world that are "agreeable" or "disagreeable" to a being of a particular species. Although one type of event may be agreeable to one man and disagreeable to another (or

agreeable and disagreeable to different animals), the difference between the values of agreeable and disagreeable as such is an *absolute*
difference, clearly given prior to any cognition of things.

The proposition that the agreeable is preferable to the disagreeable
(*ceteris paribus*) is not based on observation and induction. The preference lies in the essential contents of these values as well as in the
nature of sensible feelings. If a traveler or a historian or a zoologist
were to tell us that this preference is reversed in a certain kind of animal, we would "a priori" disbelieve his story. We would say that this
is impossible unless it is only *things* different from ours that this animal feels are disagreeable and agreeable, or unless its preferring the
disagreeable to the agreeable is based on a value of a *modality* (perhaps unknown to us) that is "higher" than that of the agreeable and
the disagreeable. In the latter case the animal would only "put up
with" the disagreeable in preferring the value for the extra modality.
There may also be cases of perverted drives in this animal, allowing it
to experience as agreeable those things that are *detrimental* to life. The
state of affairs in all of these examples, as well as that which our proposition expresses, namely, that the agreeable is preferable to the disagreeable, also serves as a *law of understanding* external expressions
of life and concrete (e.g., historical) valuation (even one's *own*, e.g., in
remembering); our proposition is a *presupposition* of all observation
and induction, and it is "a priori" to all ethnological experience.

Nor can this proposition and its respective facts be "explained" by
way of evolutionary theories. It is nonsense to say that values (and
their laws of preference) "developed" as *signs* of kinetic combinations
that proved purposeful for the individual or its species. Such a theory
can explain only the accompanying feeling-*states* that are connected
with impulsive actions directed toward things. But the *values themselves* and their *laws* of *preferring* could *never* be thus explained. For
the latter are independent of all specific organizations of living beings.

Certain groups of consecutive values (technical values[9] and symbolic values) correspond to these self values of the modality of the
agreeable and the disagreeable. But they do not concern us here.

2. The essence of values correlated to *vital feeling* differs sharply
from the above modality. Its thing values, insofar as they are self values, are such qualities as those encompassed by the "*noble*" and the
"*vulgar*" (and by the "good" in the pregnant sense of "excellent" as
opposed to "bad" rather than "evil").[10] All corresponding consecutive
values (technical and symbolic) belong to the sphere denoted by
"*weal,*" or "*well-being.*"[11] They are *subordinated* to the noble and its
opposite. The feeling-states of this modality include all modes of the

feelings of life (e.g., the feelings of "quickening" and "declining" life, the feelings of health and illness, the feeling of aging and oncoming death, the feelings of "weakness," "strength," etc.). Certain emotional reactions also belong to this modality—(a certain kind of) "being glad about" or "being sad about," drive reactions such as "courage," "anxiety," revengeful impulses, ire, etc. Here we cannot even indicate the tremendous richness of these value qualities and their correlates.

Vital values form an entirely *original* modality. They cannot be "reduced" to the values of the agreeable and the useful, nor can they be reduced to spiritual values. Previous ethical theories made a *basic mistake* in ignoring this fact. . . .

The particular character of this modality lies in the fact that "*life*" is a *genuine essence* and not an "empirical generic conception" that contains only "common properties" of all living organisms. When this fact is misconceived, the uniqueness of vital values is overlooked. We will not go into this in further detail here.

3. The realm of *spiritual values* is distinct from that of vital values as an original modal unity. In the kind of their *givenness*, spiritual values have a peculiar detachment from and independence of the spheres of the lived body and the environment. Their unity reveals itself in the clear evidence that vital values "ought" to be sacrificed for them. The functions and acts in which they are apprehended are functions of *spiritual* feeling and acts of *spiritual* preferring, loving, and hating. They are set off from like-named *vital* functions and acts by pure phenomenological evidence as well as by their *own proper lawfulness* (which *cannot be reduced* to any "*biological*" lawfulness).

The main types of spiritual values are the following: (1) the values of "*beautiful*" and "*ugly*," together with the whole range of purely aesthetic values; (2) the values of "*right*" and "*wrong*," . . . objects that are "values" and wholly different from what is "correct" and "incorrect" according to a law, which form the ultimate phenomenal basis of the idea of the objective *order of right*, . . . an order that is independent of the idea of "law," the idea of the state, and the idea of the life-community on which the state rests (it is especially independent of all positive legislation);[12] (3) the values of the "*pure cognition of truth*," whose realization is sought in *philosophy* (in contrast to positive "science," which is guided by the aim of controlling natural appearances).[13] Hence "*values of science*" are consecutive values of the values of the cognition of truth. So-called *cultural values* in general are the consecutive (technical and symbolic) values of *spiritual* values and belong to the value sphere of *goods* (e.g., art treasures, scientific institutions, positive legislation, etc.). The correlative feeling-states of spiritual values—for instance, the feeling-states of spiritual joy and sorrow (as opposed to the vital "being gay" and "not being gay")—possess the phenomenal quality of appearing *without mediation*. That is to say, they do not appear on an "ego" as its states, nor does an antecedent givenness of the lived body of a person serve as a condition of their appearance. Spiritual feeling-states vary *independent* of changes in vital feeling-states (and, of course, sensible feeling-states). Their variations are directly dependent upon the variations of the values of the *objects themselves* and occur according to their own proper laws.

Finally, there are the reactions belonging to this modality, including "pleasing" and "displeasing," "approving" and "disapproving," "respect" and "disrespect," "retributive conation" (as opposed to the vital impulses of revenge) and "spiritual sympathy" (which is the foundation of friendship, for instance).

4. Values of the last modality are those of the *holy* and the *unholy*. This modality differs sharply from the above modalities. It forms a unit of value qualities not subject to further definition. Nevertheless, these values have *one* very definite condition of intention as "absolute objects." This expression, however, refers *not* to a specific or definable *class* of objects, but (in principle) to *any* object given in the "absolute sphere." Again, this modality is quite independent of all that has been considered "holy" by different peoples at various times, such as holy things, powers, persons, institutions, and the like (i.e., from ideas of fetishism to the purest conceptions of God). These latter problems do not belong to an a priori *phenomenology of values . . .* and the theory of ordered ranks of values.[14] They concern the *positive representations of goods* within this value sphere. With regard to the values of the holy, however, *all* other values are at the same time given as symbols for these values.

The feeling-states belonging to this modality range from "blissfulness" to "despair"; they are independent of "happiness" and "unhappiness," whether it be in occurrence, duration, or change. In a certain sense these feeling-states indicate the "nearness" or the "remoteness" of the divine in experience.

"Faith" and "lack of faith," "awe," "adoration," and analogous attitudes are specific reactions in this modality.

However, the act through which we *originally* apprehend the value of the holy in an act of a specific kind of *love* (whose value direction *precedes* and *determines* all pictorial representations and concepts of holy objects); that is to say, in essence the act is directed toward persons, or toward something of the *form of a personal being, no matter what* content or what *"conception"* of a personhood is implied. The self value in the sphere of the values of the "holy" is therefore, by essential necessity, a *"value of the person."*

The values of things and forms of worship implicit in cults and sacraments are consecutive values (technical and symbolic) of all holy values of the person. They represent genuine "symbolic values," not mere "symbols of values."

Notes

1. On the other hand, one cannot reduce this division to one of positive and negative values or to one of "greater" and "smaller" values. Brentano's axiom that a value which is the sum of the values W_1 and W_2 must be a higher value (a value to be preferred, according to his definition), that W_1 or W_2 is not an autonomous value proposition but only the application of an arithmetic proposition to values, indeed, only to symbols of values. It cannot be that a value is "higher" than another simply because it is a sum of values. For it is characteristic of the contrast between "higher" and "lower" values that an infinite magnitude of a value, say, the agreeable (or the disagreeable), never yields any magnitude of, say, the noble (or the base) or of a spiritual value (of cognition, for instance). The *sum* of values is to be preferred to single values; but it is an error on Brentano's part to assume that the higher value is in this case to be identified with the one to be "preferred." For preferring is (essentially) the *access* to the "higher value," but in individual cases it is subject to "deception." Besides, the "greater value" in this case pertains only to the act of "choosing," not to the act of "preferring." For the act of preferring always takes place in the sphere of a value series that has a specific "position" in the order of values. Finally, I cannot agree with Brentano when he leaves it up to *historical relativity* to determine what the nonformal ranks of values actually are, when, for instance, he does not wish to decide (see the notes to his *Vom Ursprung sittlicher Erkenntnis*) whether an "act of cognition" is of higher value than an "act of noble love" (as Aristotle and the Greeks held) or whether the opposite is the case (as the Christians held), in other words, when he does not make a decision on the basis of the nonformal values themselves.

2. It is false to maintain, as, e.g., David Hume does, that time belongs only to a "succession" of different contents, i.e., to assume that if the world consisted of only one and the same content, there would be no *time,* and that "duration" therefore consists only in the relation of two successions of different speeds. "Duration" is no mere difference of succession but a positive quality that can be intuited without any appearance of succession.

3. The experience of values and the value of this experience are, of course, to be distinguished.

4. Taken as phenomenological unities.

5. *Extensive* does not mean "in a spatial order" or "measurable." A pain

in the leg or a sensible feeling is, according to its nature, localized and extensive, but is in no way ordered spatially or "in" space.

6. "Cofeeling" is least possible in feeling these values. It is not possible to cofeel a sensible pleasure as one can a joy, or to cofeel a pain (in the strict sense) as one can a sorrow. See *The Nature of Sympathy.*

7. H. Cornelius, *Einleitung in die Philosophie,* Leipzig, Teubner, 1911, has attempted a subtle reduction of the higher value to the value of deeper contentment.

8. Because a "relative" value is relative does not mean that it is a "subjective" value. For instance, a hallucinated body-thing is "relative" to an individual, yet this object is not "subjective" in the way that feeling is. An emotive hallucination, for example, is *both* "subjective" and "relative" to the individual. And a "real" feeling is "subjective," but not "relative," to an individual, even when only the individual concerned has access to the cognition of its reality. On the other hand a mirror image, as a physical phenomenon, is "relative" to the mirror and the mirrored object, but is not relative to the individual.

9. They are in part technical values concerning the *production* of agreeable things and are unified in the concept of the "useful" (*values of civilization*), and in part values concerning the enjoyment of agreeable things (*luxury values*).

10. One also uses "noble" and its opposite with respect to vital values ("noble horse," "noble tree," "noble race," "nobility," etc.).

11. "Weal" and "well-being" therefore do not coincide with vital values in general; the value of well-being is determined by the extent to which the individual or the community, which can be in a good or a bad state, is *noble* or *base.* On the other hand, "weal" is superior as a vital value to mere "usefulness" (and "agreeableness"), and the well-being of a community is superior to the sum of its interests (as a society).

12. "Law" is only a consecutive value for the self value of the "order of right"; positive law (of a state) is the consecutive value for the (objective) "order of right" which is valid in the state and which lawmakers *and* judges must realize.

13. We speak of the value of "cognition," not of the value of "truth." Truth does *not* belong among the values.

14. Thus, e.g., an oath is an affirmation and a promise with reference to the value of the holy, no matter what is holy to the man concerned, no matter by what he swears.

11

The Experience of the Value Nature of the Collectivity

Just as the person discovers every psychic experience against the co-given background of a stream of such experiences, and every object of outer perception against the background of and as a "part" of a nature that is spatially and temporally endless, so also in every execution of an act is the person given to himself in self-experience as a *member* of a *community of persons which encompasses* him. Whatever the type of this community, simultaneity and succession (of generations) are at first still *undifferentiated*. From an ethical viewpoint this experience of a person's necessary membership in a social sphere appears in the *co-responsibility* for the total effective activity of the sphere. With regard to the possible factualness of community, it appears in *reexperiencing and coexperiencing, refeeling and cofeeling,* as the basic acts of inner perception of the other. At least the very *sense* of community and its *possible* existence is not an assumption that requires empirical establishment, because in certain classes of acts the intention toward a possible community is cogiven *by essential necessity* with the nature of these acts themselves. It is, rather, an assumption that is conjoined with the sense of a *person as originally* and *essentially* as it is with that of the *outer and inner worlds*.

A great deal of importance rests on this *equal originality*. For the existence or the position of "community" in general is neither ethically nor epistemologically conjoined with the existence (or the position) of a *world of bodies* (as I have shown in the appendix to my work on sympathetic feelings). And this is also the *highest* philosophical reason why the sciences of community and history and their basic givens are not dependent on the natural sciences and *their* basic givens; the former are "autonomous" with respect to the latter. The constitution of the conceptual unities of these human sciences—the unities of simultaneity as well as those of succession, e.g., family, tribe, people, nation,

Reprinted with permission from *Formalism in Ethics and Non-formal Ethics of Values,* pp. 519–38.

cultural unit, or age, period, etc.—does not require any regression to existing scientific unities of reality, for example, to those of geography (territories), or to scientific-biological theories of race. Basic details in this regard must be more closely investigated in the philosophy of history and sociology. Only a mundane *correlate* is necessarily in the essence of a social unit. . . .

However, as we have shown, the existence and assumption of a community is not founded on the existence or position of an objective *inner world* or of something psychic.[1]

Understanding and coexperiencing (including the inner self-perception of the other) necessarily preclude such objectification, although they are the first condition of knowledge of the other's psychic sphere. And one's own psychic sphere is constituted only in differentiating it from that of the other.

Hence both community and history are psychophysically *indifferent* concepts.

Thus not only does everyone discover himself against a background of, and at the same time as a "member" of, a totality of interconnections of experience which have somehow become concentrated, and which are *called* in their temporal extension *history,* in their simultaneous extension *social unit;* but as a moral subject in this whole, everyone is *also* given as a "person *acting with others,*" as a "man with others," and as "coresponsible" for everything morally relevant in this totality.

We must designate as *collective persons* the various *centers of experiencing* . . . in this endless totality of living with one another. . . .

. . . according to its meaning a social unit is a totality *without an end.* Just as it belongs to the essence of any social unit to be a partial manifestation of a concrete collective person, so also does it belong to the essence of any given *social unit* to be a *member* of a social unit encompassing it, and to the essence of any kind of a given *collective person* also or simultaneously to be a *member* of a collective person encompassing it. These are strictly a priori propositions that compel us, by virtue of their apriority, to transcend in spirit any given, factual, earthly community, i.e., to see it as a member of a community encompassing it. Whether or not this transcending act finds "fulfillment" in a factual experience is of no consequence for the sense and nature of this "consciousness-of." An imaginary Robinson Crusoe endowed with cognitive-theoretical faculties would also coexperience his *being a member of a social unit* in his experiencing the *lack* of fulfillment of acts of act-types constituting a person in general.[2] For it is by virtue of their intentional *essence,* and not on the basis of their contingent *ob-*

jects or what they empirically have in common, that these acts are factual acts, that is, *social* acts, acts that find their fulfillment only in a possible community. Among these acts are acts of the true *kinds* of love (which are listed in the above-mentioned work); such acts are capable of and require "fulfillment," and I have distinguished them from all differentiations of love resulting from the nature of factual and experienced objects.[3] Acts of commanding, obeying, ordering, promising, vowing, and cofeeling also belong to this class. In contrast to these are acts of a *singularizing* nature (consciousness of self, self-esteem, self-love, scrutinizing one's conscience, etc.) and acts that are indifferent to these two directions (e.g., judging). Therefore, the being of the person as individual person is constituted within a person and a world in general in the special essential class of singularizing acts; the being of the collective person, in the special essential class of social acts. The *world* of a community is the *total* content of all experiencing of the kind "experiencing with one another" (in reaction to which "understanding" is only a secondary kind). This is the *collective world,* which has as its concrete subject on the act side the *collective person.* The world of the individual, the *individual world,* is the content of all experiencing in singularizing acts and acts of experiencing-for-oneself. This is the *singular world,* which as its concrete subject on the act side the *individual person.* Hence an individual person *and* a collective person "belong" to every *finite* person. Both factors are essentially necessary sides of a concrete whole of person and world. Thus individual and collective persons can be related to each other *within* every possible concrete finite person, and the relation of one to the other is experienceable. The collective person with its world is not the result of any kind of "synthesis" which it or even an individual person must undertake; it is, on the contrary, an experienced *reality.* The collective person is not a kind of "sum" or a kind of artificial[4] or real collection[5] of individual persons, nor are its properties composed of properties of individual persons; the collective person is not contained "first" in individual persons, nor is the world of the collective person the sum of the worlds of individual persons, not even in some first stage. Hence *no inference* of any sort and no act of constructive "synthesis" are required in order to arrive at the reality of a collective person. Such acts come into question only for the establishment of the special world *content* of a collective person.

It is therefore *in* the person that the mutually related *individual person* and *collective person* become differentiated. The idea of one is not the "foundation" of the other. The collective or group person is not composed of individual persons in the sense that it derives its existence from such a composition; nor is the collective person a result of the merely reciprocal agency of individual persons or (subjectively and in cognition) a result of a synthesis of arbitrary additions. It is an experienced *reality*, and not a construction, although it is a starting point for constructions of all types.

If one asks whether the collective person has a "consciousness-of" that is *different* from and *independent* of the consciousness-of the individual person, the answer depends on the meaning of the question. No doubt the collective person does possess a "consciousness-of" that is different from and independent of the consciousness-of of the *individual* person.

This possession will appear paradoxical only to someone who would base the differentiation of consciousness in general on the separation of lived bodies or to someone who would base the concept of the person on the concept of a soul-substance.[6] The mistake of such assumptions was shown before. Inasmuch as the collective person is constituted in mutual coexperiencing of persons, and inasmuch as the person is the concrete act-center of the experience *in* this mutual coexperiencing, the consciousness-of of the collective person is *always contained* in the consciousness of a total finite person as *act-direction*. It is not something transcendent to it. Yet it is not the case that a certain finite total person must also have a reflective consciousness of the contents that he contingently experiences in mutual coexperiencing. Nor is it the case that his experience can encompass the *collective content* . . . experienced by the collective person and to which the person *also* belongs as a member. . . . Indeed, the person's peculiar awareness that he can never encompass the total contents of the experience of the collective person to which he belongs is a part of the *essence* of this experienced relation in which both member person and collective person are given. The collective person with its world is *not fully* experienced in *any* of its member persons; it is given as something going beyond the member persons in terms of duration, content, and range of effectiveness. Indeed, it belongs to the essence of all collective persons to have members . . . who are *also* individual persons; but the collective person's existence, with its strict continuity as a collective person, is not connected with the existence of the same individual persons. In relation to the collective person the latter are freely variable and, in principle, replaceable. Through death and in other ways they lose their membership in the collective person.[7] And the same individual persons can also belong to different collective persons, for example, to a nation and to a church.

It would appear that in making these statements we have simply sided with Aristotle in the old philosophical dispute between the Aristotelian doctrine, according to which man as a rational being is by nature a political animal,[8] and the doctrine first formulated by the Epicureans, according to which community is first constituted by some form of *contract*. But this is true only in a negative way inasmuch as we must reject the theory of a contract in any of its three possible forms: as a genetic theory, as a theory of origin, or as a theoretical standard (according to which only the type of order of a community is to be assessed against the idea of a contract). But in a positive sense our views do not confirm Aristotle's. For Aristotle, the individual person is not equal in origin to the whole. He is, rather, derived from it— essentially, not historically. The person becomes a person by being a member of a community (first of all, the state) and does not have an independent value of his own apart from his value as member. In our view, however, all persons are, with *equal* originality, both individual persons and (essentially) members of a collective person. And one's own value as an individual person is independent of his value as a member person. Second, Aristotle does not recognize the concept of a collective *person*. Also, *logos, form,* and ratio are, for Aristotle, *over and above* the idea of a *person,* a principle that is typically held by the ancients (even in their theories about God). The state, too, is viewed not as a sovereign personal will but only as the firm and rational order of a people's community based on laws. However, we remain convinced that the community has its ultimate foundation in the idea of the *person;* and we maintain that it is not values of the community but values of the *person* that are the highest values, and that the highest values *among* values of the community are those belonging to the collective *person.* And so the relation between the collective person and the individual person does not represent a special kind of relation between the universal and the individual; the collective person (apart from the concepts of it, such as state, nation, church) is as much a spiritual *individual* as the individual person, e.g., the Prussian state.[9] From an ethical point of view there is for us no relation of subordination between the individual . . . and the collective person[s]. Rather, both have a *common* ethical subordination to the idea of an infinite person in whom the division between individual . . . and collective persons, necessary for finite persons, *ceases to be.* Therefore, the Godhead, according to its very idea, cannot be conceived either as an individual person (which would be henotheism, and not monotheism) or as the highest collective person (pantheism). It can be conceived only as *the* ("singular," not numerically "one") infinite person.

From this it follows, of course, that not *all* kinds of social unit are unities that may be called collective *persons* (insofar as we use "social" to designate the most general and undifferentiated combinations of men).

One must fully develop a *theory of all possible essential social units* to be applied to the understanding of factual social units (marriage, family, people, nation, etc.). This is the basic problem of philosophical sociology and the presupposition of any social ethics. . . . Let it suffice here to mention the principles of division of such a theory of the essence of the social and its chief result, so that we may get to the deeper foundation of the concept of the collective person. The first such principle deals with the essentially different *kinds of being with one another* and experiencing one another through which a specific kind of social unity is constituted. The second principle deals with the kind and rank of *values* in whose direction the member persons of a social unit see "with one another" so that they may act according to norms that conform to those values. As is the case with all noninductive concepts and propositions, these essential social units and their interconnections are never purely and fully realized in factual experience; but since they function as the *condition* for the objective possibility of this experience, they serve in their being understood. . . .

1. A social unit is constituted (simultaneously) in so-called contagion and involuntary imitation devoid of understanding.[10] Such a unit of animals is called the *herd,* of men, the *mass.* With respect to its members, the mass possesses a reality of its own and has its own laws of effectiveness.

2. A social unit is constituted in *that* kind of coexperiencing or reliving (cofeeling, costriving, cothinking, cojudging, etc.) which reveals some *"understanding"* of the members of this unit (distinguishing it from the mass). However, this understanding is not that which would precede this coexperiencing as a separate act, but that which occurs *in* coexperiencing *itself.* In particular, here there is no "understanding" in whose acts a member coexperiences his individual *egoness* as the starting point of such acts; still less is the other being *objectified* (which distinguishes this unit from society). It is in this immediate experience and understanding, in which (as I have shown in the work mentioned) there is *no division* of any kind between the experience of self and that of the other or between bodily expression and experience in the comprehension of member *A* and that of member *B,* that the basic social unit which I call the *life community* (in the pregnant sense) is constituted. The *content* of this coexperiencing is, in the "community," truly *identical* content. Any attempt to "explain" this peculiar phenomenon of "coexperiencing something" by saying that *A* experi-

ences something that is experienced by *B*, and that both, in addition, *know* of their experiencing it, or that they only "take part" in their experiences in terms of a mere "cofeeling-with," would be a fully erroneous construction.[11] If one looks away from the *uniform actus* of coexperiencing and toward (objective) individuals and their experiences, this *actus* (and the ever-changing structure) of coliving, cohearing, coseeing, cothinking, cohoping, coloving, and cohating hovers between these individuals like a *stream of experience which has its own laws* and whose subject is the reality of the community itself.[12] Hence, given the basis of the "community," mutual understanding among members requires *no inferences* from expression to experience; their common knowledge of the truth, no *criteria of truth* and no artificial terminology; and the formation of the common will, no promises and no contracts.

Whereas there is no solidarity in the social unit of the mass because the individual does not exist at all as an experience and therefore cannot possess solidarity with others, there is a special *form* of solidarity in a life community which, in contrast to another higher form (as we shall see), may be called *representable solidarity*. This solidarity arises on the basis of the fact that, although the experiences of the individual are given *as* such experiences, they vary with regard to course and content in their total dependency on the variations of collective experience. True, the experiences of an individual are given to him as single experiences, but only on the basis of a special singularizing act that clips him, as it were, out of the communal whole. *This* solidarity implies that self-responsibility, when it is experienced, is *built upon* an experience of *coresponsibility* for the willing, acting, and effecting of the whole community. And for this reason the individual is in principle "representable" by other individuals according to law, in conformity with the firm, but nonetheless changing, structure of forms which correspond to different areas of tasks of the community, and which are called caste, class, dignity, occupation, etc., depending upon the kind of structure.

Whereas we can explain the unity of the mass, with the assistance of principles of association and their derivatives, on the basis of a common, sensible complex of stimuli, this is not possible in the case of the life community. The life community is a *suprasingular* unit of life and body that possesses a (formally) nonmechanical unity and lawfulness, as does any unity of this essence, whether considered objectively or subjectively, i.e., whether considered in inner or outer perception. Nevertheless, the life community is far from being a *personal* unit, i.e., a collective *person*. True, there is one and the same goal-determined *striving* and *counterstriving,* with a certain structure of involuntary and subconscious preferring and rejecting of values and goals of striving in the form of traditional mores, customs, cults, and costumes. But there is *no* will . . . that can be called purposeful, . . . is able to choose, . . . is unitary and morally responsible, . . . [that] would belong to a person. Accordingly, the life community's *values,* i.e., both the values . . . it experiences as the same (especially in the natural language of its dialects) and the values . . . it [bears], belong to the class of *thing* values, not to the class of *personal* values.

3. The social unit of the *society* is basically different from the essential social unit of the life community.[13] First, the society, as opposed to the *natural* unit of the life community, is to be defined as an *artificial* unit of individuals having *no* original "living-with-one-another" in the sense described above. Rather, *all* relations among individuals are established by *specific conscious* acts that are experienced by each as coming from his *individual* ego, which is experientially given *first in this case,* as directed to someone else as "another."

The plain experience of what goes in the "other," or what he thinks, wills, etc., presupposes a clear *distinction* between "self-experience" and "understanding" and, consequently, between the self-experienced and the understood (with primary retention of one's own judgments), as well as the primary experienced attribution of these contents to two *different* single men. Understanding presupposes a distinction between *bodily* gestures of expression (not given as *bodily* in the life community) and the experience in the other. It also presupposes an *analogical inference* from the self-experienced to the experienced of the other (or some logically equivalent mental process), an inference that is made on the basis of the form distinction. Moreover, common cognition, enjoyment, etc., presuppose some *criteria* of the true and the false, the beautiful and the ugly, which have been agreed upon beforehand.[14] Every kind of willing together and doing together presupposes the *actus* of *promising* and the phenomenon of the *contract* that is constituted in mutual promising—the basic phenomenon of all private law.

From ethical and legal points of view there is no longer *any* original *co*responsibility. All responsibility for others is based on unilateral *self-responsibility,* and all possible responsibility for others must be regarded as having come from a free and singular act of taking over certain obligations. There is no true solidarity (in some form of "one for all" and "all for one")—either representable or unrepresentable— but only the similarity or dissimilarity of individuals' *interests* and the "*classes*" resulting from such interests. As a whole, the essential social unit of society is not a special reality outside or above individuals. It is simply an indivisible fabric of *relations* that represent "conventions,"[15] "usage," or "contracts," depending on whether they are more explicit or more tacit. Hence there is nothing to be found in society *in* which individuals can know themselves to possess solidarity. Just as boundless *trust* in one another is the basic attitude in the life community, unfathomable and primary *distrust* of all in all is the basic attitude in society. If, however, the society is supposed to "will" something that is to be "common" to all of its individuals, it can do so only by *fiction* or by *force* unless it has the assistance of *other* essential social units. It is the so-called *majority* principle which functions here in constructing the fiction that the "common will" is (and must be, if things are to go on without force) the fortuitously identical volitional content of *all as individuals* (because the majority comes closest to this ideal). Force, however, consists in imposing the will of the majority on the minority.

In contrast to the life community, which encompasses people who are *not of age* (as well as domestic animals attached to it), the society is a unit of *mature* and *self-conscious individual persons*. Whereas the personal form of unity in general does not appear in the mass or the life community, it does appear throughout society. But it appears *exclusively* as the *individual* person who obtains in society as the person, i.e., as the individual person who is related to the value modalities of the agreeable (society as sociability) and the useful (society as the bearer of civilization), which are relative to the sensible and are, by nature, not unifying, but *divisive*.[16] The "elements" of society, however, are not individuals in the sense of the individual spiritual person described above. The elements of society are *originaliter equal* and of *equal value* because they enter the picture as such "elements" solely by virtue of their formal character as *single* persons, not by virtue of their *nonformal* . . . contents of individuality. Differences in society and differences in value between its elements come about only through different values of *accomplishment* of the individuals in the value direction of the agreeable and the useful, the value correlates of society. To this extent there is a peculiar law that applies to the elements of society, namely, that they are formally (as single elements) entirely unrepresentable, but nonformally (as individuals) representable because they are originally *equal*. Although every individual being in a life community is representable by another one who occupies the same position in the community (standing, office, rank, occupation), these options themselves are not representable, nor are the individual beings insofar as they exercise functions in different positions.

However, this peculiarity of the societal structure does not preclude the possibility that the single being *as* single being, and not as an "element" of society, perfects an awareness of his incomparable *individuality*. This occurs in a manner that is impossible in the life community. On the level of the pure community the individualistic principle is realized only for the concrete *community*, not for the individual being. In a (pure) society it is realized *exclusively* for the *individual being*. An individual being of a life community is *primarily* given to himself as an *X*, a *Y*, or a *Z* of mutual living-with-one-another or of a specific form of this. In society these *X*-, *Y*-, and *Z*-places are filled with an original content, so that instead of mutual living-with-one-another, there is *mediate mutual accord* concerning what is experienced by anyone "for himself." The primary seat of all moral responsibility is the *whole* of the communal reality in a life community (the real subject of mutual living-with-one-another), and the individual being is only coresponsible for the will, actions, and doings of the whole.[17] By contrast, it is in (pure) society that the principle of the *exclusive self-responsibility* of each for his actions is realized.

Yet there are interconnections of a quite determinate character *between* society and life community (as essential structures of social unity). The basic nexus is this: there can be *no society without life community* (though there can be life community without society). All *possible* society is therefore *founded* through community. This proposition holds both for the manner of "*accord*" and for the kind of formation of a *common will*. Mutual living-with-one-another and *its* content are the origins of the nonformal premises that serve in society as bases for analogical inferences establishing the "inner" life of the "other." These premises cannot be derived from any inferences.[18] In what concerns the obligating character of "*promising*" as the *actus* of formation of the will and as the ideal ought-to-be of "promising" in the sense of *what* has been promised, the (former) duty does *not* have its source in *other* acts of promising (e.g., in the promise to keep one's promise), but solely in the moral *faithfulness* whose roots are in the norm according to which original willing-with-one-another cannot be changed without an additional and sufficient reason of value. For the ought-to-be of what has been promised and of what has been accepted as such by the one who has been promised something has its foundation in the ought-to-be of this content as something *identical* for a willing-with-one-another. And the duty to keep mutual promises that are in a contract, the basic form of the formation of a uniform will in society, does *not* have its source in *another* contract to keep contracts. It has its source in the *solidary* obligation of the members of the community to realize the contents that ought to be for the members. A so-called contract *without* this foundation would be nothing but a fiction.

It would be only the expression and statement of a momentary, hypothetical volitional readiness to do something on the condition that the other do something, while the other expresses this momentary and hypothetical readiness. But the content of the *genuine contract* (as something to be realized in the future) is *plainly* willed by the contractual partners, and not in terms of this merely hypothetical volitional readiness. And the hypothetical obligation of A to do something when B does something belongs to the mutually willed *content* of the contract, not to the will of one of the partners.[19] Furthermore, what is mutually *willed* in the contract is plainly given as something to be realized (and thus it is given as present or future); only the *execution* lies in the sphere of the future within specified dates. Just as the contractual principle has its *roots* in the principle of solidarity, so also conventions and artificial terminologies that support the societal form of *mutual cognition* have their *roots* in the *natural language,* where they can be established in the first place, and on whose *categories* of meaning they remain dependent.[20]

To say that all societal unity (in all walks of life, religion, art, knowledge, commerce) has its foundation in the unity of the life community is not to imply that the *same* groups of real individuals bound together in a society must also (in another direction) form a community. This law of foundations obtains only for the two *essential structures* of social unification. However, in its application to *factual* relations, this law means two things. First, individuals who enter into societal relations must at some time have gone through a union of the structure of the community in order to be able to enter into the forms of mutual accord and volitional formation that characterize the societal unit. For A to be able to make a contract with B, it is not necessary for A to be communally related to B; but he must have been so related to C, D, or E at some time (e.g., in terms of the family in which he grew up) in order to be able to understand the sense of "contract." Second, all societal combinations of individuals A, B, and C or groups G, G_1, and G_2 can occur *only* when A, B, and C or G, G_1, and G_2 simultaneously belong to another totality G_3 of a community—one which is not necessarily formed by A, B, and C or G, G_1, and G_2, but which nevertheless contains them as members. Thus the individuals of all families of *one* lineage form a community vis-à-vis the individuals of all families of another lineage; within the lineage they form a community only as members of their families, and among themselves they form only a society. Thus all nations belonging to the cultural circle "Europe" form a community in relation to all nations of the Asian cultural circle. The members of each cultural circle are coresponsible for the well-being of the whole of the circle; but within Europe and among themselves the same nations form only a society. In this . . . and analogous [cases] our proposition implies that the character of obligation and the sanction of the contracts into which individuals or groups enter always presuppose a *further* communal whole to which they simultaneously belong, and that this sanction stems from the unitary collective will of this whole. The idea of the contract thus does not presuppose the unit of the *state*[21]—as some have erroneously maintained in criticism of the contract theory—but a *further* community to which the partners to the contract belong.

4. From the essential types of social unity thus far mentioned, namely, mass, society, and life community, we must distinguish the highest essential type of social unity, with whose characteristics we began this chapter: *the unity of independent, spiritual, and individual single persons "in" an independent, spiritual, and individual collective person.* We assert that this unity, and it alone, is the *nucleus* and total *novelty* of the true and ancient Christian idea of community, and that this Christian idea represents, so to speak, the historical discovery of this unity. In quite a peculiar manner, this idea of community unites the being and indestructible self-value of the individual "soul" (conceived in terms of creation) and the person (contrary to the ancient theory of corporation and the Jewish idea of "people") by means of the idea of the salvational solidarity of all in the *corpus christianum,* which is founded on the Christian idea of love (and which is contrary to the mere ethos of "society," which denies moral solidarity).

For on this level any finite person is an individual person *and* at the same time a member of a collective person. It simply belongs to the essence of a finite person (fully known as such) both to *be* so and to *experience* himself so. Thus responsibility-for (someone) and responsibility-to (someone) are *essentially* different in orientation. In the life community the bearer of *all* responsibility is the reality of the community, and the individual is *co*responsible for the life community; in the collective person every individual *and* the collective person are *self*-responsible (= responsible for oneself), and at the same time every individual is also *co*responsible for the collective person (and for every individual "in" it), just as the collective person is coresponsible for *each* of its members. Hence coresponsibility between the individual person and the collective person is *mutual* and does not preclude self-responsibility on the part of both. As for the responsibility-to (someone), it must be said that there is *neither* an ultimate responsibility of the individual to the collective person, as is the case of the life community, *nor* an ultimate responsibility of the collective person to the individual (or to the sum or a majority of individuals), as is the case in the society (principle of the majority). Nevertheless, *both* the collective person and the individual person are responsible to the person of persons, to *God*, and, indeed, in terms of self-responsibility *as well as* coresponsibility. But here the principle of solidarity, which diminishes and disappears in a pure society but obtains *exclusively* in the life community, takes on a new sense. It changes from a principle of *representable* solidarity into one of *unrepresentable solidarity*: the individual person is coresponsible for all other individual persons "in" the collective person not only as the representative of an *office*, a *rank*, or any other positional value in the social *structure*, but also, indeed, *first of all*, as a *unique personal individual* and as the bearer of an individual conscience in the sense defined above. In moral self-examination at this level, not only must everyone ask, What of positive moral value would have occurred in the world and what of negative moral value would have been avoided if I, as a *representative of a place* in the social structure, had comported myself differently? But everyone must also ask, What would have occurred *if I, as a spiritual individual, had grasped*, willed, and realized the *"good-in-itself-for-me"* (in the sense described before) in a *superior* manner? The principle of solidarity is thus not *precluded* by the proposition that there is, in addition to the universally valid good-in-itself, an individually valid good-in-itself. On the contrary, this proposition raises the principle to the *highest* level that it can possibly attain.

Hence in *this* sense the principle of solidarity is for us an eternal component and a *fundamental article of the cosmos of finite moral persons*. The *total* moral world—no matter how far its sphere may extend in space and time, here on earth or on discovered and undiscovered planets or even beyond these—becomes *one encompassing whole* through the validity of this principle. This whole *rises and falls as a whole* whenever this principle suffers the slightest change, and as a *whole* it possesses at every moment of its existence a *unique* moral *totality value* (a total evil and total good, a total guilt and total merit) that can *never* be regarded as the *sum* of individuals' evil and good or as the sum of their guilt and merit. But *every* person, both the individual ... and the collective ... , participates in this according to his special and *unique* membership. Suppose that we find ourselves in a world court. No one *alone* would be tried by its highest judge; all would have to answer to him in the unity of *one* act, all taken together would have to listen to this judge in *one* act. He would not sentence anyone until he had heard, understood, and valued *all* others *with* this one. In *each* he would cosentence the *whole* no less than the whole in each.

What are the essential elements on which this great and sublime principle rests?[22] Ultimately it rests on two propositions. The first is a proposition that we stressed before, namely, that a community of persons belongs to the evidential *essence* of a possible person—regardless of the real and, . . . [necessarily], fortuitous causes of the *empirically real connections* between certain persons and certain others—and that the possible unities of sense and of value of such a community possess an a priori structure independent in principle of the kind, measure, place, and time of the realization of these unities. This is the *foundation* that makes moral solidarity *possible*. What makes moral solidarity *necessary* is the formal proposition concerning the (direct or indirect)[23] *essential reciprocity and reciprocal valueness* of all morally relevant comportment and the corresponding nonformal propositions concerning the essential nexus of the basic *types* of social acts. This reciprocity is *not* based on the contingent reality of these acts, on specific persons who execute these acts, or on the presence of real mechanisms and factual forms of conveyance in which this reciprocity gains *reality*. It rests on the ideal *unity of sense* of these acts as acts of the *essence* of love, esteem, promising, giving orders, etc., acts that require as ideal correlates responses of love, esteem, accepting, obeying, etc., in order to bring about a fact of uniform sense. These and analogous propositions *cannot* be established by inductive methods for two reasons: first, because they are presupposed by every possible understanding of these acts (including every inductive investigation of their factual occurrence); and, second, because they could not in the least be as well founded inductively as inductive propositions are required to be. The possible understanding of a love—for instance, of an act of kindness to me—at least implies coexperiencing the *requirement* of a response of love which belongs to the nature of this act and which is realized psychically (be it in terms of an actual response or a real tendency toward its execution which is disturbed by other motives, or in terms of a merely emotionally represented response of love).[24] It is, I say, the mere *understanding* of this act that implies this. One who does not see this does not look with precision at the *experience*. However I may deny esteem to him who esteems me and whose esteem I understand, however I may refuse any response of love to a felt love, or obedience to an understood command, or acceptance of a promise, I must somehow "*deny*" this to him and "*refuse*" this. I cannot on the one hand understand the sense of his intention and on the other comport myself as if nothing had happened. Of course it may be that the responding act of love and esteem, based on the experienced demand for an act of response remains a mere act *stimulus* or, if executed, hits any empty spot, so to speak, in which no *value* of the other person is given that would *correspond* to this act of response. I am then not "able" to esteem and love the other despite *his* esteem and love. But in this case this tendency or this inability or the nonfulfillment of this responding intention in the value of the other is experienced as something positive. Of course this does not in the least mean that in love and esteem there is an *intention* toward a response of love or esteem, or any conditional act with a reservation such as "I will esteem and love you *if* you love and esteem me." For precisely this is *evidentially* precluded by *true* love and esteem of the person. And even the sight of such an intention *destroys* the *experience* of the demand for response in love and esteem. The demand for the response to love lies in the *sense* of love *as* love, *not* in subjective intentions and desires (which may accompany love in X or Y); and in the mere understanding of this sense of love one finds the stimulus of the act of response to love, without which not even the experiential *material* for such understanding would be given. This holds analogously for correlative negative acts of hate and disrespect, when they occur. This *fact alone* grounds the co-responsibility of every (otherwise variable) bearer of these acts for the moral values and disvalues of the acts of the (otherwise variable) bearers of responding acts. One who loves not only realizes a positive act value in himself but also realizes, *ceteris paribus,* such a value in the beloved. Responding love, *as* love, also bears the positive act value of love.[25] He who refuses an act of love of ideal oughtness, which is to correspond to the other's *worthiness* to be loved, possesses *coresponsibility* for the negative value lying in the nonbeing of the positive value of responding love. He does not simply possess self-responsibility for having refused this act. In addition to this there is another proposition . . . which confers upon the principle of solidarity the *complete* fullness of its *extension.* Because the spiritual person, as the concrete act center of all his executions of acts, is related to his acts, not as an unalterable substance to its changing properties or activities or as a collective whole to its members or as a whole to its aggregate parts, but as the concrete to the abstract, and because the whole person is and lives in *each* act without exhausting himself in one act or the sum of these acts, there is no act whose execution does not change the content of the person's *being,* and no act value that does not increase or decrease, enhance or diminish, or positively or negatively determine the value of the person. In every moral individual act of positive value the ability for acts of the kind concerned increases; in other words, there is an increase in what we designated as the *virtue* of the person (which is very different from the habituation and practice of *actions* related to the virtue in question), that is, the experienced power to realize the good that ought to be. Thus mediated, every moral act effects changes in the being and value of the person himself. In relation to our question, this means that it is *not* by virtue of *fortuitous* causes or circumstances but by virtue of the *essence* of the state of affairs concerned that the virtue value implicit in *B*'s act of love in response to *A*, or the increase in personal value, obtains not only for *A* but also for *any other persons, C, D, E, . . . X* and can become fruitful for them. This also means that *A* possesses original coresponsibility for the presence or absence of *this*, quite apart from the fortuitous causes that lead *C, D, E, . . . X* to meet in space and time. One who has become more lovable in responding to love with love, or one who has become more filled with hate in responding to hate with hate, will become so, *ceteris paribus*, for all *possible* "others," not according to rules of experimental association, but according to essential laws.[26]

Notes

1. See *The Nature of Sympathy.*
2. For more details, see ibid., pp. 96–105.
3. For example, a mother's love, sexual love, love for one's country and home, and also love of humanity and God. These kinds of love are essentially different from one another independent of their objects and the discovery of their objects; they only find their "fulfillment or "nonfulfillment" in such objects (ibid., pp. 73–87).
4. Like a statistical unity.
5. Like the collective *thing* of the heaven of stars.
6. A collective soul-substance is, of course, nonsense.
7. Above all, one must be careful not to regard the collective person as an individual person of only wider scope, whether consciously or implicitly, and thus attribute to it the kind of consciousness which can be attributed *only* to individual persons. If one does this, it is easy to show that the collective person cannot have a consciousness, or that this assumption is but a "mysterious" assertion. This mistake would be analogous to the one with which Husserl rightly charged Berkeley. Berkeley maintained that it is necessary to represent to oneself "one" triangle which is neither right-angled nor oblique-angled and yet both at the same time in order to demonstrate the existence of the species. If one does not consider the fact that special singular acts are necessary to reveal the givenness of the individual person, one is easily led into a metaphysical hypostatization of the individual person which does not allow one to ac-

cept a collective person unless the latter is falsely interpreted simply as an individual person of wider scope.

8. Aristotle's expression means something very different from what historians and economists (especially those of the historical school), with their complete lack of knowledge of philosophy, say that it does: the mere trivial recognition of the (questionable!) fact that there is no isolated living man—a fact never denied by the subtle representatives of the theory of the contract. Aristotle means that it belongs to the essence "man" bearer of νοῦς (*anima rationalis*) to be a member of a state community and to know himself as such, no matter to what extent he may *in fact* live alone.

9. It is the tension between Christianity (especially its theory of individuality and the infinite value of every "soul," as well as its incorporation of each person into *two* basic communities, state *and* church) and the ancient idea of community and partnership that historically led to the *depth* of this problem—a depth which those who want to return to the ancient idea of the state in some form and those who want to renovate the theory of contract in some form on Christian bases (e.g., the Calvinists) completely miss.

10. On the psychological mechanism of these processes, see *The Nature of Sympathy.*

11. Ibid., p. 9.

12. The colorful and changing hypostatizations of communal subjects in history, such as units of family gods, tribal gods, and gods of common people, exist as long as religion is tied to community, i.e., to the *vital* (factual blood communities can always be replaced by the many kinds of *symbolizations* of them).

13. It is to the credit of Ferdinand Tönnies to have first established the difference between life community and society as essential forms of human togetherness. But the above characteristics of these two social forms deviate a great deal from his; in our opinion he does not sufficiently separate a priori and historical factors.

14. All philosophy using criteria is essentially philosophy of *society.*

15. Hence conventions and mores, like fashions and costumes, must be sharply distinguished. Conventions and fashions belong entirely to society; mores and customs, to the life community.

16. "Divisive" in contrast to "unifying" higher value modalities of vital values, spiritual values, and values of the holy. It is the localizable relatedness to a lived body that accounts for their being essentially "divisive."

17. All institutions, mores, and moralities conforming to the principle of solidary responsibility, for example, blood-revenge (within families, tribes, and clans), belong to the predominantly communal ethos. The community itself is responsible, while every one of its members remains coresponsible to the degree of his importance within the community.

18. See *The Nature of Sympathy,* ch. 3.

19. Naturally, willing with reservation is to be clearly distinguished from the willing of reservations.

20. There is an analogous relation between natural symbols and artificial allegory, between artistic willing and works of art in a community and in a society, between a traditional, communal, religious content of faith and religious education, etc. But the *criteria* which must be presupposed in collective cognition in a society if an understanding of the sameness of something is to be possible must themselves be seen by all. . . . Otherwise an infinite series of criteria would be necessary to establish the sameness of a proposition as a criterion.

21. The idea of a contract *between* states is for this reason precluded.

22. See *The Nature of Sympathy*, pp. 65–84.

23. By virtue of the co-originality of individual and collective persons in the nature of the uniform finite person, the individual acts mentioned earlier (self-love, self-perfection, self-happiness, etc.) "indirectly" possess this essential reciprocity and reciprocal valueness, and all social acts "indirectly" possess an essential relation to self-sanctification and self-ruin (in the end)—without any *intention toward* community or one's own self in either case.

24. We have discussed so-called emotive representations earlier.

25. Even though this act, as a reactive act, would not be equal in height to the spontaneous act.

26. In *The Nature of Sympathy*, I also showed that neither spiritual acts of love nor the genuine *kinds* of love are genetic products of drive impulses or empirically contingent feeling-states, and, furthermore, that drive impulses have only a *selective* significance for the contingent real objects that become the factual object of love or the type of love concerned. Accordingly, I showed, too, that real history, in which there occurs a gradual enlargement and extension of the domain of objects of love and its types (family, tribe, people, nation, etc.), only "fulfills" original intentional goals, which do not grow out of real history itself. As to the first of these two points, it follows, concerning the principle of solidarity, that not only the act of hate (bad *in itself*) but also the *absence* of the act of love determines coresponsibility for all evil deeds and for all that happens—and this *prior* to any empirical demonstration of even the possibility of a factual and indirect cooperation in the realization of evil. Yet these principles are maxims that obligate us always to *find out* the evil that would not have happened in the world had *we* only comported ourselves differently. The second point has this consequence for the principle of solidarity: that its sense and validity are not somehow *produced* by history or by changes in communities in factual contact with each other, that this sense is, in part, *fulfilled* only in history, and that this principle itself is a *moral a priori of all possible history and all possible community*.

12

The Structure of Values and Their Historical Variations

In order to *compare* peoples or other groups in terms of their moral values, it is first necessary to *reduce* such peoples or groups to the *same* conditions in terms of their intellectual culture, their techniques of action, the levels of expression of their value estimations and their extramoral estimations, their degrees and types of solidarity of interest, their ability to suffer, etc.[1] For the variations and developments of moral value estimations are in principle never direct consequences of all the other variations; and, more particularly, they are not consequences of the level of intellectual culture. A very highly developed, differentiated intellectual culture can have very primitive moral feeling, and vice versa; the increased dovetailing of interests, which is the driving wheel of civilization, with the resulting security of life, property, and commerce, can go hand in hand with a very low level of moral culture.[2]

It is necessary to get behind all the costumes and disguises in which the moral value sphere appears to us in history in order to find the material of problems concerning the dimensions of the relativity of morals.

Within this material, however, there are five strata which must be sharply differentiated for all historical considerations of moral affairs.

First, there are variations in *feeling* (i.e., "cognizing") values themselves, as well as in the *structure* of *preferring* values and *loving* and *hating*. Let us take the liberty of calling these variations as a whole variations in the "*ethos*."[3]

Second, there are variations which occur in the sphere of *judgment* and the sphere of rules of the *assessment* of values and value ranks given in these functions and acts. These are variations in "*ethics*" (in the broadest sense of the term).

Third, there are variations in *types* of unity of *institutions, goods,*

Reprinted with permission from *Formalism in Ethics and Non-formal Ethics of Values,* pp. 298–311.

and *actions*, i.e., the quintessences of institutions, goods, and actions, the unities of which are founded in moral value complexes, e.g., "marriage," "monogamy," "murder," "theft," "lying," etc. These types must be clearly differentiated from the (positive) definitions that are valid on the basis of mores and positive law, i.e., what shall *obtain* as "marriage," "monogamy," "murder," or "theft." Yet these types lie behind these changing definitions as the foundation of the definability of these things. They represent unities of *states of affairs,* but as such they can be distinguished only on the basis of certain *value complexes* as these or other . . . unities. Thus murder is never = killing . . . a man (or killing with intent and deliberation), a lie never = conscious statement of an untruth, etc. The essence of such unities of states of affairs is such that in each case a peculiar, morally negative value complex which is basic to each case must be given if such an action is to become a lie or murder. Variations of this kind can be called variations in existing *morals,* to which a science of morals corresponds.

Fourth, and very different from all of these variations, are variations in *practical morality.* Practical morality pertains to the value of the factual comportment of men, that is, comportment on the basis of norms which belong to the relations of value ranks recognized by *these men,* and which correspond to *their own* structures of preferring. The value of such practical comportment is completely relative to its *"ethos"* and can never be measured by an ethos of another epoch or that of another people. Only *after* we take possession of an ethos of a certain age can we judge the actions and types of comportment of the people of that age; such judgment also requires preliminary knowledge of their unities of moral *types.*[4] On the other hand, we can assess historical being and action *itself* (in terms of a refeeling understanding of the ethos of the epoch). In so doing, we can disregard the principles of the *ethics* of this age, as well as the factual assessments made by people in this age and the instances which they regarded as authoritative.[5] On the other hand, an action that is "bad" in relation to the ethos of its age can nevertheless be absolutely "good" if the acting person surpasses, in *his* ethos, the ethos of his time. Indeed, according to the nature of the relation between morality and ethos, and not according to the fortuitous immorality of contemporaries or their insufficient ethics, the *moral genius,* who is superior to the ethos of his time, i.e., who has made a new advance into the realm of extant values by being the first to comprehend a higher value, is assessed and judged as morally inferior by the extant ethos, "legitimately" and *without* deception or error. The broad transitions in the history of an ethos are therefore replete with individuals who are necessarily victimized by this *tragic* which is essentially immanent to moral development itself, but not because they are subject to the moral disapproval of a historian.[6]

Fifth, and finally, it is necessary to distinguish the variations in moralities from variations belonging to the areas of *mores* and *customs*, i.e., forms of action and expression whose validity and practice are rooted solely in (genuine) traditions, and whose nature is such that a deviation from them presupposes an act of willing. Mores and customs *themselves* can be morally good and evil, and their origins can almost always be found in morally immediate and relevant acts and actions. They can "transmit" what is morally of positive and negative value. An action against mores, insofar as it is without reason, i.e., without insight into their moral deficiency, is practically immoral because the ethos is already coeffective in the very *selection* of actions within a tradition and is also the measure of practical morality. With this insight, however, it becomes moral. . . .

Every future investigation into the manifold systems of moral value estimations that are found in history must . . . look into the great *typical forms of ethos itself,* i.e., the experiential structure of values and their immanent rules of preferring, which lie *behind* both the morality and the ethics of a people (primarily those of larger racial groups); and it must proceed with the aid of concepts drawn from this historical material, concepts which the theory of the *dimensions of the relativity of value estimations* provides.[7] It is necessary to investigate the extent to which the ethos also conditions ways of looking at the world[8] . . . , i.e., the structure of knowing world experiencing as presupposed in all judgmental activities, especially the formation of the levels of the experienced relativity of the existence of objects. It is not the changing *ideas* about love and justice that must be investigated, but the forms of *moral attitudes themselves* and their experienced order of ranks; not the action that is considered noble or useful or conducive to well-being, but the rules by which such *values themselves* were preferred or placed after.[9] Who would not be convinced by a detailed analysis that the ethos of the ancient Indian caste system and religion is radically different as ethos (and not as ethics or as adaptation to the changing historical realities of this people) from the ethos of the Greeks or from that of the Christian world? The Romans before Ennius found usury more reproachable than theft, and the old German moral and legal value estimation deemed plundering better than theft; who would not admit that this points to basically different rules of preferring for certain kinds of the vital values (courage, manliness) and the value of usefulness—and not to changes in value estimations of different actions

according to the same rule of preferring? Of course, there is also a
change in the simple adaptation of an ethos to changing historical realities, a change that is expressed, for instance, in changing positive
definitions of *what* is considered profiteering, theft, or robbery. But
these are as different from the variations in the ethos as are ethical
theories, any number of which can be found within *one* ethos. The
ethos lives *in* the structure of this historical life reality itself and is
therefore not an adaptation to this reality. It serves as the basis of this
reality and has also guided the construction of the nonarbitrary forms
of its structure. We must learn to distinguish moral change in the
ethos, which is one of the *first* order, from differences in adaptation—
just as the history of art has at last begun to *separate* typical basic
forms of the artistic representative penetration into the world of intuition, which is guided by a specific structure of aesthetic value experiences, from differences that are based on changing abilities and levels
of artistic technique and available materials, as well as from the objects determined by the ethos and worldview of a ruling class as objects
to be glorified in art, and also from consciously "applied" aesthetic
and technical laws.

Nevertheless, this *most radical* relativity of moral value estimations
gives us no reason to assume a relativism of moral *values* themselves
and their order of ranks.[10] One can only say that a complete and adequate experience of the cosmos of values and its order of ranks, and,
with this, the presentation of the moral sense of the world, is *essentially* connected with the *cooperation* of the different forms of ethos
which unfold historically according to its laws. It is precisely a correctly understood *absolute ethics* that strictly *requires* these differences—this value perspectivism of values among people and their
times and this openness in the formative stages of the ethos. Because
moral value estimations and their systems are more manifold and
richer in their qualities than the diversity of mere natural dispositions
and realities of peoples would allow one reasonably to expect, one
must assume an objective realm of values which our experiencing can
enter only gradually and according to definite structures of the selection of values. On the other hand, the origins of *ethical relativism* are
to be found in the fact that it takes values to be mere *symbols* of its
own culturally dominant value estimations of certain goods and actions (or even mere theories about these) and arbitrarily construes all
history simply as the increasing technical adaptation of acting to factual values that are posited in its own age and taken to be absolute and
thus as "progress" toward such values. Thus value relativism always
rests on an absolutizing of value estimations which depend on the idio-

syncrasies and culture of the observer concerned. That is to say, it rests on the narrowness and blindness of the horizon of moral values, an outlook that is conditioned by a deficient sense of awe and humility vis-à-vis the realm of moral values and its expanse and fullness. It rests on the arrogance of taking only the moral value estimations of one's *own* time as a "matter of course," without scrutiny, and assuming that these values underlie all times; or of "empathizing" one's own experience into men of the past instead of indirectly overcoming the narrowness of this pride by understanding the types of ethoses of other times and other peoples in an experience of the objective realm of values, shaking off the blinders that the value experiences of one's own time impose. . . .

But what are the *special dimensions* in which . . . change in the ethos takes place? The most radical form of renewal and growth of the ethos occurs in the movement of *love* and its power, in which "higher" values (with regard to existing ones) are discovered and disclosed. This happens first within the limits of the highest value modalities, which we mentioned earlier, then within those of the others. Thus it is to the *moral-religious genius* that the realm of values opens up. In such a variation the rules of preferring among old and new values become altered by themselves. Although the rules of preferring among the old values and their mutual objectivity are not necessarily affected, the old realm of values as a whole is nevertheless relativized.[11] It is now a matter of blindness or deception to prefer the old values to the new, and it is practically "evil" to live according to the old values as the highest ones. The virtues of the old ethos now become "glittering vices." *But* the rules of preferring among the old values are *not* affected by this. It remains "better" to retaliate, for instance, or even to seek revenge, than to prefer one's own usefulness (in regard to retaliation) or the common weal to the value of retaliation and revenge—even when these are subordinate in their value to forgiveness as the most valued and therefore the *only* morally "good" comportment in cases of experienced offenses and guilt. The rules of preferring that belong to an old ethos are not abolished as a new ethos "grows." Only a relativizing of the whole of the old ethos occurs. . . .

From the times when human beings were sacrificed to deities and in sacred services, through the times of deeper and more spiritual ideas of sacrifice, which belong to the core of the Christian religion, to the present time, in which it is considered "good" to devote one's life to spiritual values (of cognition, faith—be it in dangerous work or as martyr—freedom, or patriotism), the value of human life was not given to any ethos as the "highest" value. That human life is "not the highest of goods" corresponds to humanity's common ethos. This fact is undoubtedly incomprehensible to all biological ethics.[12] For according to this ethics, all values that are "higher" than life in its most valuable form, i.e., human life, must be illusions, or, as Friedrich Nietzsche says, their acceptance must be a symptom of declining life, and they themselves "values of *ressentiment*" of the disadvantaged of life, or it must be a result of false obsessions with values that were mistakenly considered absolute because their relativity to life was not known. But his basic conception fails in the light of the clear fact that the value of human life is *not* the highest value, and that the being of other values (those which belong to the modalities of the spiritual and the holy—among these, values of oneself and values of the other, individual and collective values, values of the person, and of states of affairs) is preferable to the being of this value.[13]

Notes

1. These points are only examples and are not meant to be exhaustive.
2. See *The Nature of Sympathy,* pt. B, ch. 6.
3. To the ethos there corresponds: (1) in the *intellectual* sphere, the *Weltanschauung* (= structure of looking at the world, which every man and every people has, no matter whether they "know" this reflectively or not); (2) in the *religious* sphere, the structure of a living faith, with its contents, which is to be distinguished from the dogmatic and theological (i.e., normative, defining, and judgmental) wording of the contents given in faith, the former being the foundation of the latter.
4. It is not, as Hegel maintains, moral assessment in general but the direct moral assessment according to the ethos and the morality of one's time that makes historical representations like Schlosser's so intolerable.
5. Thus the killing of Socrates, for example, remains judicial murder, even though he was "legally" sentenced by the Greek people.
6. See "Zum Phänomen des Tragischen," in *Vom Umsturz der Werte,* especially the remarks on the concept of "guiltless guilt." The eternal source of "tragic" guilt in general lies in the fact mentioned above.
7. There is to be mentioned here the problem of how the large families of language form *value units*—the faces, as it were, which the world of values assumes by and through meanings of words, and the structure which this world acquires by and through syntax. A detailed investigation of this promises most fruitful results. I hope to develop an exact indication of the methods of such investigations (with examples) in a planned work on the foundations of historical cognition.
8. Here I do not use the term *Weltanschauung* as it is frequently used, i.e., to indicate a premature termination of the essentially infinite scientific process through some ultimate conceptual result of a science, from which derives what

today is called monism, energetics, panpsychism, etc. In this sense of the word Husserl was correct in rejecting all "philosophy of *Weltanschauung*" (see his *Philosophy als strenge Wissenschaft* ["Philosophy as Rigorous Science," in *Edmund Husserl: Phenomenology and the Crisis of Philosophy* (New York: Harper & Row, 1965), trans. with notes and an introduction by Quentin Lauer, p. 71]). I use the term *Weltanschauung* in W. von Humboldt's and W. Dilthey's sense (if I understand it correctly), namely, to characterize the kind of selection and structurization which factually governs both a whole cultural unit and a person, and with which the person receives the pure whatness of physical, psychic, and ideal things (no matter whether the person knows this reflectively, and, if he knows it reflectively, no matter how he has arrived at this knowledge). In this sense of the term every historical phase of a "science" is always already *conditioned* by a *Weltanschauung* and an ethos with regard to goals and methods. Therefore a science *never* changes a *Weltanschauung*. See my address "Die Idee des Todes und das Fortleben," and my "Phänomenologie und Erkenntnistheorie." . . . [Both are in *Gesammelte Werke*, 10:9–64, 377–430.]

9. For a concrete example, see my *Ressentiment*.

10. By way of analogy, I could say that the discovery of new geometries with different axiomatic systems, which is to be sharply distinguished from the discovery of new propositions within each system, does not make geometry any more relative than it was from the very start.

11. I know of no more grandiose evidence for such a discovery of a whole realm of values which relativizes an older ethos than the Sermon on the Mount, whose very form repeatedly announces evidence of the relativizing of the old values of the "law": "But I say unto you, . . ."

12. This is not the case in the ethics of Wundt, who finds the highest principle of moral value estimation in the "promotion of spiritual goods of culture."

13. It is true that the Indian ethos (and especially the Buddhist . . .), which prescribes benevolence "toward all things alive" and derivatively toward human life, relativizes this difference. But this is because in this ethos love and benevolence are only a way "toward the deliverance of the heart" (Buddha's Sermons). This contradicts biological ethics, which regards the value of life not only as a positive value but also as the highest value, whereas the Buddhist ethos considers the value of life a negative value. The full moral meaning of the Buddhist idea of love is not "toward a positive value" but "away from oneself." Concerning the feelings and values that ground the moral relatedness to living nature and their underivability from our moral-human relations, see *The Nature of Sympathy*.

Bibliography

The following works of Max Scheler have been translated into English.

Books and Collections of Essays

The Nature of Sympathy. Translated by Peter Heath, introduced by Werner Stark. London: Routledge & Kegan Paul, 1954. Reprinted, Hamden, Conn.: Archon Books, 1970.

Philosophical Perspectives. Translated by Oscar Haac. Boston: Beacon Press, 1958.

On the Eternal in Man. Translated by Bernard Noble. London: SCM Press, 1960.

Man's Place in Nature. Translated and introduced by Hans Meyerhoff. New York: Noonday, 1961.

Ressentiment. Translated by William W. Holdheim, introduced by Lewis A. Coser. New York: Free Press, 1961.

Selected Philosophical Essays. Translated and introduced by David Lachterman. Evanston, Ill.: Northwestern University Press, 1973.

Formalism in Ethics and Non-formal Ethics of Values. Translated by Manfred S. Frings and Roger L. Funk. Evanston, Ill.: Northwestern University Press, 1973.

Problems of a Sociology of Knowledge. Translated by Manfred S. Frings, edited and introduced by Kenneth W. Stikkers. London: Routledge & Kegan Paul, 1980.

"Exemplars of Person and Leaders," "Repentance and Rebirth," and "Shame and Feelings of Modesty." In *Person and Self-Value: Three Essays/Max Scheler,* edited, partially translated, and introduced by Manfred S. Frings. Dordrecht, Netherlands: Martinus Nijhoff, 1987.

Separate Essays

"Future of Man." Translated by Howard Becker. *Monthly Criterion* 7 (February 1928).

"On the Tragic." Translated by Bernard Stambler. *Cross Currents* 4 (1954), 178–91.

"The Thomist Ethic and the Spirit of Capitalism." Translated by Gertrude Neuwith. *Sociological Analysis* 25 (Spring 1964).

"An *a priori* Hierarchy of Value-Modalities." Translated by Daniel O'Connor.

In *Readings in Existential Phenomenology,* edited by Nathaniel Lawrence and Daniel O'Connor. Englewood Cliffs, N.J.: Prentice Hall, 1967.

"Towards a Stratification of the Emotional Life." Translated by Daniel O'Connor. In *Readings in Existential Phenomenology,* edited by Nathaniel Lawrence and Daniel O'Connor. Englewood Cliffs, N.J.: Prentice Hall, 1967.

"On the Positivistic Philosophy of the History of Knowledge and Its Laws of Three Stages." Translated by Rainer Koehne. In *The Sociology of Knowledge: A Reader,* edited by James E. Curtis and John W. Petras. New York: Praeger, 1970.

"Metaphysics and Art." Translated by Manfred S. Frings. In *Max Scheler (1874–1928): Centennial Essays,* edited by Manfred S. Frings. The Hague: Martinus Nijhoff, 1974.

"The Idea of Peace and Pacifism." Translated by Manfred S. Frings. *Journal of the British Society for Phenomenology* 8 (October 1976), 154–66; (January 1977), 36–50.

"Reality and Resistance: On Being and Time, Section 43." Translated by Thomas Sheehan. *Listening* 12, no. 3 (Fall 1977).

"On the Idea of Man." Translated by Clyde Nabe. *Journal of the British Society for Phenomenology* 9 (October 1978).

"Concerning the Meaning of the Feminist Movement." Translated by Manfred S. Frings. *Philosophical Forum,* Fall 1978.

"Humility." Translated by Barbara Fiand. *Aletheia II,* 1981.

"The Psychology of So-Called Compensation Hysteria and the Real Battle against Illness." Translated by Edward Vacek, S. J. *Journal of Phenomenological Psychology,* 15, no. 2 (Fall 1984).

"Sociology and the Study and Formulation of Weltanschauung." Translated by R. C. Speirs. In *Max Weber's "Science as a Vocation,"* edited by Peter Lassman and Irving Velody with Herminio Martins. London: Unwin Hyman, 1989.

"Max Weber's Exclusion of Philosophy (on the Psychology and Sociology of Nominalist Thought)." Translated by R. C. Speirs. In *Max Weber's "Science as a Vocation,"* edited by Peter Lassman and Irving Velody with Herminio Martins. London: Unwin Hyman, 1989.

"Love and Knowledge." Translated by Harold J. Bershady with assistance of Peter Haley. This volume, ch. 7.

"The Meaning of Suffering." Translated by Harold J. Bershady. This volume, ch. 5.

Index of Names

Index of Subjects

(For proper names cross-referenced, see Index of Names, above)

Bourgeois outlook, 14, 23, 30, 138, 147. *See also* Ressentiment
Buddhism, 8, 17, 97–104, 148–54. *See also* Love; Suffering

Catholic: Bavaria, 5; bishops, 23; businessmen, 22; Intellectual Union, 22; Scheler's break with church, 22
"Catholic Nietzsche," 14
Christianity, 14, 15, 23, 31, 99–102, 110–13, 156–64. *See also* Augustine; Aquinas; Love; Lutheran doctrines; Ressentiment; Suffering; Values
Community: and values, 235–39; types of, 236–38, 240–46; versus the individual, 237. *See also* Ressentiment; Values
Cybernetic hierarchy: of leaders, 24; of values, 18, of relation of ideal to real factors, 30. *See also* Durkheim; Freud; Parsons, Talcott; Weber

Demian, 21
Dispute over methods, 30. *See also* Habermas; Hanneth; Joas; Rickert; Sullivan

Economic factors, 29, 167–72, 190–93. *See also* Sociology of knowledge
Emotions. *See* Ressentiment; Sociology of emotions; Suffering
Ethos: changes in, 257; typical forms of, 255. *See also* History; Values

First World War, 15, 18; and "The Genius of War," 18, 19
Formalism in Ethics and Non-Formal Ethics of Values, 17

German maladies, 20, 21
Grand Illusion, 21

Hands Around, 21
History: values in, 253. *See also* Sociology of knowledge; Values

Ideal and real factors, 30. *See also* Dispute over methods; Sociology of knowledge
Institute of Political Studies, 26

kinship: historical predominance of, 29. *See also* Sociology of knowledge

"Law of three Stages," 36. *See also* Comte; Sociology of knowledge
Leaders: typology of exemplary, 24–25; dangers of exemplary, 26; Rathenau as one of the exemplary, 27. *See also* Values
League of Nations, 25
Life community, 242–43; and society, 244–45. *See also* Values
"Logic of Heart," 6. *See also* Augustine; Love; Pascal
Lutheran doctrines, 29
Lutheran legacy, 5. *See also* Suffering
Love: androgynous, 155; Christian view of relation of to knowledge, 156–64; and epistemology, 147, 162, 163; Greek view of relation of to knowledge, 148–55; Indian view of relation of to knowledge, 148–54; romantic, 154. *See also* Aristotle; Aquinas; Augustine; Buddhism; Christianity; Plato; Socrates; Spinoza

Magic Mountain, 21
Material Factors, 29, 167–72, 195–96
Metaphysical impulse, 31–33, 167–68, 173, 186, 228. *See also* Comte; Sociology of knowledge; Suffering; Values

Nature of Sympathy, The, 17, 18